WELCOME
to
MUNCHKIN LAND
in the
City of Oz

BROOM RIDES

The
BROWN
DERBY

BROWN
DERBY

Weird

Hollywood

Your Travel Guide to Hollywood's Local Legends and Best Kept Secrets

By Joe Oesterle

**Mark Sceurman and Mark Moran,
Executive Editors**

STERLING

New York / London
www.sterlingpublishing.com

WEIRD HOLLYWOOD

STERLING and the distinctive Sterling logo are
registered trademarks of Sterling Publishing Co., Inc.

Published by Sterling Publishing Co., Inc.
387 Park Avenue South, New York, NY 10016
© 2010 Mark Moran and Mark Sceurman
Distributed in Canada by Sterling Publishing
c/o Canadian Manda Group, 165 Dufferin Street
Toronto, Ontario, Canada M6K 3H6
Distributed in the United Kingdom by GMC Distribution Services,
Castle Place, 166 High Street, Lewes, East Sussex,
England BN7 1XU Distributed in Australia by Capricorn Link (Austra-
lia) Pty. Ltd. P. O. Box 704, Windsor, NSW 2756, Australia

10 9 8 7 6 5 4 3 2 1

Manufactured in China.
All rights reserved.

Photography and illustration credits are found on page 239
and constitute an extension of this copyright page.

Layout and production by bobsteimle.com

Sterling ISBN: 978-1-4027-5460-9

For information about custom editions, special sales, premium
and corporate purchases, please contact Sterling Special Sales
Department at 800-805-5489 or specialsales@sterlingpublishing.com.

CONTENTS

DEDICATION

I'd like to thank all the people who contributed their words to the pages of this book: Greg Bishop, Mike Marinacci, Donna Lethal, Julie Ann Ream, Scott Michaels, Steve Goldstein, Jacy Young, and Jonathan Crellin.

A Note from the Marks

Welcome to this new volume in the famous Weird series'. This is quite a book and Hollywood is quite a city—I'm so lucky to be an integral part of it all my adult life. Over the past four decades I've worked with thousands of stars in TV, movies, radio and cartoons, live events, the Grammys, the Emmys, and the Golden Globes, and so on.

There has always been a kaleidoscope of bizarre and wonderful activity in this fantasy town. We remember when Clinton Feemish of Hollywood used to be afraid of flying, so he went to a hypnotist on Sunset Boulevard—and then became afraid of eyes. Billionaire Howard W. Wealthy Jr. was so rich he wrote a check and Warren Buffett bounced (and on this date the group Sha-Na-Na lost a "Na") Edgar Allan Poe used to eat pancakes at the International House of Usher (in the Fall). A member of the Hollywood Chamber of Commerce traced his family's origin back to his famous ancestor Alexander the Okay. Blanche Gooberman, my secretary, had a swimsuit that was so tight she became immune to the Heimlich Manuever. Brother Kreebly became the first monk to establish a mission in Orson Welles's pants.

Certainly some events in this happy city are weird—but much of it has a superb magic that is only Hollywood. This new book spotlights the silly, charming, goofy and awesome events that you should know. The talented Joe Oesterle has etched this magnificent compendium in a narbling way to meet those ever-present deadlines. We salute him. Now, start your Chapsticks and thank you.

Love to you all.

—*Gary Owens*, a regular on Laugh-In and 16 other wonderful series

Our weird journey began a long, long time ago in a far-off land called New Jersey. Once a year or so we'd compile a homespun newsletter to hand out to our friends called *Weird NJ*. The pamphlet was a collection of odd news clippings, bizarre facts, little-known historical anecdotes and anomalous encounters from our home state. The newsletter also focused on the kind of very localized legends that were often whispered around a particular town, but seldom heard outside the boundaries of the community where they first originated.

After about a dozen years of documenting the bizarre we were asked to write a book about our adventures, and so *Weird N.J.: Your Travel Guide to New Jersey's Local Legend and Best Kept Secrets* was born. When the publishers of the book asked us what we wanted to do next, for us the choice was simple: "We'd like to do a book called *Weird U.S.*, in which we could document the local legends and strangest stories from all over the country," we told them.

After the release of *Weird U.S.*, we set out to document ALL the oddities this weird land of ours had to offer in a series of books, each focusing on the peculiarities of a particular state. Naturally California was high on our list of priorities. To us the Golden State had always seemed like a strange and exotic place, well left of center, both literally and figuratively, from the rest of the country. One of the first people we got in touch with to work with us on our *Weird California* book was an old friend of ours named Joe Oesterle. Joe is originally from New Jersey, but was living in Huntington Beach, California, and working as a writer, editor, and illustrator for *National Lampoon*. Over the years he had provided our Weird magazines and books with hilarious artwork based on local characters and offbeat attractions. We knew he'd be a perfect field scout to track down all of California's unique and unusual oddities.

When the opportunity arose to create a *Weird Hollywood* book we jumped at the chance. Hollywood is almost inherently weird by design. It is a make-believe land where fabricated fantasies are juxtaposed with stark reality, and where the lines blur between who a person really is versus the role that he or she is playing. And once again, there was really only one choice for us as to whom we wanted to work with on the book. In Joe we knew we had found a kindred spirit in weirdness who possessed what we refer to as the "Weird Eye."

The Weird Eye is what is needed to search out the sort of stories we were looking for. It requires one to see the world in a different way, with a renewed sense of wonder. And once you have it, there is no going back–you'll never see things the same way again.

So come with us now and let Joe take you on a tour of his favorite place in the world—with all of its cultural quirks, hidden history, colorful characters and strange sites. It is state of mind we like to call Weird Hollywood.

—*Mark Sceurman and Mark Moran*

First of all I would like to thank the two guys who made this all possible—Mark Moran and Mark Sceurman. I will be forever thankful to these fellow Jersey boys for allowing me to contribute to dozens of their "weird" projects over the years, and I truly hope I am lucky enough to be involved in many more of their unusual endeavors for years to come. Thanks so much, Marks. It's great to work for a couple of like-minded artists.

For over a year, I have had the unique privilege of traveling all around one of the most famous and unusual cities in the entire history of civilization, and document my strange findings. No small task in a municipality known for its eccentricities.

From speaking and meeting some of my childhood idols, hunting for ghosts, investigating mysteries and urban legends, recording remarkable roadside attractions, interviewing some of Hollywood's most colorful characters, and of course sitting in the same Batmobile as Adam West, this book has been a dream come true for me. So while I may never get to hold an Oscar high above my head, and thank all the little people I stepped on along the way, I'd like to believe that someday, some laundromat or Thai food place on Sunset Boulevard will be kind enough to hang my eight-by-ten glossy somewhere between Geena Davis's smiling face and Gabe Kaplan's happy Afro.

When I was a little kid in New Jersey, I remember hearing all about this hip, edgy, adult-only sketch comedy television show called *Laugh-In*. I believe I became aware of it by listening to the older kids on my school bus quoting some of the show's more popular catch phrases. They all seemed 100 percent certain that a "bippy" was a breast, and the idea of breasts being discussed in any situation was enough to fill this Catholic school first-grader with the desire to watch this program at all costs.

My parents were devotees to the show, and while they would not allow me to watch it (for fear I might develop an unnatural obsession with bippies, I suppose) I would sneak out of my bedroom and down the hall every Monday night to listen to the mellifluous tones of announcer Gary Owens as he would boom, "From beautiful downtown Burbank . . ."

Many times the opening was all I ever heard, as my parents became more and more vigilant of my hallway espionage, and they'd squire me back to my bedroom. Other nights I'd manage to deftly slip their attentions, only to have them eventually discover me asleep in the hall after the show was over. Somehow, though, I was always able to avoid their detection for at least the duration of the introduction from Mr. Owens.

Gary Owens has done it all in this town, and his knowledge of all things Hollywood is unrivaled by anyone I've ever met. He is truly the voice of Hollywood, and one of the nicest people I've ever had the pleasure to meet in the process of writing this book.

I really should ask him what the hell a bippy is.

For more *Weird Hollywood* stories, photos, illustrations, video, audio, and animations, please check me out on my Web and blog sites, www.JoeArtistWriter.com and www.JoeArtistWriter.wordpress.com. You can follow me on Twitter (JoeArtistWriter), and if you want to write me with weird stories from wherever you've been, contact me at Joe@JoeArtistWriter.com. I want to hear from each of you.

—*Joe Oesterle*

Local Legends

The beauty of legends is that sometimes they are word-for-word fact. Sometimes these stories have a basis of truth, but when told time after time, bits and pieces get added, while other portions of information are discarded. Still other tales are entirely made up.

No other town in the history of the world has as many legends as Hollywood—which is quite a feat when you consider that Rome is pretty legendary. It's been around for a few thousand years longer than Hollywood, too, and those Romans threw some pretty scandalous parties.

Still, it's a fair bet that more people are familiar with the story of the ghost of *Three Men and a Little Lady* than they are of the marriage of Roman emperor Claudius to his much younger niece. For the pop-culturally uninitiated, the ghost of a nine-year-old boy is supposedly seen in the window drapes in the *Three Men and a Baby* sequel. It is in fact a cardboard cutout of one of the movie's leading men, Ted Danson. And if you don't know who Claudius is, Google him.

The Life and Death of Michael Jackson

On the afternoon of June 25, 2009, it was reported that the undisputed King of Pop, Michael Jackson, died of cardiac arrest in his Los Angeles home. Almost immediately thousands of fans made a pilgrimage to Michael Jackson's star on the Hollywood Walk of Fame. The pink terrazzo star they gathered at, however, did not belong to the deceased enigmatic entertainer. Instead, the star belonged to a local, conventional, and alive British-born radio host of the same name.

The confusion was due to the premiere of Sacha Baron Cohen's comedy *Bruno*. Jackson's star, along with many others, were covered up for the red carpet event, leading many of Jackson's fans to assume the star of the radio talk show broadcaster of the same name belonged to the singing sensation.

Strangely enough Jackson's older sister LaToya made a humorously awkward cameo in the Cohen movie, but she was removed from the final cut of the film at the absolute last minute, out of respect for the Jackson family. As was often the case in life, Michael Jackson was making weird news even in death.

Much of the publicity the singer made in the last sixteen years of his life was not the kind he sought. Beginning in 1993, Jackson was haunted by a series of alleged child molestation incidents. It is rumored he lost fortunes of money to accusing families to buy their silence. Whether or not these allegations were true, we may never know, but Jackson's own words (he

admitted to journalist Martin Bashir, "I have slept in a bed with many children") and actions (he allegedly allowed small children to drink wine, or "Jesus Juice," as he called it) were enough to convict him in the jury of public opinion.

Not all of Jackson's headline grabs were so shocking, and it's fair to say some were utterly incorrect. Autopsy reports verified that Jackson did indeed have vitiligo, a chronic disorder that causes depigmentation in patches of skin, and that he did not intentionally bleach his skin to make himself appear more Caucasian, as was often rumored. It is said Jackson's trademark white sequined glove was originally meant to cover up a portion of vitiligo on his hand.

The same autopsy offers that Jackson was completely bald at the time of his death, his head covered in little more than peach fuzz, and that he had a hairline tattooed on his scalp. Geraldo Rivera once divulged that the reason Jackson was seen with a Band-Aid across the bridge of his nose was because the nose was prosthetic. The same autopsy validated Rivera's claim.

It has been reported that after suffering a broken nose during one rehearsal and after his infamous pyrotechnic mishap while filming a Pepsi commercial in which he suffered second and third degree burns to his face and scalp, Michael Jackson became addicted to both plastic surgery and pain killers.

Jackson's home Neverland was seen by some as a rightful indulgence for a wealthy man cheated out of his youth; to others it was viewed as a pedophile's parlor, complete with amusement park rides and animal attractions to lure in youngsters.

He was frequently seen in the company of child stars such as Emmanuel Lewis, Macaulay Culkin, and Corey Feldman, but apparently the friendships did not remain as strong as the children approached puberty. Even though each of them went on record that Jackson never made sexual advances toward them, the public still speculated about the molestation charges against him.

In even more bizarre behavior, Jackson threw a towel over the head of his own six-month infant while visiting Berlin and dangled the child off a three-story balcony. "I got caught up in the excitement of the moment. I would never intentionally endanger the lives of my children," he later said.

Quite often, though, Jackson invented his own news, such as claiming to sleep in an oxygen tank, or that he was interested in buying the bones of Joseph Merrick, also known as the Elephant Man.

Vanity Fair reported in 2000 that Jackson attended a voodoo ritual in Switzerland in which a witch doctor promised to end the lives of movie director Steven Spielberg, music mogul David Geffen, and twenty-three other people on the entertainer's "enemies list." Jackson purportedly underwent a "bloodbath" as part of the ceremony and paid a voodoo chief named Baba $150,000 to sacrifice forty-two cows for the curse. He also had a bitter feud with music exec (and ex-husband of Mariah Carey) Tommy Mottola.

In the summer of 2009, after numerous sexual allegations and some disappointing album sales, Jackson decided to perform a comeback/farewell tour at London's O arena. The tour was to be entitled, "This Is It."

Two months after Jackson's death, the L.A. County coroner found the pop star's death to be a homicide brought on by lethal doses of physician-supplied medications. Michael Jackson was fifty years old.

Walt Disney Is Frozen

Walt Disney. He was a true twentieth-century renaissance man—a visionary, artist, and businessman all rolled into one. But the question remains decades after his death in 1966: For all his foresight and imagination, did Walt Disney have himself cryogenically frozen in hopes that he might someday become reanimated?

The rumor may have been started by one of his own animators a few years after the king of the Disney empire expired. The scuttlebutt suggests that the cartooning pioneer was obsessed with the idea of immortality. Disney discovered that he was dying of lung cancer, and supposedly had his body systematically refrigerated in the hope that future scientists would find a way to resuscitate him once a cure was found so that he might live forever.

Weirder still, the yarn continues, because of his deep love of his theme park, Disney decreed that his icy remains be buried in Disneyland, deep below what is now the Pirates of the Caribbean ride. Other versions have his decapitated head entombed beneath a bust of a graveyard statue in the Haunted Mansion.

It's simple to understand why the public would believe that, like Snow White and Sleeping Beauty before him, the plucky, good-hearted hero could cheat death. If not with love's first kiss, then at least with the assistance of a low-temperature preservation process that enables the molecular-level repair and regeneration of damaged tissues and organs.

During the golden age of television, Disney made a personal connection to almost every American who grew up in front of that magic box. Always smiling, dapper, and impeccably groomed, Disney came across as the affable rich uncle millions of viewers wished for. Not surprisingly, he was known as Uncle Walt throughout

his studios. It's also not surprising that some people refused to admit to themselves that he would no longer be a weekly guest (via the airwaves) in their living rooms.

The Disney family, as well as the Walt Disney Company, are quick to point out the obvious flaw in this often told canard. According to his death certificate, Walt was cremated two days after his demise. While scientific knowledge has grown leaps and bounds in the time since Disney passed away, even the most out-of-the-box thinkers in the community do not believe that it is possible to revive the burnt remains of the legendary animator.

Of course, if you were a fabulously wealthy entrepreneur, philanthropist, and film producer with an irrational fear of death, that's exactly what you'd want people to think.

Sowden House and the Black Dahlia Connection

Part Mayan, part Art Deco in design, the Sowden House is arguably one of Frank Lloyd Wright's most famous structures. The home, completed by the architect's son in 1926, has recently been featured in movies (2004's *The Aviator*) and on television (2006's *America's Next Top Model*).

The dramatic entrance to the interior courtyard is made of decorative earth blocks stacked in geometric patterns and is evocative of ancient Mesoamerican temples. Antediluvian artifacts and artwork have been placed throughout the mansion to suggest an authentic jungle ruin smack in the middle of Hollywood.

In his 2004 book, *Black Dahlia Avenger: A Genius for Murder*, former LAPD homicide detective turned author Steve Hodel wrote that his father, Dr. George Hodel, one-time owner of the Sowden House, may have committed the infamous Black Dahlia murder inside this distinctive domicile.

The younger Hodel claimed to have stumbled upon some personal pictures of Elizabeth Short (the Black Dahlia murder victim) in a photo album belonging to his parent. Hodel uncovered his father's passion for violent and illegal sadomasochistic sex acts and later discovered that his own half-sister, Tamar, had been raped by their father. Hodel claims that it's not difficult to imagine that both the warped mind and the surgical skills required to commit such a horrific murder make his deceased father a prime suspect. Short's naked body was found in a vacant lot, clinically bisected, drained of all blood, and intentionally posed like many of the illicit photographs found in Dr. Hodel's collection.

Hodel's critics dismiss the book as the poorly researched work of either a man who was disgusted by his father's dark sexual history, or a writer looking to make a sensationalistic buck. However, the fact remains that the doctor was part of a twenty-man suspect list immediately after the crime, and, according to Hodel's 2009 book, *Most Evil*, he "fled" LA for Manila later that same year.

Dark mysteries aside, the Sowden House is still a hot property for Los Angeles–area renters. As of 2008, the Sowden House can be rented out at $3,900 per night (three-night minimum required). That's just under $12,000 for those of you not sure how you were going to spend your next three-day weekend.

The Address of the Beast

Love or hate his politics, most Americans would agree that former Hollywood star Ronald Reagan seemed like a pretty nice guy. Thanks in part to his theatrical training, he certainly knew how to speak with eloquence and play to the camera—plus, the guy's hair was always perfectly coiffed.

Neither Reagan nor any other of his presidential colleagues has been nominated for sainthood, but there is a small percentage of people who hold that Reagan was evil incarnate, the dark prince of lies, Mephistopheles himself. The proof, they whisper, is right in front of you if you care to examine the facts.

His very name is said to be a sign of the archfiend's arrival. Ronald Wilson Reagan. Six letters in his first name, six in his middle name, and six in his surname. For the uninitiated, that translates as the number of the beast: 666. According to Revelation 13:18: "Here is wisdom. Let him that hath understanding count the number of the beast: for it is the number of a man; and his number is six hundred threescore and six."

These advocates of the absurd gladly point out another piece of evidence. Upon retiring from the White House, Reagan and his wife, Nancy, moved to an exclusive Bel-Air address: 668 St. Cloud Road. But wait, you say, that's two numbers off.

Ah, they agree, but that's before Nancy changed the address for fear the demon and his hell-bride would be discovered. (Which is actually true—not the hell-bride part, the number switch.)

Need more proof, Doubting Thomas? Reagan survived an assassination attempt, and a devil would survive that too. And Nancy Reagan wore a lot of red dresses. Red is Satan's favorite color.

Phyllis Diller—Naked!

Phyllis Diller has done it all. She has worked with everyone from Bob Hope to Scooby-Doo, and has inspired generations of women to venture into the male-dominated world of stand-up comedy. Diller may be getting on in years, but while she confesses that her hearing isn't what it used to be, her wit is as sharp as ever, and she wants to set some things straight for *Weird Hollywood* readers.

"First of all, I invented bed-head," the feisty old dame proudly proclaims. "You see it everywhere nowadays, but I started that. They have gels for it now, I just rolled out of bed and went on stage."

Second, she is not Susan Lucci's mother. The seasoned funny lady has no idea how her name was ever maternally linked to Daytime's Leading Lady. "I am not, and have never been, Susan Lucci's mother," Diller cracked, then conceded, "Nothing is going to stop that rumor. I suppose the reason it's so persistent is because it's so, so weird."

We thanked Diller for tying in the "weird" theme of the book so early in the conversation, and then we asked her if she'd heard the one about how a torrid affair between her and Stan Laurel produced a love child who went on to become Clint Eastwood. The ninety-one-year-old comic cackled her famous cackle for a good seven seconds. "Oh, my God! I have never met Stan Laurel, let alone did anything else with him. Ha!" She continued, "And I never met Clint Eastwood either, so it would have been extremely difficult to mother him. I would be proud to be Clint Eastwood's mother, though."

Diller informed us that she was thirty-seven years old and the mother of five children before she ever stepped foot on the comedy stage.

We'd heard that *Playboy* published naked photos of "Mama" Cass Elliot, the plus-sized lead singer of the sixties folk-rock quartet the Mamas and the Papas, and there was a rumor that Phyllis Diller had also posed for the men's magazine in her birthday suit.

The veteran humorist never missed a beat. "Yes, sometime in the sixties, they did a centerfold with Mama Cass, and I think they were looking to do another funny foldout with somebody terribly skinny this time. They brought me down there and found out I had a normal figure, and sort of an ugly face—that was before my face-lift. My body was good, but it wasn't what they wanted. They thought my body would be hideous, I guess, but for some reason they called me back. They did two shoots but never ran any of the pictures. I did ask them for one of the photos. Remember those old-fashioned baby pictures, with the baby on the rug? Well it's just me naked on the rug."

It was hard for us here at *Weird Hollywood* to say goodbye to Diller. We usually interview guys who trim their hedges into the shape of giant poodles, or people who swear the spirit of silent screen stars give them dating advice. Nothing against them, but this woman is a bona fide Hollywood legend.

Maybe the weirdest thing about this story was that we actually got the great Phyllis Diller to speak to us.

Poise and Repose

For a time, two nude figures stood in separate gazebos, divided only by a beautifully manicured garden of roses. One stood upright and calmly dignified, arms bent slightly at the elbows, palms turned upward. She was named Repose.

The male, just as alluring, is said to have possessed a self-confidence with arms outstretched, as if yearning quietly for the loving embrace of his feminine companion. He was known as Poise.

However, romance, it seems, was never meant for this pair of star-crossed lovers. In 1946, sculptor Caroline A. Lloyd rendered this scene of love unattainable, yet she never meant for this relationship to be so utterly doomed.

Records are hazy, but sometime in the late 1970s or early 1980s, Poise was spirited away, never to be seen again. But not all of him, actually—just everything above the ankles.

It was a common practice for thieves to remove bronze plaques and lamps from nearby museums and churches. These items were often melted down and sold. But the weight of the statue must have been prohibitive, let alone the time-consuming to saw through each leg. Regardless of the exertion, Poise was stolen.

The plan must have been to take the pair. Repose still carries the scar of a hacksaw blade just above her right ankle.

Today Repose is left alone to stare at the pedestal her Poise once stood upon, longing for tender admiration from a partner who is no longer there and, sadly, is never to return.

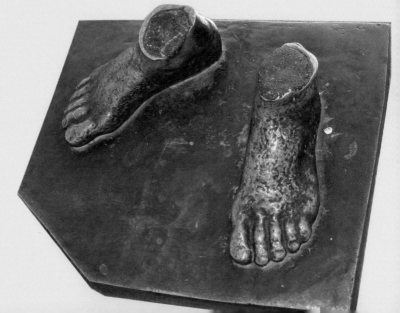

Loretta Young's Swear Jar

Loretta Young's "swear jar" was known throughout the industry. Any time a naughty word reached the virginal ears of the deeply religious actress, Young would rattle her famous swear jar, and the offending party would feel obliged to pony up the five-cent fine, for fear of chastisement from the self-righteous leading lady.

Hollywood bad boy Robert Mitchum could not have been any more the opposite of the straitlaced Young. Straight-talking Mitchum was no stranger to colorful language—or unlawful behavior for that matter. The sleepy-eyed leading man had been known to participate in the occasional alcohol-fueled fistfight, and had just served forty-three days in prison for possession of marijuana when he was paired up with Young for 1948's *Rachel and a Stranger*.

© John Springer Collection/CORBIS

After watching his co-star castigate one of the set's technicians, the unconventional actor approached his castmate. Mitchum whipped out his wallet, and stuffed a bill into Young's jar. Staring sweetly into her eyes, the Hollywood tough guy shot, "Here's a twenty, Loretta. This ought to cover me for the rest of the picture."

It must be addressed that despite all her openly pious convictions, Young had a child out of wedlock with Clark Gable in 1935. Young left the country for ten weeks, and, upon returning, announced to the world she had adopted a baby girl, Judy Lewis. Lewis was in her early twenties by the time she found out Gable was her biological father. ("That would explain my enormous ears," Lewis later recounted.) A number of years later, Lewis confronted her mother, and Young reportedly admitted it was true, and immediately threw up.

Shenanigans, Three Stooges Style

Fearing that decades of eye pokes, hair pullings, and heads clonked together like cymbals were all in vain, Moe Howard, Larry Fine, and Curly Joe DeRita hatched a plan in 1964 that read like a classic Three Stooges short.

The comedy trio had been privately frustrated. Despite an impressive array of work and millions of fans worldwide, the Stooges' slapstick schtick was thought to be too lowbrow to garner a star on Hollywood's celebrated Walk of Fame. A plan—no, a hair-brained scheme—was hatched. At midnight, Moe, Larry, and Curly Joe, dressed in overalls, planned to cordon off the intersection of Hollywood and Vine. There they would paint a huge golden star in the middle of the famous crossroads—so large that four of the five points of the symbol would touch each street corner. Inside the star they would all sign their individual names under the heading "The Three Stooges."

Apparently it was Moe who backed out of the plan at the last minute, concerned that he and his wisenheimer cronies might get pinched by the coppers. Years later it's easy to see that Moe's apprehension was misplaced. No numbskulls in the hoosegow would be crazy enough to mess with the Stooges' ringleader if they'd ever seen him twist a nose 360 degrees with a plumber's wrench.

Knickerbocker Hotel Ghosts

It's a building with a rich and storied past.

In the glamour days of Hollywood, the Knickerbocker Hotel was the place to see and be seen. Many celebs resided for a time at the once swanky tower.

It was here that Marilyn Monroe and Joe DiMaggio consummated their wedding vows. There was no other place Rudolph Valentino preferred to dance the night away, and Elvis Presley both worked and played in the ritzy halls of this superstructure. The King of Rock and Roll even posed for a photo shoot in support of his hit record "Heartbreak Hotel"—and for all its glory, this hotel has witnessed its share of heartbreak.

The Knickerbocker was the scene of some of Tinseltown's saddest moments. Police dragged a half-dressed Frances Farmer from her hotel bathroom through the lobby, humiliating the already mentally unstable actress beyond repair. An all but forgotten D. W. Griffith, it has been said, could be found getting stewed on a nightly basis at the bar, bending the ear of any unfortunate who happened to have the misfortune of resting his rump on a neighboring stool.

Then there's the tragic tale of Irene Gibbons. A former actress turned costume designer, Gibbons, inconsolable over the passing of her one true love, Gary Cooper, checked in to the hotel under an assumed name and checked out of life by jumping from a tenth-story window.

If it weren't for death, of course, we wouldn't have ghost sightings, and the Knickerbocker has had plenty of those over the years. Monroe and Valentino are probably the most active spirits in this town today, and one of their favorite haunts, living or dead, has been the Knickerbocker.

Harry Houdini enjoyed the comforts this once great accommodation had to offer during his mortal existence, so it stood to reason that the brilliant magician would attempt to make a return visit in the afterlife. Harry and his wife, Bess, made a pact before Harry died. Bess was to conduct a séance on each anniversary of Harry's death (Halloween 1928), and if Harry were able to return to this plane, Bess would know by a special phrase. The tenth of ten of these services was conducted on the rooftop of the Knickerbocker, and while it was reported that there was a mighty thunderclap, the heavens opened, and rain poured above and only above the Knickerbocker immediately following the ritual, Bess considered the event to be a disappointment. Harry never shared their secret code.

Today, after years of neglect, the Knickerbocker is an apartment building for the elderly. Sara, the building manager, is a woman with a gravelly voice and no time for ghosts. When called for a comment, it was apparent she'd been down this road a number of times before. Her tone revealed that she was no longer amused with the constant questions about celebrity apparitions. Sara said plainly, "Take my word for it—I've been here for fourteen years. There's no ghosts here. It's all BS." That's exactly the kind of thing you'd expect to hear from a woman who was obviously possessed by the spirit of a surly phantasm who has no desire to share her ethereal secrets with a mere "fleshy" like myself.

The Ghost in the Garret

In 1912, twenty-seven-year-old Milwaukee housewife Walburga "Dolly" Oesterreich couldn't get her sewing machine to work. She complained to her husband, Fred, who owned the Oesterreich Apron Company, and asked him to send over a repairman. Seventeen-year-old Otto Sanhuber showed up, and Dolly took an immediate shine to him.

After ten years of matrimony, Fred and Dolly's marriage had lost whatever passion it once had. A daily pattern emerged: Fred would come home from a grueling day, hit the bottle, and then hit the hay. Full of carnal desires, Dolly Oesterreich lay in wait for her appointment with the juvenile repairman.

Over time, Dolly began to worry that the neighbors would wonder why Otto's truck was always parked in front of their house. Even in 1912, sewing machine repair was not a month-long ordeal. Dolly cooked up a plan for Otto to secretly live in the Oesterreichs' attic. During the day, while Fred was toiling away at work, Dolly would unlock the attic door, and Otto would clean the home and fulfill Dolly's other needs. At night, before Fred returned home, Otto would return to his confined living quarters, quietly writing romance adventures by candlelight until he fell asleep.

One day five years later, Fred returned home unannounced and caught Otto raiding his refrigerator. Fred gave chase, but Otto escaped. Using Fred's "discovery" as an excuse to move away, in 1918 the couple relocated to Los Angeles. Dolly managed to find a home with an attic, overlooking Sunset Boulevard. Otto snuck his belongings in when the coast was clear.

The living arrangement went swimmingly, until one night, after an evening out, Dolly and Fred returned home in the middle of a loud and heated argument. As tempers flared, the pale, slender Otto crashed from his secret dwelling place, a .25 caliber pistol in each hand. Fred, outraged, went for the guns, but in the struggle was shot dead.

Quickly staging a burglary, Otto removed Fred's expensive watch, locked Dolly in the closet, then scurried back to his covert hideaway. Fred's murder went unsolved.

Although Fred was now out of the picture, Otto continued to live in secrecy in the attic, serving Dolly during the day. Meanwhile, Dolly enjoyed a new pair of suitors: her estate attorney, Henry Shapiro, and local businessman Roy Klumb. At Dolly's request, Klumb ditched one of the guns in the La Brea Tar Pits. A neighbor buried the other gun in his backyard.

Juggling multiple lovers eventually got the best of Dolly. Klumb and the neighbor informed the police about the guns, and Dolly was arrested. But both guns were so rusted, it was impossible to tell if they had in fact been the weapons that had killed Fred Oesterreich. Dolly's court case was thrown out.

Otto left the house and Shapiro moved in. When Shapiro moved out in 1930, seven years later, he blew the whistle. Dolly and Otto's decade-long affair became front-page news. Both were arrested, Dolly charged with conspiracy and Otto with murder.

Found guilty of manslaughter, Otto, forty-three, was released because the statute of limitations had run out. Represented by Jerry Geisler, who eventually became a famous defense attorney, Dolly was acquitted.

Dolly remained in LA until her death in 1961; but ironically, during her last years, she lived in a small room over a garage in one of Los Angeles's seedier neighborhoods.

The Curse of *The Conqueror*

Imagine Jerry Seinfeld in the title role of Spike Lee's *Malcolm X*, then visualize, if you will, Nicole Richie portraying Dr. Betty Shabazz. Now you have an idea of the poor casting choices in the 1956 epic flop *The Conqueror.*

The film is part combat movie and part love story between twelfth-century Mongolian warlord Ghengis Khan, played by John Wayne, and his less-than-willing bride-to-be, Bortai, portrayed by the lovely, yet obviously Caucasian, Susan Hayward. The last film ever produced by RKO Pictures, *The Conqueror* was another in a long losing streak of big-budget films that tanked for the Howard Hughes–owned studio. It is often honored along with Ed Wood's *Plan 9 from Outer Space* and the George Lucas–produced *Howard the Duck* as one of the worst films of all time.

In an effort to save the studio large travel expenses, the decision was reached to film in Snow Canyon, Utah. Aesthetically, Utah is not exactly the mystic Orient, but it is physically closer to Hollywood. It is even closer still to Yucca Flats, Nevada, the home of close to a dozen military atomic bomb tests in the early to mid-fifties. About one hundred miles upwind of the quaint Utah town, which is known for its red and white Navajo sandstone and its extinct lava flows, Yucca Flats was the base of operations for many of the government-approved atomic blasts that were prevalent at the time. The gigantic mushroom clouds that formed after each explosion drifted across to Utah, bringing with them enough radioactive dust to contaminate an abundance of animal life and vegetation between Nevada and Utah.

The cast and crew worked, slept, and ate in this infected location for more than three months, and, to make matters worse, RKO had sixty tons of the poisonous soil shipped back to Hollywood for retakes and studio lot shots. The staff that worked on *The Conqueror* had little knowledge of the risk that they had taken (although a picture of John Wayne holding a Geiger counter during the filming is said to exist). According to the sobering numbers, however, the members of that production were placed in a severely toxic setting.

In 1980 *People* magazine reported that of the 220 persons who worked on the picture in 1955, 91 had contracted cancer. That's 41 percent of all the people who worked on the set, and it does not take into consideration guests and family members who visited. Of the 91 victims, 46 had died from the malady. Among the deaths were both headlining stars, Wayne and Hayward, along with Agnes Moorehead and director Dick Powell. Costar Pedro Armendariz committed suicide after being diagnosed with the disease.

Sadly, the death toll didn't stop there. Thousands of residents of nearby St. George, Utah, also died of the deadly disease, but they rarely get mentioned. That sad detail is probably because none of the residents of St. George ever became Hollywood icons.

The Culver Hotel

Built in 1924 and billed as a six-story skyscraper, the wedge-shaped Culver Hotel is one of the more legendary buildings in all of Los Angeles County. Rumors of high-stakes poker games, secret underground Prohibition-era tunnels, famous ghosts, and drunken Munchkins have all added to the lore of this truly historical structure.

In the early days of film, the building had been *the* place to stay. During its heyday, the lodging boasted Clark Gable, Greta Garbo, Buster Keaton, and Ronald Reagan among its part-time residents. However, real estate speculation caused the hotel to be left to deteriorate in the fifties, and it became a sad eyesore for the next few decades.

General manager Douglas Newton is proud to say that the Culver has been restored to its former majesty, and the building does have the feel of a Hollywood long since gone. This sense of a more glamorous era may have attracted at least one person who had a connection to its glory days: its first owner, the late Harry Culver.

Newton explains his strange experience with the first man to occupy his current workstation. "In Harry's [second floor] office, when I first took over the hotel, there was a window that kept opening up. I'd close it, and, mind you, I'd lock the door so no one else can get in, but every morning when I'd arrive, the window would be wide open. So then, finally, this one day I had new locks put on, and I put a heavy chair in front of the windows. I figure whatever it is won't come in again through these French windows. And that morning, the window's open, and the chair's on the floor."

Harry Culver hasn't been the building's only proprietor. Rumor has it that the title has also belonged to a jungle king, a little tramp, and the most macho cowboy of all time. City historian Julie Lugo Cerra admits that the official paperwork is hard to find, but she believes that Johnny Weissmuller was at least a partial owner at one time, as was Charlie Chaplin. Rumor has it that Chaplin lost the deed to the hotel in a poker game to John Wayne. The hotel bar, Duke's Hideaway, was named in the rugged actor's honor.

While the hotel is famous for housing some larger-than-life characters, it is probably best known for providing room and board to many of film history's smallest stars. In 1938 the Culver Hotel was home to the Munchkins during the filming of *The Wizard of Oz*. The event even inspired the 1981 Chevy Chase comedy *Under the Rainbow*. Tales have come and gone over the years, but according to Lugo Cerra, a couple stories have held up. Here's one.

First, the hotel was not entirely prepared to house 124 little people, so many of the tiny actors had to sleep sideways, three to a bed. But they did not complain about the accommodations: "They considered themselves lucky to have a job," says Lugo Cerra.

The building is as elegant today as it was when Garbo hung a DO NOT DISTURB sign on her stylish doorknob. The Culver Hotel is located at 9400 Culver Boulevard, in Culver City.

Charlie Chaplin Studios

The sprawling English-style village on the corner of La Brea and Sunset is one of Hollywood's most important and treasured landmarks. Although the property is no longer surrounded by acres of orange groves, it has diminished in size since its initial construction, and there is a huge statue of an amiable hobo frog on the roof, it is still likely that the charming cottage community and vast entertainment empire would still be recognizable to its original owner, Charlie Chaplin.

Chaplin constructed the studio on five acres of land in 1917, and he filmed many of his silent movie classics within these faux colonial walls, including *The Gold Rush*, *City Lights*, and *Modern Times*. Chaplin also erected a home on the premises and imprinted his famous "duck walk" footprints in the cement outside Sound Stage 3 (possibly inspiring the Grauman's Chinese Theater footprints years later). There are even occasional sightings of Chaplin's ghost.

Politically left of center, Chaplin had long been suspected by FBI director J. Edgar Hoover of being a Communist. While Chaplin was flying back to England in 1952 for the premiere of what proved to be his last American film (*Limelight*), Hoover ordered the Immigration and Naturalization Service to refuse re-entry to the comic icon.

Exhausted from having been involved in a number of court cases and political controversies during the forties and early fifties, Chaplin opted not to challenge Hoover, gave up his US residence, and moved to Switzerland. He sold the studio in 1957, and it was sold again two years later to comedian Red Skelton, who removed the famous duck walk cement footprints and placed the impressions in his home in Palm Springs.

The studio was sold again in 1961, this time to CBS studios. Raymond Burr, star of the network's hit *Perry Mason*, lived on the lot for a number of years.

Changing hands once more in 1966, the studio was purchased by Herb Alpert and Jerry Moss, the "A" and "M" of A&M Records. Soon Quincy Jones, the Carpenters, the Sex Pistols, and the Police were working at the house Charlie built.

For years, the recording studios would close between 2:30 A.M. and 3:00 A.M. because of relentless hissing and feedback. Some say this was the scheduled time for the ghost of Karen Carpenter to lay down her latest tracks.

In 1985, the one-time-only supergroup USA for Africa left their egos at the door and recorded the popular single "We Are the World" there. The band members, which included Bruce Springsteen, Ray Charles, Bob Dylan, Stevie Wonder, Michael Jackson, Waylon Jennings, Billy Joel, Paul Simon, and others, donated their profits to the relief efforts of the Ethiopian famine victims.

The Henson family bought the building in 1999, and the Jim Henson Company lot has set up shop there since. In a fitting homage to the property's first landlord, as well as to creative visionary Jim Henson, the Jim Henson Company erected a twelve-foot-tall statue of Kermit the Frog, decked out in Chaplin's famous Little Tramp costume. The sculpture stands proudly on top of the building today and at night is spotlit for a very dramatic effect.

Caioti Restaurant: A Pizzaria That Really Delivers!

When chef-owner Ed LaDou opened Caioti (pronounced *kai-oh-tee*) restaurant in 1986, he had no idea that his place would become a hotspot for overdue mothers. LaDou learned his craft at world-class eateries like Spago, where he made the now ubiquitous "California pizza," using ingredients like roasted eggplant and barbecued chicken, but it was one of his salads that was destined to put Caioti on the map. Originally located in North Hollywood in Laurel Canyon, the restaurant moved to Studio City in the late 1990s.

But what do buns in the oven have to do with an upscale Italian bistro tucked between equally chi-chi boutiques on this quiet residential street?

Sometime in 1993 a pregnant woman who was well past her due date stopped by

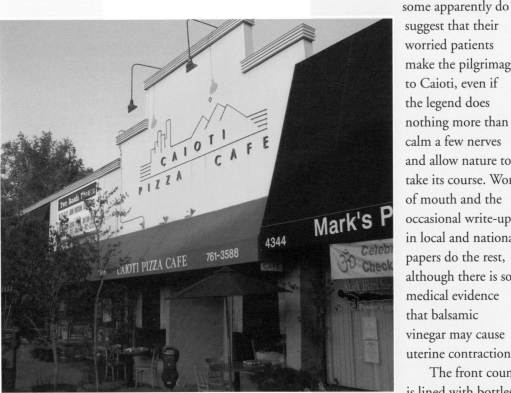

and ordered the romaine and watercress salad. The next day, she went into labor. She told a friend, and the same thing happened. A local legend (and apparently quite a few babies) were born. "We get pregnant women in here every day, sometimes twenty or more," says one of the waitresses.

Over just half an hour on a recent weekday afternoon, five women waddled in with their friends to give the salad a whirl. "We don't even have to ask what they want. We just bring it out," she added.

Although he was at first a little miffed that his humble salad was the thing that kept butts in the seats, LaDou eventually embraced his dubious celebrity. Although doctors are reluctant to prescribe the balsamic vinaigrette, some apparently do suggest that their worried patients make the pilgrimage to Caioti, even if the legend does nothing more than calm a few nerves and allow nature to take its course. Word of mouth and the occasional write-up in local and national papers do the rest, although there is some medical evidence that balsamic vinegar may cause uterine contractions.

The front counter is lined with bottles of the famous vinaigrette ready for takeout, and the staff even provides a notebook for customers to leave testimonials, which run the gamut from cautiously hopeful to effusively joyful.

Do Ed a favor when you go, and at least order a pizza. They are really very good.

Bronson Caves

If you've seen the 1955 sub-basement-budget sci-fi laffer *Robot Monster*, or even watched any of the old 1960s *Batman* TV shows, you've seen the Bronson Caves. Some location scout decided the place was great (and very convenient) for filmed exteriors, and the area began a legacy in 1919 as a filming site for a forgotten silent Western called *Lightning Bryce*. The Batmobile screamed out of the largest existing tunnel every time the commissioner rang up Bruce Wayne, and exteriors for two of the episodes of the original *Star Trek* series were filmed in this desolate gravel bowl ringed with sagebrush.

Hollywood has made the site more famous than it ever should have been. The three-hundred-foot-deep scar wouldn't be here but for the Los Angeles Stone Company, who bought the hillside in 1903 and proceeded to dig, blast, and crush the rock for the paving material used on Sunset Boulevard, Highland Avenue, Wilshire Boulevard, and other less-storied thoroughfares. Much of the Bronson bowl also

made it into track beds for the Red Car trolleys, which, as we all know, were shut down by a conspiracy of oil and automobile companies, as recounted in the animated masterpiece *Who Framed Roger Rabbit?*

The "caves" are actually tunnels blasted into the granite hill that were left vacant when the quarry was abandoned in the late 1920s. Rains leave the dark passages wet with mud puddles and dripping ceilings. The place is currently favored by dog walkers, death rockers, and Trekkies making the obligatory pilgrimage. We recently tried a shortcut straight up the hill to reach another

trail and became hopelessly trapped on a crumbling outcropping while a middle-aged woman and her golden retriever watched from two hundred feet below. A pair of screeching crows landed on a ledge nearby and commenced telling jokes to each other.

I threw a rocks at them. Forty-five minutes later, at the bottom of the rockslide with my shoes full of dirt and pebbles, Dog Woman informed me that testosterone-addled climbers are airlifted off the cliffs a few times a year.

The last film costarring the Bronson Caves was the testosterone-addled flick *The Scorpion King*, starring The Rock (aka Dwayne Johnson).

The caves are accessed by a short walk from the parking lot at the end of Canyon Drive in Hollywood. —*Greg Bishop*

The "Lost" Batman Script

ROBIN: *(Pounding his gloved fist into the other, very excited)* Holy standing-at-the-entryway-of-television-and-movie-history, Batman! It's the Bronson Caves!

BATMAN: *(Speaking as if he's drawing out each and every syllable, establishing overly dramatic pauses where none seem to be needed, ensuring the maximum amount of air time possible.)* Very perceptive, old chum. Very perceptive indeed.

ROBIN: *(Furiously typing away on the Bat Computer laptop)* Holy Information Highway! According to these clues I found on Bat-Google, it seems the Bronson Caves have been an integral backdrop to some of the most beloved movies and TV shows of all time!

BATMAN: *(Pacing back and forth, his index finger studiously tapping his chin)* So it would seem, Boy Wonder. So it would seem.

ROBIN: Holy filmography, Batman! Did you realize these caves have been featured in such movies as *The Scorpion King, Star Trek VI: The Undiscovered Country*, and the original *Robin Hood*, starring Douglas Fairbanks?

BATMAN: *(Spinning on his heels)* Good work, Robin. What about the small screen?

ROBIN: Holy weekly episodics, Batman! The Bronson Caves have been used as atmospheric scenery in *The Lone Ranger, Fantasy Island, Little House on the Prairie*, and some campy show in the sixties starring Adam West and Burt Ward.

BATMAN: And what of the history of this cave? When was it discovered? How deep is the actual cavity? How accessible is this hollow mountain opening to the public? And, most importantly, who is this Bronson fellow?

ROBIN: Holy interrogations, Batman! That's a load of questions, but here's the info. The caves are definitely man-made. They were probably created specifically for the entertainment industry, but some speculate they were used in the early 1900s, when the surrounding area was a rock quarry.

The actual distance of the Bronson Caves itself isn't that long. Less than one hundred feet, that's for sure. The tunnel actually splits off into two exits. One exit is roughly seven feet tall (like the entrance), and the other is closer to four feet high.

You can't drive up to this location, because there's a gate blocking the road that leads here, but parking is not much of an issue. It's in Griffith Park, off of Bronson Avenue. It's a bit of a hike from the main road, but nothing the Penguin couldn't handle.

Fetuses Found at Hyperion Waste Treatment Plant

A lot of strange things have been found in urban sewage effluvia. New York City has its alligator scares, which crop up every few years; the stories can be traced to a newspaper report from the 1930s. But things like stuffed toys, bicycles, and the ubiquitous rats turn up with almost boring regularity in sewer lines all over the world.

Los Angeles's Hyperion Treatment Plant (as it is officially known) has seen all this and more. The prevailing local legend about the place says that workers find more than three hundred human fetuses each month in the pipes. Of course, management denies this, and it is only partially true, but we'll get into that later. From the colorful variety of junk flushed down millions of toilets and sinks in this great megalopolis, it would seem that no find should be a surprise by now.

In the late nineteenth century, the city's first sewage "treatment" system consisted of a few hollowed-out redwood trees strung together to pipe the flow straight into the breakers at Santa Monica. Methods gradually improved, and when California's population exploded in the 1950s, the plant was expanded and retooled to meet demand.

Today, all over the city, storm drains bear a message stenciled onto the curb by the LA Department of Public Works: WARNING: DRAINS TO OCEAN. The first heavy rain of the season washes months of contamination into the sea. Warning signs go up, the water turns brown, and locals don't even bother to make the trip to the beach. The Hyperion facility actually treats a small amount of gutter runoff during dry months, but shuts off the flow when it starts to rain. The resulting influx would tax the system like an overflowing septic tank, sending untreated sewage into Santa Monica Bay. The plant typically processes about 350 million gallons of disgusting, soupy gray water per day from a nexus of 6,500 miles of sewer line, most of it from homes and apartments. The treated water is not fit to drink, but meets EPA standards for release, and it is piped five miles offshore and released 190 feet below the surface.

Hyperion is the second largest complex of its kind in the United States (the biggest is in Chicago), and over the years it has seen some pretty scary, uh, crap caught in the main intake gates. In what has to be the most disturbing step in the process, raw sewage flows through bar screens to prevent larger objects from clogging up the works down the line. A sort of mechanical rake drops fifteen feet below the floor into the murky depths to comb objects from the steel bars before dumping a congealed mass of partially decomposed toilet paper, empty pharmaceutical blister packs, and other unidentifiable gunk into a hopper. Also screened out is a heaping helping of feminine hygiene products, condoms, and the occasional rubber glove. A large bank of these contraptions sits at the northern end of Hyperion, housed in a gigantic room behind closed doors. Imagine the smell when the toilet backs up, and multiply it by a thousand.

Unflappable tour guide Nancy Carr enjoys taking visitors to this part of the plant first. Asked about the fetus rumor, she says, "Well, I know that one was found about four years ago. After I heard that, I told the guy who found it that I didn't want to hear any more." She doesn't know where the three-hundred-a-month fetus story came from. What else has turned up, apart from the obvious? "We've had bowling balls, two-by-fours, hypodermic needles, and a few body parts. When that happens, by law we have to call the police, so that they can investigate," says Carr. She adds that she usually doesn't ask for the juicy details.

Although there is an obvious public fascination with what turns up in the sewers, the day-to-day operations of the Hyperion facility are nearly as interesting. The sterile solid waste, politely referred to as biosolids, left over from various bacteriological purification processes, is used to fertilize a 4,600-acre farm in Kern County (incidentally called Green Acres) that was purchased by the city in 2000. "LA bought the farm. I love saying that," jokes Carr. The land is used to grow barley, alfalfa, corn, and other crops, but calm down—the product is fed only to livestock. In 1972, parts of the vast underground labyrinth that lies below the Hyperion Plant were used for location filming on Soylent Green, which predicted a dystopian future in which dead people are recycled into food.

To complete our list of wacky things flushed down the toilets of Southern California, Paul Young notes in his 2002 book L.A. Exposed that "staff members admit that they've found other . . . curious items, including bags of money, a finger, a mattress, various sex toys, a full set of kitchen cabinets, a complete motorcycle, a five-foot grease ball, and a fully intact, adult male horse."

For tours of the Hyperion Plant, contact Public Relations at 310-648-5363. —*Greg Bishop*

Parkyakarkus: A Show Legendary Business Death

Parkyakarkus was the stage name used by comic entertainer Harry Einstein, whose sons Robert and Albert are better known as Super Dave Osborne and Albert Brooks. And yes, Albert Brooks's real name is Albert Einstein.

Einstein, known to friends and family as Parky, had been diagnosed at an early age with a disease that fused his spinal cord to his vertebrae. He created the character Parkyakarkus, a play on the phrase "park your carcass," pronounced in faux broken English. His humorous malapropisms caught the ears of comic actor-singer Eddie Cantor, who persuaded the funnyman to move to Hollywood and costar on Cantor's radio show.

The move led to acting, writing, and performing from 1936 to 1945. Concerned for his health, Einstein had all but given up performing when he was asked to speak in 1958 to roast Lucille Ball and Desi Arnaz.

Einstein's performance consisted of a number of nods to Desi Arnaz's reputation as a ladies' man. He also made light of the fact that Lucille Ball was allowed at a roast at all, since the Friars Club prided itself on its chauvinistic fraternal roots. Einstein finished his set to wild applause.

As Einstein took his seat, he leaned against Milton Berle's shoulder and slumped forward with his head on the table. An alarmed Berle shouted, "Is there a doctor in the house?"—only fueling the laughter of the crowd, which mistakenly assumed this was still part of Einstein's shtick. Harry "Parkyakarkus" Einstein died after giving perhaps the greatest performance of his life.

Albert Brooks was eleven when his father passed away. "What always impressed me was that he finished. He didn't die in the middle of a line. That's what makes you believe in something."

My Dinner with Angelyne

There are people who become icons because their body of work is so identifiable with their persona. There are Hollywood icons whose horrific actions and behavior are burned into our collective psyche. And then there is a Hollywood icon whose legend involves posing seductively and showing off ample cleavage in skin-tight pink Saran Wrap mini-dresses (or less) on forty-eight-foot billboards on Sunset Strip. That would be Angelyne.

When I first got the call from my editors asking if I'd be interested in writing this book, all I could think of was how I'd need to interview Angelyne. To do a book like this and not mention her would have been a travesty of the highest order.

We agreed to meet at one of Angelyne's favorite restaurants, Casa Escobar in Malibu Beach. She was a vision in pink, a happy pattern of smiley faces adorning her very low-cut pink micro-mini dress. Pink

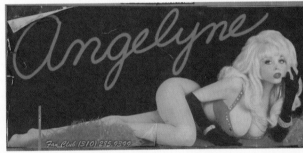

feathery earrings dangled from her lobes, and she was using some other pink feathery thing as a hair ornament. She wore pink platform stripper shoes, and on top of each rested a pink faux flower. Her well-manicured fingernails and her big pouty lips matched the rest of her ensemble. She ordered the cheese enchilada.

"My parents died when I was five," she told me. "I was in and out of adoption homes, passed from one to another." She said she often played with Barbie dolls and dreamed of living in a Barbie Dream House and having "tons of boyfriends."

The curvaceous kitten had been hanging around the Whisky, the Roxy, and the Palladium in the late seventies and early eighties. "One day I was hanging out backstage with my boyfriend at the time, who was a guitarist. The band was posing for pictures, and one of the photographers pointed to me and asked, 'Is she in the band?' Before I could answer no, my boyfriend pipes up and says, 'Yes!' and pulls me into the pictures." Shortly after, Angelyne started singing with the band and taking guitar lessons.

Being the new face of the group, Angelyne's sexy image was used to market the band. This was the start of Angelyne's billboard revolution—but giant billboards cost money, and many giant billboards cost even more money.

Angelyne openly admits she's more than comfortable using her feminine wiles to get the president of a printing company to do her bidding. It wasn't long before image-conscious Los Angeles noticed her. In seemingly no time at all, Angelyne's oversized portraits were paying dividends. Suddenly she was appearing in eighties music videos with Mötley Crüe and Sheena Easton. Legendary musician Neil Young even paid homage by including her one-hundred-foot-tall mural in his video for "This Note's for You."

In the decades that have passed since the enterprising glamour gal first peeked over her Wayfarers and glanced down on Los Angeles motorists, she has appeared in thousands of television shows and magazines worldwide. She has recorded four albums and tells me still receives offers to star in feature films. Angelyne spends what little downtime she has painting.

After our meal, she presented me with an extra large Angelyne Fan Club T-shirt. We hugged goodbye, wished each other well, and down the Pacific Coast Highway sped one of Hollywood's most enigmatic figures.

Count Smokula

His IMDB page boasts a starring role in the Stan Lee television brainchild *Who Wants to Be a Superhero*, a couple of appearances on *The Tom Green Show*, and a writing credit on the soundtrack to the movie *Poultrygeist: Night of the Chicken*. He's a member of the Rockabilly Hall of Fame, and he's been described as the greatest undead burlesque performer alive today.

We walked into the Taste of Thai restaurant, sat down at a booth, and received more than a couple double-takes from patrons and employees alike—no easy feat considering its proximity to "anything goes" Venice Beach. Count Smokula ordered the pad Thai and we got on with the interview.

WEIRD HOLLYWOOD: You must miss Smokesylvania. What did you do over there?

COUNT SMOKULA: Ehhhh, what did I do? I rocked and rolled. I played da Shlabozz, vhich vere da bean-eating festivals. Vee played skveezebox [accordion] all da time. It vas great times.

WH: Well if everything was so great, why did you leave?

CS: I come to the Hollyvood of the California to become a big cable access TV star.

WH: What's a typical day for Count Smokula?

CS: Vell, I like to get up, and compose zum music with my skveezebox. It's qvite a vorkout—the skveezebox—so by the time I'm done, I'm strong like a bull, and then I'm hungry like an ox, and den I eat maybe a moose."

WH: What about drinking blood. Is that something you enjoy?

CS: Enjoy? Who could enjoy? I dabbled, I von't lie, I dabbled, but to enjoy, no, not so much. Plus my doctor told me tree hundred years ago, da cholesterol vas getting high, so now I do cranberry juice, I do grape juice. It's sveeter.

WH: We hear vampires sleep in coffins that contain native soil from their place of birth. Do you sleep this way?

CS: I don't do much coffin' vhen I sleep, it's mostly snorin', you zee, so no. No coffin. And as for da native soil, I can't say I sleep in my native soil, but dere is some doit in my bed, I must confess.

As we ate we also spoke of politics, art, and alien abductions, but before too long we finished our lunch, and the Count had to take his leave. We shook hands, and as he strolled down Venice Boulevard, he vanished in to thin air . . . possibly into the Zone of Erotica gift shop.

Davy Jones's Monkee Business

Before there was American Idol, or boy bands in shopping malls, or even Fat Albert and the Cosby Kids playing rusty bedsprings and garbage cans, there were the Monkees—Micky Dolenz, Davy Jones, Mike Nesmith, and Peter Tork—whose television show ran for only two memorable years in the late 1960s but whose legend continues.

Davy Jones, the cute Monkee and the Englishman in the group, no longer calls Hollywood home, but he recalled his days here.

WEIRD HOLLYWOOD: What was your first impression of Hollywood?

DAVY JONES: I came to Hollywood in sixty-five. I was on Santa Monica Boulevard with my manager, and [saw] my idol Jan Berry, from Jan and Dean. Next time I saw him we were recording in the same studio, and soon after that he got into that crash [in 1966, that left the surf rocker with brain damage and partial paralysis]. I took him on tour with us in sixty-seven.

WH: What were you doing in Hollywood?

DJ: I auditioned for *The Wackiest Ship in the Army* and *Hogan's Heroes.* They were considering me for Robin in *Batman.* I'd done *Bewitched*, *Ben Casey* . . .

WH: Robin with an English accent. Weird. But you had already made a name for yourself and were in New York as the Artful Dodger in Broadway's *Oliver.* You must have hung around plenty of celebrities.

DJ: I sang with Judy Garland, went to lunch with her . . . I saw her go around the revolving door three times trying to find a way out after sixteen margaritas, or whatever she was drinking then. I was just a kid at the time. I wanted to be just like them—go out to Fire Island on the weekend. It was a strange world.

WH: You and Frank Gorshin, of *Batman* fame, performed on the *Ed Sullivan Show* the same night as the Beatles debuted in America.

DJ: Yeah. The Beatles were the first manufactured band in America, the ones who wore the same suits and the same hair and the Capezio boots. They were presented in a very organized and merchandisable way.

WH: Obviously you've hung around some real musical legends. What can you tell us about some Hollywood rockers?

DJ: The last time I saw Jim Morrison, he was standing naked in Peter Tork's pool over in the Valley, with two chicks, one at either side, and a bottle of bourbon in each hand. . . . I read Eric Clapton's book recently, and he said the first time he ever took LSD was with the Monkees. Well,

www.JoeArtistWriter.com

I wasn't there, and I don't know if the other guys were or not, but maybe he had some good stuff, and he was just seeing Monkees.

WH: Tommy Boyce, half of the great songwriting duo for the Monkees, Boyce and Hart, died of an apparent suicide. He was suffering from depression, brought on by a brain aneurysm, but there are some who wonder if he really shot himself.

DJ: Tommy Boyce—a dear, dear friend of mine—shot himself in Nashville, but . . . he hated guns for one thing. He was still sitting up and had the gun in his hands, so I'm not sure about that one either.

WH: Tell us the real story about Jimi Hendrix and the Monkees.

DJ: I used to socialize with him, but here again, I had no idea he was into drugs. I always saw this guy in this purple outfit with his scarf flowing, and bandana, but this was the same thing he wore when we went fishing in Florida too, you know? Got on the boat, it was a hundred and ten degrees and he'd still have his show clothes on.

WH: There's a famous story of him warming up for a Monkees concert, and he flipped the audience the finger and walked off the stage.

DJ: That was at Forest Hills Stadium. [The audience was] shouting, "We want Davy!" or "We want the Monkees!" and he threw his guitar at the audience and left. That's got to be worth a lot of money—I wonder who has that? It was still attached to the amplifiers when he threw it.

He played down in the Village, and Micky had seen him and said, "This guy pees on his guitar, sets it on fire, plays behind his back, plays it with his teeth." It was variety, it was fun. We didn't realize he was a serious, serious, serious person. At that time he was a backup player.

WH: The four Monkees reunited in Europe in '97 to sellout crowds, then in '98 Mike Nesmith refused to tour America. What happened?

DJ: It's a shame, really, we didn't come back into America, because it left a bad taste for me and I lost respect for Mike Nesmith. I don't imagine the four of us will ever get together again.

WH: What do you remember most fondly about your weird Hollywood days?

DJ: The times we spent together in the sixties, swimming in Micky Dolenz's pool after the baseball games with Alice [Cooper], who was living next door to Micky at the time.

WH: Whenever we do karaoke, we get up and sing "Daydream Believer" and do the Davy dance. What's the origin of that dance?

DJ: When my kids first saw me doing it, they said, "Dad, why are you dancing like Axl Rose?"

Unexplained Mysteries

Drugs, *alcohol, homicidal tycoons,* brutal murders, superheroes, hidden Nazi camps, underground lizard people, unusual religious practices, and a healthy dose of UFOs—it sounds like the latest movie from *Grindhouse* duo Quentin Tarantino and Robert Rodriguez, but it's not. It's simply the introduction to our next chapter.

When it comes to inscrutable secrets, this town is an inexhaustible wellspring of the stuff. Hollywood is the only place in the world where you can find so much bizarrely inspirational material in your own front yard, and have the ability to film it in your own backyard.

Who killed television's Superman? Is it true that an ancient subterranean empire once flourished under what is now the city of Los Angeles? And did director-producer Thomas Ince die from indigestion, or was that bullet hole in his head a sign of what did him in?

Brace yourself for some truly disturbing puzzles and unfathomable acts of immorality as we examine Hollywood's unexplained mysteries.

Open Case: Black Dahlia Black Dahlia Murder

It's a story as old as Tinseltown itself. A troubled, attractive small-town girl, dissatisfied with her humble surroundings and station in life, decides to move out West and hit the big time in the motion picture game. Capitalizing on her God-given charms, innate acting ability, and sheer determination, Elizabeth Short hoped to become a Hollywood legend. Tragically she did just that: as a murder victim in 1946.

The nickname Black Dahlia is one Short garnered in death. She typically dressed in black from head to toe. She also was frequently seen with a flower tucked in her raven-dyed hair, just behind her ear. A film noir titled *The Blue Dahlia*, starring Alan Ladd and Veronica Lake, was popular at the time, and it is assumed the posthumous moniker was an outgrowth of both the film's recognition and Short's everyday appearance in the news.

The immediate cause of death, according to the coroner's report, was hemorrhage and shock from concussion of the brain and lacerations to her face, but that doesn't paint much of the gruesome picture. Elizabeth Short was kidnapped, tortured, and most likely sexually violated before her severed body was left in a vacant lot where a house now stands on Norton Avenus (see facing page).

The murder of Elizabeth Short has baffled police and amateur sleuths for decades. The case is undeniably intriguing. Why was this attractive young woman killed in such a horrific manner, and what kind of monster would commit such cruel acts on another human being? As each new day passes, it becomes less and less probable this vile crime will ever be solved.

Short has been inaccurately described as a prostitute in a number of books and articles written about her. Though she enjoyed the attention of men and understood the power she possessed, she seems to be guilty only of underage drinking (see mugshot, from 1943).

What does ring closer to the truth is that the financially strapped thespian dated a number of men, but often it was for the free dinner, which might be repaid by a peck on the cheek, and no more. In her letters there is evidence that Short and her one-time military fiancé were waiting to marry before consummating their love. Tragically, he was killed in a plane crash, and the event left Short mentally shaken to the point she would occasionally make up stories about her late "husband" and a child who had died at birth.

Short has also been referred to as a dance girl, which brings to mind lurid images of lusty frolicking, but she was a showgirl in a reputable supper club called Florentine Gardens. It was at there that Short may have originally met a young Marilyn Monroe; the two were said to have been friends. Monroe had her first wedding reception at the club when she was just sixteen years old, but she allegedly never again entered the dance hall after Short's murder. Was Monroe frightened of someone connected to the Florentine Gardens who might also be connected to the Black Dahlia murder?

We know that on January 15, 1947, Betty Bersinger and her three-year-old daughter were walking along LA's Norton Avenue when the young housewife noticed something in the overgrown weeds. Shielding her young child's eyes, Bersinger ran to the closest house and phoned the police.

Officers Will Fitzgerald and Frank Perkins were the first to arrive on the scene, and the pair immediately noted that the body had been scrubbed clean and drained of all blood, and that the victim's hair was freshly shampooed. Her body had been purposefully arranged in a chillingly seductive manner.

Rope marks were found on her wrists, ankles, and neck, indicating to investigators that she had been tied and tortured for days. The autopsy later revealed more horrifying surprises. The contents of her stomach contained human feces, which it is surmised she was forced to consume, and her reproductive organs were missing, leading some to speculate that perhaps she was pregnant at the time of her death and had refused to have an abortion.

Not long after the story hit the press, dozens of "Confessing Sams" came out of the woodwork, claiming they were the killer. The police had a long list of suspects, but sadly were never able to pin the horrendous deed on anyone. The case has gone officially unsolved and will undoubtedly always remain one of the darkest tales ever to come out of Hollywood.

The Death of George Reeves

"Great Caesar's ghost!" shouts Perry White, the lovable but gruff editor-in-chief of a great metropolitan newspaper. "We've got a story here! I want my top reporter on this! Where's Kent?"

Eager to please, but wary of his boss's infamous temperamental mood swings, cub reporter Jimmy Olsen meekly squeaks, "Mr. Kent hasn't been seen all day. I could send in Ms. Lane if you'd like, Chief."

"Fine, Olsen, send Lane in," the old man blusters from behind his five-dollar cigar, "and for Pete's sake, stop calling me Chief!"

In sashays Lois Lane, the sharpest dame to ever walk the city beat. She's got more moxie than a lot of fellas. Brains to beat the band, and the rest of her ain't so bad either.

Lane is wearing a form-fitting blazer and skirt with a pillbox hat perched fashionably atop her head. Appearances to the contrary, she's all business. "You called me, Mr. White?"

"Yes, Lois, it seems we have a puzzling murder on our hands. A good-looking, successful actor was found dead in his home in Benedict Canyon last night around 2 A.M. The cops are calling it suicide, but I'm not so sure." White strolls nervously behind his desk, chewing on his stogie as if it were a tough piece of meat.

"Why so skeptical, Mr. White? It's not like you to doubt the police," the attractive yet savvy reporter inquires.

"It just doesn't add up Lois, it just doesn't add up. . . ."

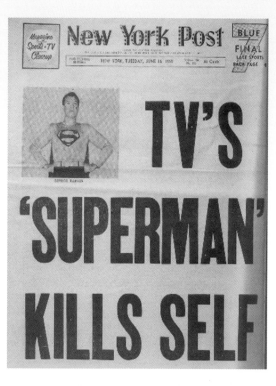

If this sounds like the beginning of a 1950s movie serial, the actual death of George Reeves, the actor who portrayed the Man of Steel in *Adventures of Superman*, is far more sinister than anything the popular weekly episodes would dare broadcast. And the ending is far too ambiguous to leave audience members satisfied.

On June 16, 1959, George Reeves had been up drinking with his girlfriend Lenore Lemmon and several houseguests. Reeves's blood alcohol level was 0.27. Couple that with the painkillers he had recently started taking, as the result of a suspicious car accident, and George Reeves was in no shape to fend off potential evildoers.

Reeves's death was called a suicide, but no fingerprints were found on the murder weapon, and, as we can surmise, it's hard to effectively wipe down a pistol after recently blowing your own brains across a room. No residue or powder burns were found on the victim's body.

The bullet shell was found underneath Reeves's body, and the gun itself was discovered on the ground between the actor's feet.

Two additional bullet holes were found in floor of the room where Reeves died, covered by a throw rug before police entered the house. And why was his death not reported to the authorities for close to forty-five minutes after the shooting?

In the decades since Reeves's death, there have been multiple theories on how the charismatic actor died, but most assumptions usually end up as one of three possible scenarios.

Eddie Mannix and the Mob

It was a well-known Hollywood secret that George Reeves had been carrying on a longtime romantic affair with Toni Mannix, wife of former MGM studio executive Eddie Mannix. Eddie was rumored to run with an unsavory crowd. Eddie had been suspected of killing his first wife in a "high-speed chase," and his name had been thrown around a number years earlier in the "suicide" of producer Paul Bern.

Reeves had at least one strange car accident just months before his death. He was driving on Benedict Canyon Road when his brakes failed. This mishap left Reeves with a number of scrapes and severe back pain. The mechanic who later inspected Reeves's vehicle found the brake system to be in perfect condition, and suggested to Reeves that perhaps someone had drained the fluid.

Did Mannix, frustrated with the botched brake job, order a hit on George Reeves that night, and did the gunman (gunmen?) frighten the potential witnesses so effectively that the terrified houseguests kept their silence forever?

The Girlfriend

According to Lenore Lemmon, the brawny actor had been known to occasionally point an empty gun to his head and fire a few invisible rounds after a few drinks. Lenore is reported to have joked to friends in the house when Reeves retired to bed on the night in question, "He's probably going to shoot himself." Minutes later, Reeves was found naked on the bed, dead of a single bullet to his head.

Lemmon admitted the extra bullet holes in the floor were caused when she was "fooling around" with the gun. Was she getting a feel for the Luger? Or, more dastardly, knowing that Reeves enjoyed holding an empty pistol to his temple, did Lemmon load the firearm with live ammo, hoping that Reeves, in a pharmaceutical- and booze-induced haze, would one day unintentionally end his own life?

Suicide

Some of Reeves's friends thought the actor was the happiest he'd been in years, while others found him to be often depressed. The role of Superman had been a blessing and a curse to Reeves.

Reeves desperately yearned to be taken seriously as an actor, so after the cancellation of the show in 1957, he was initially optimistic he'd be given weightier roles. Unfortunately, he found himself typecast as the Kryptonian superhero, and respectable work was hard to come by.

Weeks before his death came news that the studio ordered a new season of the Superman show and was willing to raise Reeves's salary. It seemed that Reeves had finally come to grips with his acting legacy, and not only saw the financial upside of filming more Superman episodes but also was extremely excited about his upcoming lucrative exhibition boxing match against light-heavyweight champ Archie Moore.

A former amateur boxer, Reeves is believed to have tried out for the 1932 Olympics. The athletic Reeves was eager to show off his actual fighting skills to the public. He was quoted by numerous sources as saying, "The Archie Moore fight will be the highlight of my life."

By all accounts, Reeves was looking forward to marrying Lenore Lemmon in just two days, even though the two had what many would describe as a volatile relationship.

Did George Reeves take his own life, or was he murdered in cold blood? Unfortunately, this mystery really does look like a job for Superman.

What's Buried Beneath Brentwood Rec Center?

In the late 1970s, UCLA professor Dan Hirsch heard from some of his students that the future site of the Barrington Recreational Center in the tony LA suburb of Brentwood was hiding a dark secret. There was talk that Veterans Administration (VA) doctors and staff were quietly dumping nuclear waste from the hospital in a secret landfill, and had been doing so for almost twenty years.

Hirsch started a coalition to look into the charges and soon found that the rumors were true. Wealthy parents were lobbying at the time for soccer and baseball fields on the radioactive real estate. Most didn't believe the stories, or perhaps thought that some developer had planted them, Scooby-Doo-like, to scare away the competition.

Hirsch and his students investigated and found a paper trail indicating that the VA had indeed used the area as a dump for waste from the radiation therapy program, "secret" human experiments, and perhaps even from a small reactor. Some "hot" items were even buried in plastic garbage bags. Hirsch, of course, was concerned that radiation could have gotten into the soil and would affect vegetation for hundreds of years.

The Brentwood parents' group absolutely insisted that the playing fields be built. The Nuclear Regulatory Commission (NRC) was called in to investigate. After a perfunctory sweep of the area with a Geiger counter, the NRC pronounced the area safe. Not satisfied, after repeated delays Hirsch was finally able to secure an LAPD helicopter to fly him over the property with an infrared camera, which would possibly reveal hotspots that the NRC had perhaps willfully ignored.

Hirsch arrived on the appointed day to find that someone had gone over the area with a bulldozer, wiping out any vegetation that would show up "hot" on the infrared pictures.

If the waste is buried more than a few feet underground, the radiation should be well contained, and the NRC can be trusted in this case, even though they didn't take the simple and obvious route to obtain soil samples. If you are the cautious type, though, it might be a good idea to limit visits to the Barrington Recreation Center to a half-hour or less.

In late September 1999, someone filed a Freedom of Information Act request with the NRC to see the secret findings on the Barrington property. You can read them, but to do so you need to get to Rockville, Maryland, where the NRC headquarters' public reading room is located. Request "Landfill site at 330 S. Barrington Ave., Brentwood, CA, permit/license & inspection reports, FOIA/PA 99-374." Good luck. —*Greg Bishop, with grateful acknowledgment to Paul Young, whose research was featured in the book* L.A. Exposed

The Bizarre Death of Thomas Ince

William Randolph Hearst was once quoted as saying, "News is something somebody doesn't want printed; all else is advertising." The news of how movie producer Thomas Ince died was certainly newsworthy, but the somebody who didn't want this particular piece of news printed was the billionaire newspaper magnate himself.

Hearst wanted to use one of Ince's studios as the headquarters for his own production company, so the sixty-one-year-old tycoon offered to throw the soon-to-be-forty-three-year-old a little birthday party to help sweeten the deal. This party was to be located on the *Oneida*, Hearst's 280-foot yacht and would be the social event of the year. It turned out to be much more sinister.

Among the guests were many of Ince's friends and business associates, including comic actor Charlie Chaplin, whose romantic charm was almost as renowned as his comedic timing. Chaplin was rumored to be having an affair with Hearst's mistress, Marion Davies. Hearst supposedly wanted to see for himself if he could detect a romance between the two.

Ever the workaholic, Ince missed the ship as it sailed from San Pedro, and took a train to San Diego to join the party there the next day. Later that night, he was greeted with much fanfare and a spectacular dinner. Some say Ince was forced to skip breakfast the next morning because of a severe stomachache; others whispered it was foul play.

One account of the legend tells that while strolling the deck, Hearst spotted his lady and Chaplin in a compromising position. Enraged, the wealthy industrialist ran to fetch his pistol. Coincidentally, Chaplin, who had been a bundle of nerves the entire cruise, bid his paramour a well-timed good night and slunk back to his room. Ince happened to be taking in the fresh sea air and happened to be wearing a hat similar to Chaplin's. Ince chanced to run into Davies, and the birthday boy struck up an innocent conversation with the twenty-seven-year-old star. Hearst returned, gun in hand, spotted the fedora-wearing fornicator, and shot him in the head. Ince was declared dead the next day.

The related stories that ran nationwide in Hearst's newspapers claimed Ince (above, with his wife, Nell) had grossly overeaten and expired at his home from a case of acute indigestion. But Chaplin's secretary claimed she saw Ince's bullet wound as he was removed from the luxury vessel.

Both the San Diego and the Los Angeles police had reason to question Hearst, but neither law enforcement agency seemed too eager to thoroughly interrogate the almighty mogul or his guests.

It would seem that determining whether a man died of a case of critical heartburn or a bullet through the skull would not be too taxing a task for an experienced coroner, but no autopsy was performed and Ince's body was cremated just hours after he was pronounced dead.

The Battle of Los Angeles

With Pearl Harbor fresh in the nation's mind and war jitters at a fever pitch, Los Angelenos were jarred out of their comfy beds early on the morning of February 25, 1942, by the sound of air raid sirens and anti-aircraft fire. It was the first time in history that an airborne enemy had been engaged in the continental United States, but officials and civilian witnesses were not entirely sure about what they had seen beginning at about 2:15 A.M. Defense batteries opened up from their bases in Inglewood, Santa Monica, and other south bay locations that were never pinpointed in daily papers, because "loose lips sink ships." Shrapnel and a few unexploded shells fell from the skies, smashing into sidewalks, driveways, and even a few homes. Miraculously, only five deaths were reported, and those were due to traffic accidents and a couple of heart attacks.

The term "flying saucer" would not be invented until more than five years in the future, when Kenneth Arnold would see a group of objects from his plane in Washington State and described their movement as "like a saucer skipped across water." Although newspapers continually referred to the invaders as "planes" or possibly "blimps," no one could agree on their size or even the number of targets. Reports ranged from one object to perhaps fifty. At 2:25 A.M., a general blackout was ordered and lights began going off from northern LA down to the Mexican border. Though residents were asked to stay indoors, many could not resist the free show and crowded out onto sidewalks and balconies. There was even a "blackout murder," as one killer took advantage of the darkness to beat a forty-year-old woman to death in a rooming house.

Army observers looking at the celestial fracas through binoculars from atop a tower in Culver City thought they saw a group of silvery objects, which they assumed were airplanes. All witnesses agreed that the things came in from the northwest (probably from the ocean) near Santa Monica and moved in a leisurely fashion until they disappeared somewhere south of Long Beach. Because all lights in the city had been turned off, stars shined on the moonless night with an intensity most had never seen.

Just before the firing started, a woman identified only as Katie said that she received a call from the local air raid warden at her home near Santa Monica, telling her to look out the window and see if she could report anything. "It was huge! It was just enormous! And it was practically right over my house. I had never seen anything like it in my life!" she said. "It was just hovering there in the sky and hardly moving at all. It was a lovely pale orange and about the most beautiful thing you've ever seen. I could see it perfectly because it was very close. It was big!"

When the "attack" began, powerful searchlights lit up the early morning sky, converging on the object (or group of objects) so that the gun batteries could get a good bead on the thing. The UFO never changed direction or speed, even with the combined firing of hundreds of anti-aircraft guns, many of which scored direct hits. The whole thing lasted for about a half-hour, as the "mystery planes" took their sweet time traveling twenty or so miles across the night sky.

Optical physicist Bruce Maccabee performed a detailed analysis of one of the dramatic original negatives from the *Los Angeles Times*. Taking into account the size of the searchlight beams, the angle of incidence from the ground, and reported altitude of the target, he estimated that the UFO measured anywhere from one hundred to three hundred feet from end to end. The strange thing about contemporary news accounts is the glaring lack of any concrete guess as to what exactly was floating over a metropolis of three million people that night.

William Randolph Hearst's jingoistic and sensationalized *L.A. Herald Express* summed everything up with section featuring the glaring headline "Was It a Raid?"

An analysis of the first report on the firing in the Los Angeles area early today fails to give convincing proof that any enemy planes were over Los Angeles during the disturbance. It is significant that "no bombs were dropped and no planes were shot down." It may be also stated that persons equipped with powerful glasses failed to discern a plane or planes at the apex of the searchlight beams where many people feel sure they saw a moving object or objects under the fire of our batteries. If a moving plane or object was caught in the light beams, it seemed to move too slowly across the sky to have the speed of a modern airplane, such as our own planes which flash across the sky so rapidly. The newspaper, at that time, was unwilling to hazard even a guess on exactly what transpired in the skies above Los Angeles last night, but certainly the city was given a splendid practical lesson on what to do in case of attack.

A quick-thinking advertiser in the *Herald Express* placed an ad for bargain "blackout window shades" next to stories about the raid, and Hearst's editors reported on a "rising chorus of demands that the U.S. government immediately evacuate from Southern California all Japanese—alien and American-born alike." Curiously, the only quotes from the "chorus" were attributed to two congressmen from Santa Monica calling for "concentration camps." This of course actually happened a few months later. The paper also quoted unnamed civilians who had observed Japanese people signaling to the sky with flashlights and flares.

As for the mysterious flying objects, perhaps the "persons equipped with powerful glasses" didn't know how to get their minds around what they were seeing until later sightings and popular culture provided them with a mental box labeled "flying saucer" in which to place their observations and memories.

One writer noted that a number of Japanese citizens were arrested and questioned, "including several aliens." The aliens were probably mistaken for Japanese and sent to the camps as well. The answers were right under the noses of the authorities! —*Greg Bishop*

The Mysterious Death of Bobby Fuller

The 1960s produced a bumper crop of untimely rock star deaths. Leading the pack in LA was the unfortunate destiny of Robert "Bobby" Fuller. Fuller is best known for his chart-topping hit "I Fought the Law," a 1965 cover version of a 1959 song by Sonny Curtis and the Crickets. The song has since been covered by many more bands, most notably the Clash in 1979.

Whether his life was cut short just shy of superstardom by his own hand, or something more sinister is still an open question—but not by much. The Los Angeles Police Department called it a suicide, despite the fact that Fuller's body was found slumped over the front seat of his car, doused in gasoline.

Fuller was from Texas, and he recorded some of his first hits in the same studio as his idol, Buddy Holly, and his band, the Crickets. "I Fought the Law" was in fact written by former Crickets member Sonny Curtis and recorded by the band after Holly's death. Riding the crest of his popularity, Fuller moved to Los Angeles to make a run at the big time. He restyled his band as the Bobby Fuller Four, and on July 17, 1966, he was hanging out in preparation for a big meeting at Del-Fi Records the next day.

At around 5 P.M. on the eighteenth, the band arrived at Fuller's Hollywood pad, just around the block from Grauman's Chinese Theater. Fuller's mother, who was visiting from El Paso, was out checking the mailbox. On her way back to the apartment (shown on previous page), she saw the family car in the parking lot. Fuller had taken the Olds out the night before after receiving a call at about 1 or 2 A.M. Opening the driver's door, she was nearly overcome by a wave of gasoline fumes. She fought her way through the odor to find her son lying on the front seat, dressed only in his pajamas. He looked like he was asleep, but Mrs. Fuller couldn't wake him up. "He was lying in the front seat," she recalled. "The keys were in the ignition, and his hand was on the keys, as if he had tried to start the car. I thought he was asleep. I called his name. When I looked closer, I could see . . . he was dead." Friends and associates were shocked, to say the least. Fuller was known to have down periods, but nothing that screamed "suicide" to anyone who knew him.

The coroner later determined that Fuller had numerous cuts and bruises in various areas of his body, as well as a hairline fracture on his right hand. He also had dried blood around his chin and mouth. Despite all these problems and the aforementioned gasoline poured liberally around the interior of the car (and, as the autopsy found, even in Fuller's throat) the LAPD stuck to its suicide theory. Because an opened book of matches was left on the front seat, this was offered as proof that Fuller had tried to soak himself in gasoline and swallowed some for good measure, and then asphyxiated on the fumes.

Why would the cops stick to such a ridiculous theory? The coroner's report doesn't even mention the location where Fuller's body was found. Muted in death, Fuller had no way to fight the LAPD, and the cops won.

The murder had all of the earmarks of a mob hit, which leads to the obvious question of what a budding star from Texas was doing messing with organized crime. He wasn't, but Bob Keane, the owner of Del-Fi records, was not so smart. Keane was reportedly angry with Fuller over his decision to rebuild his band. He also held a $1 million policy on Fuller's carcass. Many conspiracy theories focus on Keane's (or his business partner's) mob connections and guess that Fuller's death may have been some kind of warning or was a way to collect on the insurance policy.

Keane later offered his own weird theory about the demise of his new find, and it's even stranger than the LAPD's: Fuller was doing acid at a party, fell and killed himself, then was taken back to his place by frightened comrades and left in the car. Nothing has been uncovered so far to back up this story.

Del-Fi's fortunes had peaked when another of its stars, Ritchie Valens, died in a plane crash, creating a huge demand for his catalog. Although most seem to agree that Keane had little or nothing to do with Bobby Fuller's death, his comments about the incident tend to leave a bad taste. The official records of the investigation are still sealed. Bobby Fuller Four drummer Dalton Powell probably put the whole thing best when he said, "Anyone who can write it off as a suicide is either totally incompetent or totally scared to death."

Bobby Fuller's apartment was at 1776 North Sycamore Avenue, a half-block north of Hollywood Boulevard. The building still stands. —*Greg Bishop*

Builders of the Adytum Temple

At first glance you may not even notice this brick building on North Figueroa Street in Los Angeles amid the mini-malls and Mexican restaurants. This otherwise nondescript little building in the Highland Park district houses what might be the most unusual church in Los Angeles.

The Builders of the Adytum (BOTA), is, in their own language, a "mystery school."

The church is the world headquarters of the religion, which was founded in 1920 by writer, lecturer, vaudevillian, and magician Paul Foster Case. Case was a precocious expert in both the use of and the symbolism of tarot cards, and in Kabbalism, the ancient, complex system of Jewish mysticism. He taught willing pupils such subjects as tarot (a system of divining future events based on a deck of mystical cards), Qabalah (an ancient Jewish cult that revolves around the doctrines that were supposedly revealed to Adam by the archangel Gabriel), and alchemy (a medieval chemical philosophy having as its asserted aims the transmutation of base metals into gold, the discovery of the panacea for all known diseases, and the preparation of the elixir of longevity).

At the tender age of twenty-six Case assumed leadership of the legendary Order of the Golden Dawn, a seminal occult society whose members included Aleister Crowley, Arthur Machen, and W. B. Yeats. But Case became embroiled in a scandal during his term and resigned his post to found his own Kabbalistic mystery school, Builders of the Adytum, in New York City. Case moved back to LA in 1933.

Here, it thrived under the ministry of Ann Davies, who was Case's star pupil. Davies, who took over the organization after Case's death in 1954, was an intelligent, charismatic woman who expanded and complemented Case's doctrines, and drew many people to the Builders through her services and correspondence courses. She established the Highland Park building in 1959 as a temple for BOTA public worship and an administrative center for what was to become an international organization.

The Builders' beliefs are based in solidly Western symbolism and teachings, such as the six-pointed Star of David and the Kabbalistic Tree—the representation of universe, consciousness, and body in Jewish mysticism. The word *Adytum* comes from ancient Greece referring to the holiest part of the temple: "That which is not made with hands." *Builders* refers to both Jesus as a carpenter and has a connection to esoteric Freemasonry.

The Builders' temple holds Sunday morning services for the general public and is decorated with bright tarot paintings and Hebrew lettering. Services feature organ recitals, singing, censing, angelic name chanting, and hand-raising prayers. The highlight of the ritual is the silent meditation, when the lights dim and the assembled worshippers meditate and send out healing energies while the illuminated Kabbalistic Tree glows in the incense-hazed darkness.

BOTA sells its famous tarot pack and other items by mail, and maintains a Web site at www.bota.org.

The Land of Mu: Lost City of the Lemurians

On the western edge of the Santa Monica Mountains National Recreation Area, not too far from the tiny beach houses of Malibu, lies what one researcher believes may be the most spectacular hidden archeological site in North America.

Robert Stanley, a journalist and publisher of *Unicus* magazine, had traveled around the world in search of ancient mysteries and lost ruins. But he never suspected that he would find the remnants of a lost world (almost) literally in his own backyard, on the slopes of these chaparral-covered mountains that bisect the Los Angeles basin.

In 1985, Stanley was hiking through the Santa Monicas when he noticed odd and unnatural-looking formations in their western reaches, around the Los Angeles–Ventura county line. He noted gulches that looked like sculpted ramparts, stone walls on rocky hills never occupied by houses or livestock, and floorlike flat surfaces at the tops of windswept peaks. There was also a huge rock outcropping that resembled the outline of a human face staring out to the Pacific, which Stanley dubbed "the Sphinx."

Researching the history and lore of the area, Stanley found a local Chumash legend of a "First People" who had lived in the mountains long before the Chumash arrived in around 3000 B.C. The Chumash said that these mystery people were long gone, but certain of their artifacts—crystalline sculptures of strange animals and the like—could be found in certain mountain caves. As with the Anasazi ruins of the Southwest, the First People's remnants were avoided by the local Indians.

What was most intriguing about the Chumash legend, to Stanley, was the story of the First People's demise. The Chumash claimed that the civilization had been called Mu, and had been wiped out in a catastrophic flood. This exactly paralleled the legend of Lemuria, the lost continent of the Pacific.

Geologists and oceanographers believe that at the end of the last ice age, the Malibu sea level was at least two hundred feet lower than it is today. This would have made the Channel Islands a far-western extension of the Santa Monicas and allowed for a large lowland region—the Mu of the legend—to exist in what is now the California coastal shelf of the Pacific Ocean. That prehistoric peoples lived in this area is beyond dispute: one of North America's oldest human remains—the 13,000-year-old Channel Islands Woman—was found on Santa Rosa Island, twenty-five miles west of Malibu.

Stanley thinks that Mu's lowlands were wiped out by the rising post–ice age sea levels. The higher regions of the civilization, whose traces he says still exist in the Santa Monicas, may have been destroyed by a tsunami—a fast-moving, powerful tidal wave created by an earthquake or a collapse of the submarine ocean floor shelf. Such a wave would have devastated coastal hillside settlements and left countless tons of silt and debris in its wake.

Mu may be the Californian equivalent of underwater archeological sites like Japan's Yonaguni, Egypt's Alexandria, or Wisconsin's Rock Lake. Stanley believes that the Malibu site most closely resembles Peru's Marca Huasi, a strange, ancient place high in the Andes that boasts a giant stone "Face of Humanity" that resembles Mu's "Sphinx."

Although he has become an expert on the Mu site and has involved both professionals and laypeople in explorations of the area, Robert Stanley has not revealed the exact locations of the area's most peculiar features, fearing their destruction by vandals or curiosity seekers. —*Mike Marinacci*

A Secret Nazi Camp in Rustic Canyon?

In 1933, a widow named Jessie Murphy made plans to build a self-sufficient redoubt in Rustic Canyon, complete with a 295,000-gallon spring-fed water tank and a 20,000-gallon tank for diesel fuel, as well as electric generators and a twenty-two-bedroom mansion. Just when the basic amenities were finished, there was a disastrous fire, and Murphy gave up, depressed and disgusted, in 1938. The property passed to Norman and Winnona Stephens, who finished the work by 1942.

Around that time, one of the workmen at the property mentioned seeing "troops dressed in paramilitary outfits" and someone who apparently ran the show, whom he referred to as "an overbearing German named Herr Schmidt." Schmidt had convinced Mrs. Stephens either that

Topanga Canyon—UFO Hotspot

For four years, from 1988 to 1992, I lived in Topanga Canyon, where huge objects glided silently between the steep slopes of ravines, structured craft hovered over isolated cabins and homes, and a rash of abductions startled researchers. Strange, unearthly animals were also sighted.

Often, while driving home from work at 2 A.M., I got the uneasy feeling that something was watching me and had designs on landing in the road before pulling me out of the car. Early one morning while driving Topanga Canyon Road in a thick fog with a friend, we saw a blinking yellow light that seemed to come from everywhere. It was so bright that we could see the outline of sagebrush crowning a hill ahead of us. We braced for our long-awaited encounter. As we rounded a corner, the glow became almost blinding. I slowed the car to a crawl until we saw the light coming from

behind a tree near the road. We shielded our eyes and peeked out between our fingers at . . . a beer sign that had been left on at the local bar.

Topanga became known as a hotspot for saucer spotters. Two teenagers were driving through a nearby canyon one night, chasing a black, diamond-shaped object that they had seen earlier, and happened upon a group of people staked out in lawn chairs, waiting for the reliable UFOs. Most of the sightings tended to cluster near the town center or the state park area just up the hill.

Author and investigator Preston Dennett wrote a book on the period titled *UFOs over Topanga Canyon*, published in 1999. He described hundreds of sightings and closer encounters that began in June 1992 (barely two months after I moved out) and continued unabated for almost two years. He wrote the original story in the local Topanga *Messenger*.

the Third Reich would win the war or that the United States would be turned into a post-apocalyptic nightmare, and with her acquiescence began teaching survivalist classes. The Stephenses were later cleared of any charges.

It's best to allow a full day to explore the canyon. The hike begins from the end of Queensferry Road in Pacific Palisades among multimillion-dollar homes that hug the hillside, many with elaborate security systems and high walls to keep out the hoi polloi. Head up the fire road until a fence bordering the street disappears down the steep slopes of the canyon. The massive concrete water tank appears on the right, littered with charcoal from what used to be a gargantuan wooden cover.

Ruins of the old Stephens complex are not hard to find, although they are overgrown with trees, brush, and ivy. The entire length is lined with cypress and eucalyptus trees, and it's not difficult to imagine shiny black Model Ts and Pierce Arrows making their way through the compound, dropping off more recruits for Herr Schmidt. Keep an eye out for square concrete holes along the way—entrances to underground passageways full of debris, seemingly leading nowhere.

Recent floods have uprooted horse stables and other wooden buildings. Everything is covered in graffiti. Orange and avocado groves planted in the early twentieth century still bear fruit in the spring and summer months. What looks to be an old hotel blocks the path farther on. Stop and add a piece from the rusting metal building to an impromptu sculpture in the driveway.

Hikers in Rustic Canyon have all commented on the brooding and sinister nature of the place and they say, many rattlesnakes live in the valley. —*Greg Bishop*

Dennett led a television crew out to the state park area one evening, accompanied by a group who claimed to be able to summon UFOs at will. They shined flashlights and even a laser beam heavenward and waited. Some in the group became excited and called attention to a slow-moving, amber light that appeared across the valley. The TV crew managed to get a few minutes of footage before the enigmatic object sank lazily out of sight below the ridgeline. Residents also reported military-type helicopters searching the area after UFO sightings.Dennett's theory is that UFOs use the area as a base, studying the population in concealment.

Mimi Smith was driving on the main street late at night in November 1994 when she stopped to watch what looked like a sheep crossing the road. "It was shaped like a sheep, and its head was round and placed lower on its body, and it appeared almost as if it had waggled on some kind of spring. . . . It moved like it glided along. As I looked at it, I saw that its eyes . . . were like holes with nothing there. You could see through. If you looked at the thing's eyes, you could see the fenceposts in back of it." She saw the same unnerving specter a few months later in the same location.

Dennett says that sightings continue in the canyon, but the UFOs are not as predictable as they were in the early 1990s. Perhaps relocating to the area might up your chances. It also might be interesting to ask Danny Elfman, film composer and former leader of the band Oingo Boingo, if he saw anything from his sprawling home on a hill above a bump on the Topanga Canyon Road.—*Greg Bishop*

I got the uneasy feeling that something was watching me.

Moon Landing Hoax

Stanley Kubrick is considered to be one of the greatest directors in the history of cinema. His use of color, lighting, and camera angles to artfully convey emotion and drama have been studied and copied by virtuosos like Steven Spielberg and Martin Scorsese. Seven of Kubrick's last nine films were nominated for Oscars, and his film legacy includes such brilliant and diverse work as *Spartacus, 2001: A Space Odyssey, A Clockwork Orange*, and *Full Metal Jacket.* For some people, however, Kubrik's most impressive masterpiece was broadcast into the living rooms of an estimated five hundred million people via their tiny television sets in July 1969.

That is to say, there is a small but vocal minority who believe that the moon landings were a hoax, and many of them also believe this ruse was skillfully "directed" by master filmmaker Stanley Kubrick.

The question is why. Why spend billions of dollars on a space program, only to film the entire deception in a Hollywood soundstage (or perhaps a remote desert)? Why dupe hundreds of millions of tax-paying Americans into thinking we really were capable of sending a small team of men to Earth's only natural satellite? And if we were going to go through all this trouble, why use Neil Armstrong? Why not Steve McQueen?

Here are some compelling and thought-provoking questions from those who subscribe to the hoax theories:

1. How can the flag be fluttering? There is no wind on the moon.

2. In many of the photographs taken by the "astronauts" during their "walks" on the "lunar surface," why are shadows inconsistent in both size and angle? The sun would be the only light source on the moon, but many argue that the shadows cast in the photos of the Apollo landings can be explained only by using multiple light sources—similar to the big expensive kind you might find on a fancy Hollywood movie set.

3. How did the flimsy radiation protection possibly shield the spacecraft, the astronauts, and even the NASA cameras and film from burning up? Some men of science believe the capsule itself would need to be wrapped in insulation no less than two meters thick, yet *Apollo 11* is guarded by a substance that appears to be no thicker than ordinary tinfoil.

4. Why are the footprints so well preserved? With no moisture or atmosphere on the moon, the photographs of the imprints on the lunar dust of the space boots seem very well defined. Perhaps too well defined.

5. Why didn't NASA provide a direct film link from the moon to a live broadcast television feed? Film footage of the event is poor quality, but most people assume that's simply a result of 1960s camera technology in outer space. The real reason for the grainy, glowing low quality of the images is because the networks were forced to film the images from a television set in Houston.

Kubrick was working on *2001* when the U.S. government secretly approached him and asked if he would be interested in participating in this project. In return for his involvement, Kubrick would be allowed to borrow one of NASA's newest camera lenses—the exact type of lens Kubrick need for certain effects on *2001*. The government would also permit the artist to tour an exclusive collection of alien artifacts and autopsy footage at Nevada's infamous Area 51 site.

If Kubrick needed any further convincing, our government hinted that they knew that Kubrick's brother held close ties to the Communist Party USA.

The great director spent more than a year filming and creating specially built soundstages around the world. It is rumored that hundreds of hours of footage was shot during those months: establishing shots, reaction shots, and the shot of Armstrong's first small step upon the "moon" itself.

But what motive could our government possibly have for the elaborate hoax in the first place?

Well, the Cold War for one. John F. Kennedy promised America that we would beat the Russians to the moon, and the Soviets were already ahead on the scorecard thanks to Yuri Gagarin's space travels. The Americans didn't dare lose face to those pesky Ruskies.

The economy was another reason. NASA put folks to work. The space industry was a booming business, and the country's passion for the space race translated to billions in revenue. And it wasn't just NASA profiting from the nation's interest in outer space: movies, television, comic books, food service, music, advertising, and the apparel industry all cashed in on the wave of moon mania.

Finally, perhaps the most cynical reason was that the space program served as a patriotic distraction from the unpopular Vietnam War. Seeing our guy plant the old Stars and Stripes on that crater-filled galactic dustbowl filled each of our hearts with a pride in the American way we seemed to have lost in the latter half of the decade.

So now you are armed with a possible other side of the moon landing scenario. Is there any validity to the claims? You decide.

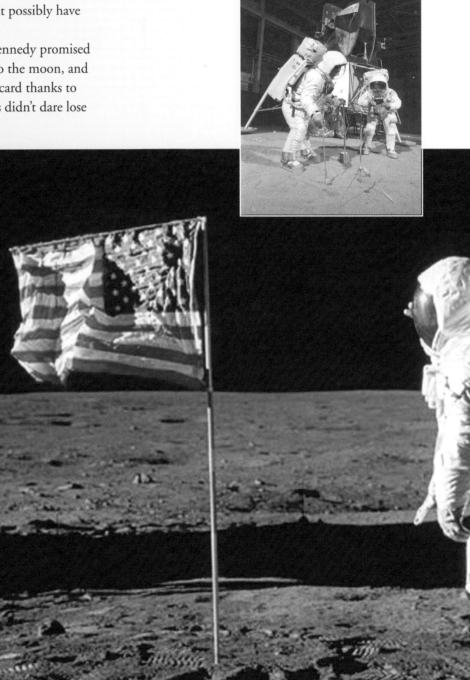

The Underground City of the Lizard People

Deep beneath the heart of Los Angeles's financial district, hundreds of feet below the huge downtown edifices that house banks, corporate offices, and government agencies, lies another city remembered only in obscure Native American legends, an underground world built by a strange race that vanished five thousand years ago.

At least that's what mining engineer W. Warren Shufelt claimed in the January 29, 1934, edition of the *Los Angeles Times*. According to reporter Jean Bosquet, Shufelt had city council's blessing to dig up downtown LA in search of this ancient subterranean civilization.

Shufelt had first heard of the city in a Hopi legend about the Lizard People, a fabled lost race that had nearly been wiped out after a meteor shower rained down on the Southwest around 3000 B.C. (Arizona's famous Winslow Crater was said to be ground zero of this fiery deluge.)

The Lizard People constructed thirteen subterranean settlements along the Pacific Coast to shelter the tribe against future disasters. These underground cities housed a thousand families each, along with stockpiles of food. As the story has it, they used a "chemical solution" that melted solid bedrock to bore out the tunnels and rooms of their subsurface shelters. They also used the tunnels to hold a trove of golden tablets that chronicled the tribe's history, the origin of humankind, and the story of the world back to creation. Shufelt was particularly interested in these tablets for both pecuniary and archeological reasons.

A Hopi chief named Little Green Leaf told Shufelt that the vanished race's capital city was located under present-day downtown Los Angeles. In 1933, after surveying the area, Shufelt occupied the Banning property at 518 North Hill Street and sank a 350-foot shaft straight down, digging for what he said was a "treasure room" directly underneath. Shufelt said that he had located gold in the catacombs below with the aid of his "radio X-ray."

Shufelt never actually found anything. Shortly after the *Times* story appeared, the project suddenly ceased, and Shufelt and his cohorts disappeared. The whole mysterious, improbable business was written off as a hoax and quickly forgotten. Since then, inexplicable tunnels have been unearthed in downtown Los Angeles, but they've usually been explained away as the work of smugglers hiding illegal Chinese laborers in the nineteenth century.

On the evening of December 22, 1933, five weeks before Shufelt's excavations hit the pages of the *Times*, the clairvoyant Miss Edith Elden Robinson envisioned that under Los Angeles lay "a vast city . . . in mammoth tunnels extending to the sea-shore," according to the highly respected *Journal of the American Society for Psychical Research*. She said that the tunnels had been constructed by a vanished race to protect themselves from danger and to provide access to the sea.

Who knows? Maybe this fabulous subterranean city really existed. Perhaps it is even populated with latter-day Lizard People who live hidden and unsuspected hundreds of feet below modern-day Los Angeles, emerging only furtively to watch the twenty-first-century barbarians slowly strangle their own surface-level civilization with smog, traffic, and urban sprawl. —*Mike Marinacci*

The Day the Clown Cried

By the early seventies, Jerry Lewis had gone through a number of public transformations. In the forties and fifties he was known as crooner Dean Martin's monkey-faced, slapstick sidekick in numerous movies and nightclub appearances. After the duo's acrimonious split in 1956, Lewis proved to be a solo box office star with such comedic hits as *The Bellboy* and *The Nutty Professor*, and with those financial successes came the clout to demand directorial control.

As 1972 rolled around, however, Lewis had built a reputation as an egotistical, bullying perfectionist with a thirteen-pill-a-day Percodan habit. To make matters worse, his brand of comedy no longer appealed to the movie-going public. *The Day the Clown Cried* was to be the triumphant return of a more subtle and nuanced Jerry Lewis. The comedian, of Russian Jewish descent, toured Dachau and lost close to forty pounds in an effort to prepare for the role.

The story centers on a World War II–era German clown, Helmut Doork, who is no longer the popular headliner he once was. After overhearing that he is to be fired from the circus, Doork shuffles sadly into a nearby alehouse and promptly gets schnockered. In his inebriated state, he dips his comb in a glass of beer and pulls his hair down over one eye. Next, he takes a fingerful of brown jam and smears it under his nose, creating a passable toothbrush mustache. Finally, to the horror of the tavern's patrons but to the seething delight of the Gestapo officers who have gone unnoticed by our drunken protagonist, Helmut mocks Adolf Hitler himself, screaming, "Ve vill conquer the world . . . Heil me! Heil me! Heil me!" Doork wakes up on the floor of a German political prison, separated from the nearby concentration camp by a few feet of property and a high barbed-wire fence.

Inside the prison Doork is ostracized by his fellow inmates and beaten by the guards. Dejected, battered, and facedown in the mud, the clown hears the distant laughter of a small child from the other prison camp. He looks at his own visage in the puddle's reflection and sees his face covered in stage makeup. He quickly fashions a big ball of sludge and sticks it on the end of his nose. As more and more children from the Jewish camp gather by the fence and laugh at his antics, Doork is filled with a renewed sense of purpose and starts performing his tired old routines to a group of new appreciative fans.

At first the Nazis are none too pleased at Doork's fraternization with the young Jews, but soon they see he has garnered their trust, and they decide to use his charismatic sway over the trusting children.

Promising Doork an easier time during his stay in the jail, Captain Runkel convinces the clown to transport the children from their detention center to the gas chamber. Below is actual text taken from the script.

RUNKEL: Are you one of them, clown?

HELMUT (*terrorized at the thought of death*): No . . . no! I'm not one of them. I'm not!

RUNKEL SMILES, MOVES AWAY FROM HELMUT.

RUNKEL: You misunderstand completely. The Judas goat is never killed. He isn't worth killing. (*Moves to cell door.*) I'm just asking you to lead them.

ANOTHER ANGLE — FAVORING HELMUT

His eyes plead, "No. I can't do it. No."

RUNKEL: Not . . . even to save your own life?

(*For a brief moment,* helmut *struggles to find the courage to stand up to* runkel—*but he has no courage and he sinks slowly to his knees, his head bowed.*)

CLOSE SHOT — RUNKEL

RUNKEL (*victorious*): I'm glad to see you're not a self-appointed martyr.

TWO SHOT — HELMUT, RUNKEL

(RUNKEL *towers above* HELMUT, *who sits back on his haunches, leaning against the wall.*)

RUNKEL: Just think! Now you're really one of us.

(*The truth of* RUNKEL'S *remark hits Helmut like a devastating blow. He turns his face to the wall in shame.* RUNKEL *walks to the door, raps on it, the guard outside swings it open.*)

In the movie's final scene, Doork is shown remorsefully leading a parade of blissfully unaware kids to the end of their brief lives. As he stops at the door, and allows his happy audience entrance to their ruin, he is met with the hand of a small child, beckoning him into the deadly enclosure with them. Knowing that crossing the threshold to the showers means certain death, Doork steps inside and begins his juggling act, much to the delight of his tiny, yet doomed, spectators. As the giant steel door slams shut behind him, a single tear rolls down along the pancake makeup of our redeemed but soon to be departed jester, and the chamber resounds with the sounds of gentle laughter.

When recalling why he chose to accept the role, Lewis was quoted as saying to producer Nate Wachsberger in his own inimitable way, "My bag is comedy, Mr. Wachsberger, and you're asking me if I'm prepared to deliver helpless kids into a gas chamber. Ho-ho. Some laugh—how do I pull it off?"

Lewis apparently sat in silence for a moment, then grabbed the script and declared, "What a horror . . . It must be told."

For decades, Lewis steadfastly refused to comment on the film, and he has been known to become volatile at the mere mention of the title. Occasionally though, he would drop hints that he planned to release the movie, even though he no longer owns the rights to the story and the authors of the original story have sworn that the film will never see the light of day.

© Owen Franken/CORBIS

Hellacious History

Is *there anything more satisfying* than the traditional Hollywood happy ending? Danger has been

thwarted, obstacles have been overcome, the bad guys are brought to justice, and true love is expressed during the long-awaited first kiss—preferably against the backdrop of a breathtaking sunset.

In reality, Hollywood endings are often more dour than some movies would have you believe. Sure, all ended well for Dorothy Gale the minute she clicked her ruby slippers together and recognized there's no place like home, but real life seemed to hold a lot fewer rainbows and Lollipop Guilds for actress Judy Garland. (Although it's possible she envisioned a flying monkey or two during one of her legendary nights of excess.)

Real Hollywood endings, or at least the type of finales you're expecting from this book, are not so much happy as laced with cruel ironies, petty jealousies, and now and then a dose of pure old-fashioned evil. Don't act shocked—this is precisely why you turned to this chapter. Most everyone loves a healthy heaping of schadenfreude.

If you are, however, the type who claims to not experience secret pleasure in the suffering of others, especially those who have more money and fame than you, we suggest you put down this copy of *Weird Hollywood* and go look for a book called *Blissful Hollywood*. (It's three pages long, printed in twenty-four-point type, and the words are double-spaced. The entire third page is a picture of a smiley face.

For the rest of you less-than-blissful types, allow us to present a hellacious history of Hollywood.

Shame on Spade

One of Hollywood's original singing cowboys, Donnell Clyde "Spade" Cooley, once held Hollywood by the tail. He acquired the nickname Spade because of his prowess at the poker table, always winning in spades.

Appearing in more than fifty films, his credits include titles such as *The Kid from Gower Gulch*, *The Silver Bandit*, and *The Singing Sheriff*. He, along with the contributions and talents of Bob Wills and others, coined the "Western swing" sound in the 1940s.

An extravagant spender, Cooley owned an estate on Ventura Boulevard in Los Angeles, a ranch in the Mojave Desert, and a fifty-six-foot yacht. He had a plan to open the first water park in Los Angeles—until he dashed his own dreams.

Born in 1910 and classically trained as a fiddler, he began his career playing square dances and such before his father, John, moved the family from Oklahoma to Los Angeles during the Depression. By the mid-1930s, he was working as an actor, having earned bit parts in several Westerns.

A talented musician, Cooley and his orchestra played the longest gig ever at Santa Monica's Venice Pier Ballroom, where they were hugely popular. The Spade Cooley Orchestra typically had more than a dozen musicians. A charismatic and consummate showman, he dressed himself and his players in handmade Western wear from one of LA's top wardrobe designers, paying as much as $500 per outfit for the most elaborate cowboy getups.

Cooley's first recording, "Shame on You," was an immediate hit. Recorded in 1944, it was number one on the folk music charts and remained his theme song for the rest of his life.

In 1945, Cooley married blond beauty Ella Mae Evans. Their marriage produced a son and a daughter.

Cooley was a complex man; these days, perhaps, he would have been diagnosed as bipolar. He jumped from being loving and thoughtful to firing his band, then trying to patch up the damages the next day. He was purported to be a heavy drinker and womanizer, conditions that at best threatened and at worst shattered many of his professional and private relationships and would eventually lead to his demise.

Perhaps because of his own dalliances, and undoubtedly fueled by his own fits of alcoholic fury, Cooley was constantly hounded by suspicions that Ella Mae was having extramarital affairs. He kept Ella Mae a virtual prisoner in her own home. His suspicions led to rage on April 3, 1961. The Cooleys' fourteen-year-old daughter, Melody, arrived home to witness the brutal beating and murder of her mother at the hands of her father.

Melody later testified in court, "When I entered, he was on the phone. He was talking to his business partner and he said, 'Don't call the police.' He was real sweaty and he had blood spots on his pants. He put down the phone and said, 'Come in here. I want you to see your mother. She's going to tell you something.' He took hold of my arm and took me into the den. The shower was running in the bathroom. Mother was in the shower. He opened the door and said, 'Get up. Melody's here. Talk to her.' He grabbed her by the hair and dragged her into the den with both hands. She was undressed. He banged her head on the floor twice. He called her a slut. She couldn't move. She seemed unconscious. He turned back to mother and said, 'We'll see if you're dead.' Then he stomped her in the stomach with his left foot. He took a cigarette which he had been smoking and burned her twice."

Melody also testified that her father picked up his pistol and aimed it between her eyes, threatening, "You're going to watch me kill her . . . and if you don't, I'll kill you too. I'll kill us all." Just then the phone rang. Distracted, Cooley left the room to answer it, leaving his frightened daughter to escape.

On August 19, 1961, after a month-long trial and nineteen hours of deliberation, the jury convicted Cooley of murder. His poor health saved him from the death penalty, and he was sentenced to life in prison. Ordered to serve out his sentence in the California state prison at Vacaville, he reportedly became a model prisoner, playing in a prison band and building fiddles in the prison hobby shop. He eventually found religion.

The state parole board unanimously recommended parole for Cooley, to become effective the day after his sixtieth birthday. However, three months before his scheduled release date, Cooley was granted a three-day furlough to perform in Oakland at a benefit concert for the Alameda County Sheriff's Department. Cooley was quoted as saying, "I have the feeling that today is the first day of the rest of my life."

He then clutched his chest, dropped his fiddle, and died. He was felled by a fatal heart attack at the age of fifty-nine.—*Julie Ann Ream*

Russ Columbo

Smoldering good looks coupled with a silky-smooth baritone quickly earned Russ Columbo the nickname the Romeo of Song. By 1934, Columbo had already been a veteran of the ballroom circuit, traveling the country with an orchestra that included Gene Krupa and Benny Goodman. His NBC radio program, broadcast from the Roosevelt Hotel (see page 193), was a hit with audiences. His records became the musical standards of the decade, and Universal had signed him to a lucrative movie contract. Not bad for a twenty-six-year-old kid from New Jersey.

But Russ Columbo would never reach the age of twenty-seven.

Columbo invited his best friend, respected portrait photographer Lansing Brown Jr., to the premiere of *Wake Up and Dream.* It was Columbo's first role as leading man. Columbo's date for the evening was actress Carole Lombard. As the film ended, the singing star and the beautiful blonde were whisked away by studio handlers from party to party and celebrated the night in a style befitting a new leading man. But in all the merrymaking, Columbo was never able to ask his good friend what he had thought of the film.

The projectile entered Columbo's left eye, lodging deep in the crooner's brain.

The next day, Columbo dropped by Brown's Los Angeles bungalow to find out if his old pal enjoyed his performance. Greeted warmly by the parents of his dear friend, Columbo headed into the library, where he and Brown often sat and talked. A pair of antique dueling pistols were displayed on the desk of the library. The two friends had played with the handguns many times in the past.

Picking up a matchstick in his right hand, Brown casually lifted the gun with his left. Nonchalantly, Brown swept the match head against the wooden stock of the weapon. Unbeknownst to Brown, the idle gun still contained enough explosive sulfur to ignite and launch a ball still left in the chamber. The projectile ricocheted off a mahogany desk and entered Columbo's left eye, lodging deep in the back of the crooner's brain.

Columbo was declared dead six hours later. At the funeral Brown was inconsolable, weeping on his knees during the entire service.

Brown was put on trial for the murder of his friend. As he took the stand on his own behalf, a grieving Brown recounted, "We were friends . . . he was my best friend . . . I didn't know there was powder and a slug in it . . . there was a noise . . . and Russ was slumped in the chair . . . I put ice on his head . . . he couldn't speak to me." The jury, believing the slaying to be an accident and moved by Brown's sincere grief, exonerated him of all charges.

But family and friends feared for Columbo's elderly mother, Julia, blind and in poor health. In the interests of their matriarch, the family concocted an elaborate ruse that involved Columbo marrying Lombard and moving to England.

Monthly checks were also sent to Columbo's mother. Though she was told the checks were from her son, in reality they were dividends from his life insurance policy. The sympathetic deception went on for a full decade before Julia Columbo peacefully passed away her own bed in 1944.

Marie Prevost

Born Mary Bickford Dunn in Ontario, Canada, on November 8, 1898, Marie Prevost broke into Hollywood at the age of eighteen as one of Mack Sennett's Bathing Beauties. The stunning ingénue became an icon of the Roaring Twenties.

Physically, Marie was the embodiment of the doe-eyed, pouty-lipped flapper girl we think of today. She capitalized on those looks when she moved from New York, where she was a chorus girl in Broadway's *The Midnight Follies*. In Los Angeles, Marie landed a contract at one of the most powerful studios in Tinseltown, Mack Sennett's Keystone Studios.

Universal Pictures noticed Marie, stole her away from Sennett, and almost overnight made Marie a full-blown star. The twenties were a good decade for Marie, as she starred in such silent-era box office bonanzas as *Kiss Me Again*, *Up in Mabel's Room*, and *Getting Gertie's Garter*.

Alas, the thirties were a much crueler decade for the young glamour girl. Her mother was killed in a car accident, and Marie turned to food and drink for solace. She found herself in a series of big-budget flops, and also found herself at the end of her contract without any offers. Talkies were making a bigger noise than many in the industry had expected, and, to make matters worse, America was just heading into the Great Depression.

With little work on the horizon, Marie's bank account and star power shrank as much as her waistline ballooned, and her drinking grew out of control.

Convinced (in her alcoholic haze) that she could make a comeback, Marie decided not to diet but to give up food entirely. Not surprisingly, she died of malnutrition in her squalid apartment at the age of thirty-eight.

Startlingly, the Marie Prevost story doesn't end there, because the gruesome footnote to Marie's short life is that when the police responded to calls of rancid odors coming from her door, they burst in to find Marie's dog had eaten most of the remains of the deceased and decaying diva.

Charles Manson and the Tate-LaBianca Murders

It's often said that the Manson murders brought an end to the sixties. Over the years, countless people have tried to clarify why and how Charles Manson orchestrated the horrific deaths of seven people he had never even spoken to before (plus an unborn baby). The truth is, there is no coherent answer, just the malevolent deeds of an evil madman and his deluded, sycophantic followers.

At the behest of Beach Boys drummer Dennis Wilson, record producer Terry Melcher met and auditioned Manson, an aspiring rock star. Melcher didn't think Manson was particularly interesting, but he gave Manson $50 for his trouble. Manson assumed the $50 was for a recording contract. With no word from Melcher, Manson decided to return to Melcher's home at 10050 Cielo Drive in Benedict Canyon to confront the music industry bigwig. Filmmaker Roman Polanski and his wife, Sharon Tate, now occupied the home and firmly asked Manson to leave the premises. Manson did retreat, but not before making eye contact with Tate.

On the night of August 8, 1969, Manson ordered Tex Watson and a few female followers to drive to Melcher's old house in Benedict Canyon, kill everyone in it, and "leave something witchy behind." There, five people were murdered, including Tate, her unborn child, and four guests. The word *pig* was written on the front door of the house in Tate's blood. Contrary to urban legend, Sharon Tate died with her child still in her womb. Killer Susan Atkins toyed with the idea of removing it and presenting it to Charlie as a gift, but for some reason decided against it at the last moment.

A week earlier, Gary Hinman in Topanga Canyon had been killed after several days of being tortured. Manson and his "Family" alleged that Hinman had stolen money from them. Hinman's killers, headed by Manson's right-hand man, Bobby Beausoleil, painted a paw print on the wall in the victim's blood, along with the words *political piggy*. Beausoleil was arrested shortly afterward while driving Hinman's car with the murder weapon inside.

Supposedly to clear Beausoleil's name, Manson staged more gruesome "copycat" murders to make the police realize they had the wrong guy in custody.

On the night after Sharon Tate, her unborn child, and her friends were murdered, Rosemary and Leno LaBianca returned to their Los Feliz home, miles from the gruesome events of the previous evening. Leno had just sat down to read the newspaper when Manson entered the house from a back door, tied up the LaBiancas, and left. Watson and the girls punctured and stabbed the pair sixty-seven times. The word *war* was carved in Leno's stomach, and the words *rise*, *death to pigs*, and *healter skelter* [*sic*] were written on the walls in the victims' blood.

> **There, five people were murdered, including Tate, her unborn child, and four guests.**

Leno LaBianca's wallet was stolen and discarded at a gas station in a primarily poor black neighborhood, with the hope that the credit cards would be discovered and used illegally by someone there. By butchering only rich white people, Manson, a white supremacist, hoped police would deduce that the crimes were committed by members of the Black Panther organization.

For several months the crimes baffled detectives and sent the city into fits of terror. Sporting goods stores couldn't keep guns on the shelves, and guard dogs were nearly impossible to acquire.

In October, a group of hippies was arrested in Death Valley for arson and auto theft. While in jail, Atkins could barely contain her excitement and continually bragged to her cellmate that she and her friends were responsible for the Tate and LaBianca slayings. Then she revealed the details in an interview with the *Los Angeles Times*, which busted the case wide open.

Begun in June 1970, Manson's trial was the longest in LA history. The jury was sequestered for nine months in the Ambassador Hotel (where, two years earlier, presidential hopeful Robert F. Kennedy was assassinated the night after having dinner with Roman Polanski and Sharon Tate). Manson and his Family were found guilty and sentenced to die in the gas chamber. (In photo below, Atkins, left, and two other Family members, after receiving the death penalty.) In 1971 the death penalty was ruled unconstitutional, which is why Manson and his Family members are still alive and periodically come up for parole.

Even today people want to know why, and there is no simple answer. A paranoid Manson convinced his homicidal crew that Armageddon would soon be started by a revolution of angry black people. He was confident that he was hearing indications of the conflict in popular rock-and-roll lyrics. District attorney Vincent Bugliosi acquired a conviction with the theory

© Bettmann/CORBIS

of "Helter Skelter," a global war between blacks and whites, which Manson was determined to instigate. While this battle was waging, the Family would hide in Death Valley in a fantastic bottomless pit, which no one had ever seen. Manson believed blacks would emerge victorious and allow him to be world leader

Manson liked to read the Bible, and he skewed its messages to prove his point: He thought himself Jesus Christ, the Son of Man. Man Son. Get it? They would even hold mock crucifixions, starring (of course) Charlie himself. In the Bible, the book of Revelations refers to the rapture and the four horsemen of the apocalypse; those would certainly be the Beatles and their breastplates of fire—their electric guitars. The Beatles' 1968 *White Album* was the soundtrack in the Manson Family home, and Manson took this as his personal note from the Beatles to start his race war, Helter Skelter. There are loads of "clues" on the album, which Manson interpreted to suit himself and his agenda.

When I put together my Helter Skelter Tour, we cover more than thirty miles and visit not only the places where the crimes occurred, but also the places where the victims spent their time, such as where Tate lived when she was working on *The Beverly Hillbillies*. We also visit where the killers hosed off in a driveway after the Tate murders. A percentage of the ticket price goes to the Doris Tate Crime Victims Bureau, a nonprofit organization dedicated to public safety and victims' rights.

A DVD version of the tour is available at www.dearlydepartedtours.com.—*Scott Michaels*

Manson's Musical Connections

Charles Manson. Dangerous convict, bloodthirsty cult leader, and wannabe pop recording artist.

That's correct. The murderous mastermind behind the Tate-LaBianca killings was also a frustrated folksinger and musician. Manson was doing time in the state pen the first time the Beatles ever shook their mop tops on *The Ed Sullivan Show*. The deranged prisoner was said to be obsessed with their fame and promised that one day he'd become more celebrated than the popular lads from Liverpool.

One of the most persistent and well-known stories about Manson and the world of music is absolutely untrue. This tale reports the orchestrator of at least nine murders was supposedly among the hundreds of hopeful young actors and musicians who auditioned for the sixties TV rock group the Monkees.

In 1965, producers Bob Rafelson and Burt Schneider placed an ad in *Variety* looking for "folk musicians" to play "four insane boys." It seems a part Manson was born to play, but during the casting cattle call since he was busy serving a stretch in the slammer that lasted until 1967. (Still, it's interesting to think of a world in which Charles Manson is referred to as the short, cute Monkee.) Other notables who really were among the hopefuls were Paul Petersen, Steven Stills, and renowned Hollywood deejay Rodney Bingenheimer.

Manson's connection to the sixties' music scene takes a strange and factual turn in 1968. One night as he was returning to his Pacific Palisades pad, Dennis Wilson, drummer for the Beach Boys, picked up two young female hitchhikers and brought them home with him. These girls were Charlie's girls, and before Wilson knew what was happening, the Manson clan had moved into his posh LA digs.

The Beach Boy and the "boy from the big house" even wrote at least one song together. Originally titled "Cease to Exist," the name and some lyrics were changed. The new title was "Never Learn to Stop Loving." The song later became the B side to a nominal Beach Boy hit, "Bluebirds over the Mountain."

Manson's version starts:

> Pretty girl, pretty, pretty girl
> Cease to exist
> Just come and say you love me
> Give up your world
> C'mon you can see
> I'm your kind, I'm your kind.

Wilson later admitted that he cowrote the song with Manson, but felt justified in not including Manson's name on the songwriting credits or allowing him to partake in the royalties because, according to Wilson, Manson was paid in cash, and, on top of that, he had stolen or damaged more than $100,000 of Wilson's property.

The Beatles came back to play an integral role in Manson's life in 1969. Under the delusion that the rock group was speaking directly to him, Charles Manson and his followers misinterpreted many of the songs on the *White Album* ("Helter Skelter," "Blackbird," and "Piggies," for example) as the commencement of an apocalyptical race war.

Manson was arrested and convicted of seven counts of first-degree murder and one count of conspiracy to commit murder for his involvement in the Tate-LaBianca murders. He was also convicted of the first-degree murders of two other people.

Manson's music is still occasionally recorded by top music acts. In 1993, Guns N' Roses covered Manson's "Look at Your Game," and a year later shock rocker Marilyn Manson included lyrics from Charles Manson's "Mechanical Man" in his song "My Monkey."

When speaking about his musical tastes during a famous interview with Geraldo Rivera, the lifelong criminal had this to say: "I'm not a generation of the sixties [*sic*] I'm a Bing Crosby fan, not a Beatle fan. You guys make me out to be something I wasn't. . . . I was a beatnik, not a hippie."

Regardless of his musical influences, Manson enjoyed creating music. In the same Rivera interview, Manson seemed despondent when he was not allowed to take a guitar into the prison.

One is left to wonder what would have happened had Manson ever made a name for himself in the recording industry. Maybe he would have gone on to write and produce dozens of hits. Maybe he would have developed a unique sound, and maybe he would have never been involved with murder at all. Maybe he could have been the next Phil Spector. (Cue ironic music.)

Man from Mars Bandit

During the spring, summer, and fall of 1951, the San Gabriel Valley was terrorized by one of the strangest criminals in the LA's history. His face was hidden behind a gas mask, his head covered by a crash helmet, and two corkscrew antennae-like wires popped out of the ears of his helmet. A little white plastic skull was affixed to the headgear; another skull was sewn on to his right breast pocket. He wore tight-fitting black shirts and pants, black leather gloves, and knee-high motorcycle boots. With a .45 pistol in a holster, a belt of ammo slung around his shoulder, and a 12-gauge shotgun on his back, he waved his .38 in the faces of petrified cashiers. Newspapers dubbed him the "Man from Mars Bandit."

On May 25, he made his first daring robbery, striking Boy's Market, now known as Hawaii Super Market, at the corner of Valley and Del Mar. He rushed into the giant grocery store, known for its many rows of cash registers, and before anyone had a chance to scream or react, he quickly emptied the contents of the tills, to the tune of $4,000, into his black leather shaving bag and escaped.

His intimidating garb made it difficult for witnesses to think about anything more than their mortal existence, much less give much of a description of the lawbreaker. Over the course of the next few months, the bandit struck seemingly at will.

On October 11, cashier Thelma Bacquet recognized the darkly uniformed figure with sofa springs affixed to his head as the same man who had robbed her at Boy's five months prior. She jumped into her car and drove to a nearby gas station to call the police. By the time the dozens of officers arrived, the costumed criminal had already made off with $13,675 in his shaving bag.

Unaware of the police presence, but always prepared for a confrontation, the bandit was making his getaway through the store by using his three hostages as human shields. Quietly camouflaged behind a pyramid of stacked canned peas, police officer Harry P. Stone fired one slug from his .38 caliber pistol into the left side of the gunman's head. Two hours later, the Man from Mars Bandit was dead.

He was identified as twenty-seven-year-old Forest Ray Colson, a former Glendora and Monterey Park police officer. He had been released from both positions for "inefficiency" and "conduct unbecoming an officer."

Colson's total take for five months of robbery was $55,000—not bad for a part-time job in 1951 dollars.

The city of San Gabriel has commemorated this infamous fugitive by erecting a set of 1950s postmodern space age–looking light fixtures across the street from Hawaii Super Market in the parking lot of a Denny's restaurant. Colson's original uniform is on display at the San Gabriel Police Department.

Headgear worn by the "Man from Mars" at the time of his death. A single 38-caliber bullet from the officers revolver entered Forrest Ray Colson's head approximately 3½ inches above the left ear. (10/11/51)

Hollywood's First Movie Star

In its infancy, the movie industry refused to give screen credits to actors for fear they would become well known enough to bargain for bigger salaries. This practice, while a shrewd bit of business, was flawed from the beginning. It was only a matter of time before some charismatic performer would shine bright enough to light up the silent screen and grab the attention of the ticket-buying public; that charismatic someone was Florence Lawrence.

Upon turning twenty years old in 1906, the Canadian-born Lawrence moved to New York to find fame on Broadway. Work on the Great White Way proved elusive for the blond beauty, but she did manage to catch on with a fledgling film studio and, thanks to her ability to ride a horse, was cast as Daniel Boone's daughter.

It wasn't long before Lawrence caught the eye of the great D. W. Griffith at Biograph Studios, and the director was instrumental in signing her for the comfortable sum of $25 a week. Almost immediately, the public was enamored. Biograph's offices were besieged with fan letters, begging for the name of the flaxen-haired actress. In a most mild form of capitulation—and a bigger dose of self-promotion—the studio decided to give Lawrence credit. She was billed as the "Biograph Girl."

By 1909 Florence Lawrence was receiving a salary double the industry norm, and her popularity soared even higher thanks to her leading role in the first comedy series in movie history, the Jones series. A year later, with Lawrence's star still on the rise, she was lured away from Biograph by the founder of Universal Pictures, Carl Laemmle.

Laemmle promised the magnetic young performer more money and promoted his new headliner with her own name not only in the screen credits but also on marquees and in print advertising. This was just the beginning for Laemmle's brand of celebrity marketing. Next he started a rumor that Florence Lawrence was killed in an automobile accident. The movie-going public spiraled into nationwide grief. Weeks later Laemmle took out ads in the major newspapers all over the country assuring the grieving country that the great Florence Lawrence was alive and well. To prove it, he had her make personal appearances. The maneuver only helped sell tickets and made Lawrence a household name.

During the shooting of 1914's *Pawns of Destiny*, Lawreance was badly burned in a staged fire. In 1916, she was paralyzed for four months. Her career never recovered from the absence, though she did have small parts in the 1920s and a string of uncredited roles in the 1930s. In 1938, the onetime golden girl of the silver screen unceremoniously ended her life by swallowing ant killer.

Destitute at the time of her death, Florence Lawrence was buried in an unmarked grave at Hollywood Forever Cemetery. In 1991, Roddy McDowell, a member of the National Film Preservation Board, paid for a marker that reads, FLORENCE LAWRENCE—'THE BIOGRAPH GIRL'—THE FIRST MOVIE STAR—1890–1938.

We hope that, with the proper billing, the world's very first movie star is now resting in peace.

Karl Dane

Danish-born comedian Karl Dane enjoyed a fair amount of success during the silent-film era. He was a blue-collar worker by trade when he auditioned for a bit part in a two-reel comedy short. To his surprise, he got the gig, and his career as a comedic actor was born. His entertainer's salary afforded him the luxury of a very comfortable Hollywood Hills mansion. All over the country, people found themselves amused by his comic antics and his giant grinning face. The former machinist quickly became accustomed to the perks of fame.

Throughout the twenties, Dane worked with some of the biggest stars of his time. Buster Keaton, Lillian Gish, and Rudolph Valentino all shared the screen with the gangly, happy-go-lucky comic. During this period, MGM studios paired up Dane with Scottish actor George K. Arthur. The duo starred in a series of low-budget comedy shorts that proved both popular and profitable.

While some had been experimenting with pairing a soundtrack to movies, talkies were seen as an expensive undertaking and a technological nightmare to most insiders. Even after the box-office success of 1927's *The Jazz Singer*, the studios did not make the immediate leap to sound. Before the thirties rolled in, however, it was clear that the days of big-screen pantomime were nearing their end.

It became just as clear to studio execs and performers alike that not everyone would be making a smooth transition. While the advent of sound helped to establish the movie-making business as *the* industry in Hollywood, it also ended a good number of careers. Karl Dane's career was among the casualties.

While Dane's was able rely on quiet slapstick and goofy faces to elicit laughter from the ticket-buying public, his thick Danish accent was said to sound too guttural and harsh to be employed for comic effect when sound became the standard of film. Dane managed a few small nonspeaking roles in talking pictures, thanks in large part to his friendship with Buster Keaton, but by 1933 he had given up hope of making a comeback.

After brief stints as a carpenter and a mechanic, Dane accepted a job as a hot dog vendor outside the gates of MGM. The cruel reversal of fortune was too much for the proud Dane to endure. In 1934, a mere nine years after his film debut in MGM's smash hit *The Big Parade*, Karl Dane spread his reviews and newspaper articles on the floor at his Miracle Mile apartment. Sitting down on a chair in the middle of the room, he raised a pistol to his head and pulled the trigger.

Fatty Arbuckle

It is said that newborn Roscoe "Fatty" Arbuckle entered this world in 1887 at a hefty sixteen pounds. By the time the plump funnyman had become a household name and formed his own film company thirty years later, he was tipping the scales at close to three hundred pounds. The extra baggage around Arbuckle's midsection both amazed and amused movie audiences during the silent era. Despite his bulk, Arbuckle moved with the fluid grace of a ballerina and possessed more athleticism than many of the stuntmen working in the back lots at the time.

It was not obesity that finally ended the brilliant career of Hollywood's first million-dollar player; it was the weight of scandal that brought him down.

From 1909 to 1921, Arbuckle had appeared in more than 150 motion pictures. In 1914 alone he starred in 49 movies, filming many of them simultaneously. Although most of these pictures were two-reel films, that's still a lot of broomsticks to the back of the head, pies to the face, and comic pratfalls that inevitably end up with landing on the seat of one's pants. So when in 1921 director Fred Fisbach, Arbuckle's friend, mentioned taking a long Labor Day weekend vacation in San Francisco, Arbuckle jumped at the chance to unwind and celebrate.

The two pals had booked a couple

suites at the elegant St. Francis Hotel in the city's Union Square district and had arranged for cases of alcohol to be delivered to their rooms. This was no easy task for ordinary folk during Prohibition, but for Hollywood's most famous comedian and his well-connected friend, it was only a matter of time before the champagne was flowing freely.

Everyone was enjoying themselves, dancing and frolicking, when Arbuckle suddenly noticed that a couple of uninvited guests had crashed his shindig: Virginia Rappe and Maude Delmont. Rappe was an attractive starlet with a dubious reputation who had badmouthed Arbuckle in the press on more than one occasion. By the time she was seventeen years old, Rappe had had five abortions, given up one out-of-wedlock child for adoption (presumably for profit), and had more venereal diseases than film credits.

Delmont was a professional con artist whose rap sheet included extortion, fraud, and racketeering. She made a name for herself as a woman who had blackmailed politicians and powerful men in Hollywood either with photos of compromising situations or by producing women who falsely claimed to have been raped. Arbuckle expressed his concerns about having the two unscrupulous women in attendance, but he let them stay anyway.

Hours passed, and Arbuckle had to leave the party early to help a friend. Upon entering his bedroom to change clothes, the entertainer discovered what he perceived to be a drunken Rappe lying on the floor of his adjoining bathroom. Her clothes were partially torn off her body. (A number of witnesses at Arbuckle's trial testified that they had seen Rappe rip off her own clothes at a number of parties after a few drinks.) Arbuckle picked up the woman and laid her on his bed, then returned with a glass of water and a bucket of ice.

Just then, Delmont rushed into the room. Arbuckle explained that her friend must have had too much to drink, and Delmont began applying the ice to her feverish cohort. Rappe then sprung from the bed, struggling again to remove her already tattered blouse and screamed, "What did he do to me, Maudie? Roscoe did this to me!"

The caterwauling sent many partygoers to Arbuckle's bedroom, and Delmont called a physician friend of hers, Dr. Melville "Rummy" Rumwell. Delmont told the doctor that she believed Arbuckle had raped the plastered actress, but the doctor found no signs of intercourse, forced or otherwise. He treated her for pain and released her to Delmont that night. Arbuckle left the party, shaken but confident his good name was clear.

Days later, an ailing Rappe was admitted into a local hospital where she soon died of peritonitis, an acute infection that was caused, in this case, by a ruptured bladder. Arbuckle was arrested and a trial date was set. Soon rumors spread that Arbuckle had forced himself on the innocent young actress and that the stress of his enormous weight fatally injured her. Headlines falsely screamed across the front page of many newspapers in the country: RAPER DANCES WHILE VICTIM DIES! Perhaps the most widespread of these yellow journalism stories was that Arbuckle had raped the woman with a Coke bottle.

The melodramatic trial lasted for a year, and, after two mistrials, Arbuckle not only was cleared of all charges, but he received what is believed to be the very first written apology from a jury. It stated: "Acquittal is not enough for Roscoe Arbuckle. We feel that a great injustice has been done him . . . there was not the slightest proof adduced to connect him in any way with the commission of a crime. He was manly throughout the case and told a straightforward story which we all believe. We wish him success and hope that the American people will take the judgment of fourteen men and women that Roscoe Arbuckle is entirely innocent and free from all blame."

The long trial took its toll on Arbuckle. He was banned from the industry by Will Hays, president of the newly formed Motion Picture Producers and Distributors of America—an organization that promised to clean up and renovate the image of the movie industry. He had lost his savings, his homes, and his cars. Through the years, good friend Buster Keaton would slip Arbuckle some uncredited film work, but Arbuckle was never the same man.

In 1930, after a considerable exile, Arbuckle started directing films under the name William Goodrich, his father's first and middle names. A year later, Warner Brothers signed Arbuckle to a feature film contract, his very first talkies. The six films, while not as mesmerizing as his early works, were well received, and they hold up even today. After filming only a handful of the shorts, the forty-six-year-old actor died in his sleep of a heart attack. Lifelong pal Keaton maintained that Roscoe died of a broken heart.

Bob Crane's Unsolved Murder

The victim had been callously murdered

while he slept in his two-bedroom apartment. There was no evidence of a break-in, despite the fact the fatally injured party was known to double-lock his door at all times. An unspecified blunt instrument had crushed his skull in two fatal blows. An electrical cord was wound tightly around the victim's throat. No money was missing from the deceased's wallet, and police quickly ruled out robbery.

Actress Victoria Berry was the first to discover the body of her friend and coworker—a body so brutalized that she first assumed the dark red puddle on the mattress behind the dead man's head was the long auburn hair of a woman. But when she noticed the distinctive left-hand wristwatch, she knew she was looking at the corpse of Bob Crane.

If the thought of one of television's most charming comedic actors lying lifeless in a pool of his own blood wasn't jarring enough for the American public to imagine, the revelation of his kinky escapades took almost everybody else by shock.

Crane's first big Hollywood break came in 1956. He had been working as a disc jockey in his home state of Connecticut when he was lured to Los Angeles KNX radio to host a celebrity-interview show. His easygoing magnetism and quick wit soon earned him the title of "King of the LA Airwaves." It wasn't long before Crane also became one of the first deejays to command a six-figure income.

A born performer, Crane dropped out of high school to play drums with the Connecticut Symphony Orchestra. Now that he was living in Hollywood, Crane was going to take a shot at stardom. He often told friends he wanted to become "the next Jack Lemmon."

After a number of television guest-star appearances, in 1965 Crane was cast as the enterprising Colonel Hogan in *Hogan's Heroes*. While filming the Nazi POW comedy, Crane divorced his first wife and married actress Patricia Olsen (aka Sigrid Valdis), who played Colonel Klink's buxom secretary, Hilda. The show was a hit for six years, and it was still performing well in its time slot when CBS decided to pull the plug because it wasn't capturing the highly desired eighteen-to-thirty-five demographic.

Financially comfortable, Crane continued to make guest appearances and made-for-TV movies. But after *The Bob Crane Show* ended after just two months on the air in 1975, the star found that work in television was increasingly difficult to find.

In 1978 his second marriage dissolved amid rumors of numerous casual extramarital encounters. Word around the studios was that Crane had developed a king-sized appetite for all sorts of "amor"—the more bizarre the better. Outlandish erotic behavior was nothing new in Hollywood, but one of Crane's favorite activities was nonconsensual photographing and videotaping of his conquests.

Crane's behavior worried TV executives. He had become consumed with this desire to record his dalliances. The nation believed Crane was the handsome, wholesome, wisecracking all-American man, and nobody in the industry wanted to be in the position to explain away his penchant for autobiographical pornography should Crane's private life become exposed to the public.

One of Crane's constant companions was an electronics expert named John Henry Carpenter, introduced to him by *Hogan's Heroes* costar Richard Dawson. Carpenter provided Crane with state-of-the-art video cameras, and at times he took part in Crane's group trysts.

But Crane tired of Carpenter's company. On the night before the murder, the two men were visiting a favorite local watering hole in Scottsdale, Arizona, but their discussion was described by witnesses as "tense." People in the know

© Bettmann/CORBIS

believe that Crane informed his long-time cohort that he was dissolving their friendship. The next day, Crane's dead body was found on his bed in Scottsdale, Arizona.

Police records indicate that Carpenter called Crane's apartment from Los Angeles a number of times the following day. Carpenter had taken an 11 A.M. flight from Arizona to LA the morning after their "tense" discussion. Investigators noted that Carpenter didn't seem surprised when he was informed the police were there.

Carpenter's rental car was examined, and tiny spots of dried blood and what may have been brain tissue were discovered on the passenger door. DNA tests were not available at the time, but the bloodstains were type B. Only 10 percent of the world's population is type B, and Crane was among that minority.

Though it looked like he had reasonable cause to file charges, the Scottsdale district attorney let the case go dormant. Then, in 1992, fourteen years after Crane's death, the case was reopened and Carpenter was subsequently arrested. Carpenter was acquitted of all charges, and he maintained his innocence until his death in 1998.

Did John Henry Carpenter beat a murder rap, or was the killer a jealous husband, a hired thug, or a scorned lover? It's likely the murder of Bob Crane will remain just another of Hollywood's sensational unsolved murders.

Local Heroes

*i*t ain't so easy to make it in Tinseltown. **This city seems to delight in crushing the hopes and dreams of the supremely talented, the not so talented, as well as the delusionally talented on a daily basis.**

For every Lana Turner discovered sipping soda at the Top Hat Café (not Schwab's Drug Store, as the popular legend goes) there have been approximately six billion would-be actors, writers, and directors who never got to experience the thrill of being seen on the red carpet . . . or of having Joan and Melissa Rivers coo and cluck over their evening attire, only to cackle cattily the nanosecond they're out of earshot.

It takes a thick skin, a resilient spirit, the patience of Job, a serious dedication to craft, a little luck, and a good amount of ability—and that's just to get a nonspeaking role on *Two and a Half Men.* Having a rich producer father also helps.

This chapter is devoted to all those who have taken their shot at immortality in this business we call show. Some are still climbing their way to the top, some recognize they've made their contribution, and others are at their peak.

Hollywood Boulevard Characters

In 1991, *Christopher Dennis* was just another frustrated waiter-actor in Los Angeles. Sick of hearing his boss tell him he couldn't have time off to go on auditions, Dennis and a couple thespian friends started dreaming up ways of becoming their own bosses.

Ever since he was a kid, Dennis knew he bore a striking resemblance to Superman actor Christopher Reeve. His pals decided that, with the proper accoutrements, they could pass for Elvis Presley and Charlie Chaplin. The enterprising trio quickly realized that there was a new, built-in audience of out-of-towners every day at Grauman's Chinese Theater, and many of them would be happy to part with a buck or two to pose for snapshots with a bona fide celebrity look-alike.

In the years since, both Chaplin and Elvis have left the building, but Dennis's Superman remains at the corner of Hollywood Boulevard and Orange Drive to fight for truth, justice, and his share of the tourist dollars. Nowadays there are dozens of recognizable figures parading and posing with vacationers, from Jack Sparrow to Freddy Krueger, but few garner the attention of Superman, and that's partly because of Dennis's dedication to and reverence for the hero. "When I'm out there in costume, I am the character of Superman. I take it seriously, and I want people, after they meet me, to walk away and go back home thinking they really did just meet Superman."

In his personal life, Dennis seems to have taken this type of method acting to a new level. He and his wife, Bonnie, live in a one-bedroom apartment building that is walking distance to his "job." The residence is literally filled to the brim with tens of thousands of Superman paraphernalia worth more than $2.5 million. His incredible collection contains everything from Superman fast-food plastic cups to an actual life mask of TV's Superman, George Reeves, to a

1978 *Superman* movie poster autographed by the entire cast. Dennis even owns (and often wears) the original athletic cup Christopher Reeve wore to protect his merely mortal private parts while he portrayed the Man of Steel.

When pressed for his favorite piece of Super-memorabilia, Dennis hesitates and explains that each is dear to him, but he does have a particular fondness for his autographed Superman cape. "It started out as this thing I would only let Superman people sign—people like Noel Neill [Lois Lane], Jack Larson [Jimmy Olsen], Richard Donner [director], and John Williams [composer]," Dennis recounts. "But we took it to the American premiere of *Superman Returns*, and as soon Dean Cain was signing it, Mike Tyson asked what it was." Dennis started to explain to the former heavyweight champ it was a sort of an exclusive Superman-only signatory club, when Tyson grabbed the pen from Cain's hand and inked his own name on the bright red material. Dennis kept his mouth shut and sagely wondered to himself, "How do you tell Mike Tyson 'no'?" Since then the cape has been signed by hundreds of other nonsuper types, including Bruce Willis, Heather Locklear, Will Smith, and Gene Simmons.

Actress Jennifer Wenger was walking by the Kodak Theater, pursuing a nine-to-five job, when she first met Christopher Dennis. He was not in his superhero costume, but she recalls he was wearing a Hawaiian shirt with the Superman insignia and a Superman watch and ring. Wenger remembers the conversation: "We got to talking. I said, 'Oh, that's cool you're Superman.' He said, 'You look like Wonder Woman.' I said, 'I was her for Halloween.'"

Wenger admitted the costume was still in her closet. Dennis assured her that she would make decent money if she showed up that Saturday dressed as Wonder Woman. "It I made pretty good cash for like three hours—definitely better than I expected to make on some eight-hour shift at a regular job. So I said, 'Screw doing a job I'm going to hate; I want to do something fun. I want to do this.' I've been doing it off and on ever since."

Wenger loves portraying comics' first super-powered heroine. She read Wonder Woman comics as a child and has been a fan of Lynda Carter (TV's Wonder Woman) for as long as she remembers. She sheepishly admits that she knew Carter only as the commercial spokesperson for Lens Express until her mother explained that Carter donned the red, white, blue, and gold getup to battle nefarious villains in the seventies. "I always thought she was so beautiful. I loved her eyes. I wanted to be her."

Conversely, Dennis was not much of a comic book reader as a kid, but that doesn't stop him from upholding his own supermoral code of ethics while in spandex. It's actually more fun to watch the children who watch Dennis than it is to watch Dennis. Preschoolers especially are in a state of awe when they come face to face with Superman. Some too astonished to speak; others relentlessly fire away questions to their favorite Kryptonian. Typically, they ask Dennis to fly, bend a street sign, or use his heat vision, and Dennis, true to character, kindly and patiently asks each youngster, "If I use my powers for fun, and someone really needed my help while I was goofing off, it wouldn't be a good thing, would it?" Invariably, the kid understands that with great power comes great responsibility, and they walk away believing they actually met the real Superman—and as far as Dennis is concerned, that's a super day's work.

Melrose Mystery Lady

In this town, if you're not famous for being famous, you can always become famous for not being famous. The late Rea Suzanne Strauss, for instance, carved out a nice little niche of Hollywood recognition for herself.

Little is known of this unconventional fashionista, and the Internet is uncommonly bereft of information regarding her. It seems all that is left are the recollections

of people who would occasionally pass this unique woman on the street during her daily excursion in the neighborhood, where some people came to know her as the "Lava Lady."

Did she live in a house made of actual lava? Was she in fact the estranged ex-wife of world-renowned children's book author Dr. Seuss? Did she, as some people have claimed, come from another planet? The enigmatic Strauss has passed, so we may never know the answers (although I will assume she was an earthling), but this quiet nonconformist made her mark on the community. Below are a few recollections about one of Hollywood's more enigmatic local personalities.

Suzanne Strauss was the woman who used to walk around on platform heels in a suede pantsuit, hands clasped in prayer, hair spun up in a twelve-inch cone, walking slowly down Hollywood streets. She was a trip. She lived in a home off Beverly that was made of black lava rock, and had children's swings and toys in the yard. That always seemed a little unsettling to me.—Chris Dye, former West Hollywood resident

I lived in the Melrose-Fairfax area from 1992 to 1994. I'd often stroll around the neighborhood and would walk past this rather tall, very skinny, and extremely elderly woman who was notable primarily for her hair, which stood up on the top of her head like a single spike protruding a good six inches into the air. Her pancake makeup and her clothes, which invariably consisted of wild bell-bottomed pantsuits, were always the most garish of colors.

It was generally accepted that this woman— who never spoke, never smiled, never looked me in the eye even once out of over a dozen encounters— made her own clothes. Everybody who lived in that neighborhood during the late eighties and early nineties had seen her and knew about her. She walked around alone almost every day, a colorful, if haunting, local character. —Mark Tapio Kines, Cassava Films

Rea Suzanne Strauss, alternately rumored as being the widow of Dr. Seuss, omniscient, clairvoyant, and/or a practicing witch, was an oft-seen LA eccentric who lived in the famous Black Lava Rock House (criminally torn down rather recently). I photographed her on assignment for the late great Glue magazine. She was very nice to me.—Jack Gould, photographer

David Liebe Hart: Renaissance Man

Church musician, sign painter, poet, puppeteer, and actor David Liebe Hart has been a Los Angeles–area cult personality since 1988 when he first gave voice to the ventriloquist dummy Chip the Black Boy on the cable public access show *The Junior Christian Science Bible Lesson Show*. Some criticized the choice of the name Chip the Black Boy, but Liebe Hart (an African American) defends his puppet's moniker. "He is a black boy. If he was a white boy, I would have called him Chip the White Boy."

The ventriloquism skills of the entire staff of the show would be much harder to defend, but the low-budget, quirky guests and puppeteering mixed with scripture and original songs by Liebe Hart are what made the show an underground hit for two decades.

Liebe Hart declares that he got into puppetry thanks to the guidance of two legendary pioneers in the field: Burr Tillstrom, creator of *Kukla, Fran and Ollie*, and the architect of the Muppets empire, Jim Henson. "They gave me some of the odd puppets they didn't really use."

While Liebe Hart has a profound fondness for puppetry, it's fair to say they are just a vehicle for his true passion: singing and songwriting. Liebe Hart chronicled his meeting with Tillstrom and Henson in his thirteen-minute autobiographical opus, *Story of David Liebe Hart*:

> I met my Sunday school teacher
> Jim Henson and Burr Tillstrom
> They gave me their puppet collection
> If I'd give them a resurrection
> To do a puppet show called
> *The Junior Christian Science Bible*
> *Lesson Show*

A deeply religious man, Liebe Hart peppers in biblical quotes during almost every conversation. He not only accepts that he has a personal relationship with the Lord, he also believes that he has made personal contact with celestial beings on many occasions. He even gets e-mail from members of alien governments. The artist is quick to point out that all German people are direct descendents of an extraterrestrial race of beings known as the Korendians. Likewise Liebe Hart maintains that all Irish can trace their true lineage back to the planet Omega.

He insists the two races have been on Earth for thousands of years, and while both outer space tribes have a secret allegiance to the United States of America, they are ironically sworn enemies to each other.

"I love the Korendians and I love the Omegans, and I'm not going to take sides," he confides. "I don't agree with the war; I just wish I knew why they hated each other. It's sad, because they have given us so much."

Indeed they have. Liebe Hart alleges the Korendians have given us cell phones and computers, while the Omegans have bestowed upon us beer, milk, cows, and mushrooms.

The generosity of the Omegans inspired the poet to compose arguably his greatest work, "Milk":

> Drink milk
> Taste milk
> Eat milk
> Like milk
> Be like the Omegans on Star Kalidan
> That are good milk fans
> They stay healthy, cause they drink milk
> That's why they are healthy still

According to Liebe Hart, the Korendians were none too pleased to learn he had written a song praising the Omegans. But then Liebe Hart was approached by Korendian elder Jessadle. "At first I didn't believe she was an alien, she looked like [forties pin-up model] Bettie Page in the face, she had a body like Raquel Welch, she was very attractive, and her skin was a pale, pale, pale white. I told her I didn't believe she was an extraterrestrial. When she took off her shoes, her main toe was in the middle, instead of on the side like ours."

That meeting prompted Liebe Hart to write the song "Korendian Honk":

> There's a Korendian
> Who knows my name
> And she looks just like
> Bettie Page
> I met her at the Tar Pits
> While I was selling my portraits
> She told me that she was in love with me

Liebe Hart insists that earthlings have done more damage to him than any alien invader ever has. Liebe Hart claims he got his first taste of how cruel Hollywood can be while performing preshow comedy before live audiences for the popular seventies television show *Happy Days*. He also maintains that he was good friends with Robin Williams, though the movie star now refuses to accept his calls. He has also never forgiven producer Garry Marshall for selecting Williams to star as Mork from Ork in *Mork and Mindy*. His feelings are perhaps best retold in his epic song, "Garry Marshall Blues":

Garry Marshall blues
Garry Marshall didn't choose
I was a struggling comedian at the Comedy
    Store
Performing with Robin Williams all the
    more
Garry Marshall chose Robin Williams and
    didn't choose me
But he said I could do the warm-ups at the
    TV show

Garry Marshall promised me I'd become a
    star
And that I would go far
He had me do the warm-ups before his
    shows came on
For *Happy Days* and *Laverne and Shirley*
    and *Blansky's Beauties*
He said if I did the warm-ups he would cast
    me in the show
But he threw me out the studio and told
    me he wouldn't use me at all
    you know

It was idiosyncratic lyrics like these that undoubtedly compelled Tim Heidecker and Eric Wareheimer to cast Liebe Hart in their own Adult Swim cult hit, *Tim and Eric Awesome Show, Great Job*. Fans couldn't get enough of Liebe Hart's eccentric appearances, but, according to the songwriter, while he still loves the two men and is proud of his work on the show, he won't be a cast member any longer.

Nowadays Liebe Hart and his puppet, Doug the Dog, can be seen and heard belting out his many songs on various street corners around Los Angeles, and if there's a big concert in town, you can guarantee he'll be performing for donations around the perimeter of the Hollywood Bowl.

David Liebe Hart is a legitimate artist. Like Dylan and Lennon before him, he writes and sings about what he sees—and like the aforementioned geniuses, Liebe Hart sees things much differently than most. Of course this is all best summed up in his uplifting ditty "Artist and Creator"

I am artist and painter
I am artist and creator
I create art
I create from the heart.

I am artist and painter
I am artist and creator
I sing about light
I sing about life

Robbie Rist: The Black Sheep Brady

For years now, Robbie Rist has been unjustly saddled with the burden of being the "shark" the Brady clan "jumped," thus ending a six-year run of prime-time family-friendly entertainment. To say that his portrayal of Cousin Oliver ruined the show—he appeared in the *Brady Bunch's* last season—is an inaccurate cheap shot, but it is one that Rist not only takes in stride but also seems to wear as a badge of perverse pride.

I met the former child star for burritos and beer at the famous El Compadre Mexican restaurant on Sunset Boulevard. Traffic from the Valley delayed his arrival by a full hour, but the bartender seemed to have no shortage of cerveza, so by the time Rist arrived, he was already three beers behind me. I believe he took that as a challenge, and he ordered himself a frosty mug.

His still cherubic face, though now hidden behind a scruffy five o'clock shadow, belies his approach to middle age. Despite the whiskers, he hasn't changed much since the seventies when he and Bobby became convinced that Alice's long-time beau, Sam the Butcher, was in fact an undercover Russian spy.

Rist's Internet Movie Database page lists a plethora of appearances in iconic seventies television: *The Bionic Woman*, *What's Happening*, *The Mary Tyler Moore Show*, and *CHiPs*, to name but a few. He is both familiar and likeable.

If you don't recognize his face, there is no mistaking the voice. It's pure laid-back, comically nasal California boy genius. You would also recognize his as the voice of Michelangelo ("the one with the orange mask") in the *Teenage Mutant Ninja Turtles* movies from the early nineties.

Rist is also a musician. He studied music since the age of three. He plays the piano, guitar, bass, drums, and mandolin, and has recorded a few albums. He credits costar Susan Olsen (Cindy Brady) for his obscure musical preferences. "Susan had a pretty eclectic taste in music for her age. She'd bring in Dr. Demento tapes and we'd listen to them in her dressing room. Loved Barnes and Barnes's 'Fish Heads,' Old Weird Al stuff—Susan really kind of started my lifelong fascination with offbeat music."

Rist, who had recently wrapped up producing and acting duties for the horror-comedy film *Stump the Band*, weighs in on the film industry today and a few other matters.

Rist on Hollywood

"In the seventies there are these great films with dour endings—you ever seen *Dirty Mary Crazy Larry*? They're like, 'We made it! We made it!' then they run into a train. But after *Star Wars* and *Rocky* everybody wanted a happy ending, and it's taken a while to get away from that philosophy."

Rist on LA Architecture

"When you consider the contribution Los Angeles/Hollywood has made to culture . . . it's contributed so much and sadly has no respect for its own history. They tore down the Ambassador Hotel. They got rid of the Brown Derby [see the Gone But Not Forgotten chapter]. Not that long ago they were talking about tearing down the Chinese Theater. Maybe it's because LA is such a transient place. . . . [P]eople come to seek their fortune, and whether they achieve that or not, they move. [T]hey need to put up something new and modern all the time."

Rist on Bowl Haircuts

"I credit the whole look to my German mother. I have this class picture of me in elementary school. There's a kid with a polka-dot shirt, a kid with a plaid shirt, a kid with a paisley shirt, and I'm the kid with the bowl cut, wire-rimmed glasses, and lederhosen. It's probably a good thing the lederhosen didn't catch on."

Rist on Glass Half Empty

"First of all, I only did six episodes of that show [the *Brady Bunch*]. They just happened to be the last six of the series." He laughs and shrugs. "I had to do a huuuge sort of emotional and intellectual reevaluation on myself, and I got depressed when I was in my late twenties. I was thinking, 'Is it possible that the only thing I'll be known for happened when I was nine, and I didn't even know what I was doing?' No one prepares you for the day it all goes away. I was nine. I had no idea that was going to be the highlight of my career, and it's tough when that attention goes away. It did do a number on me for a while."

Rist on Glass Half Full

"This dude walked up to me and said, 'when I was a kid, my mom was really poor, and she had three jobs. I was left alone in our apartment—a lot! The episodes of the *Brady Bunch* that you were on helped me get through those years.' Here was this kid, trapped in a world he didn't make, finding solace in some character I was playing. At that moment I realized it wasn't just a stupid TV show. It helped a lot of kids somehow, and once I realized that, I sort of learned to live with my past. And if that guy is out there reading this book, I just want to say thanks."

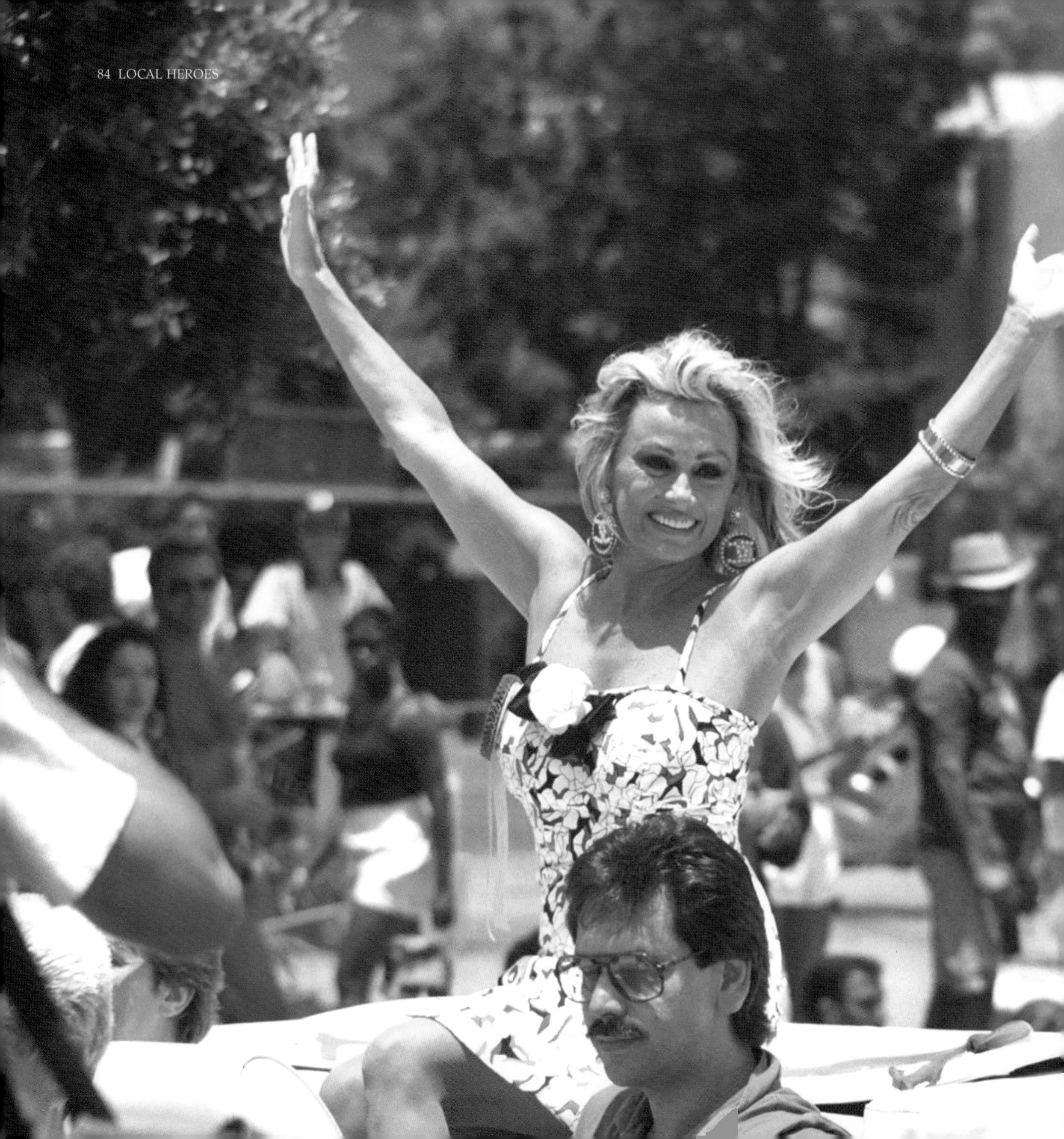

Mamie Van Doren

Mamie Van Doren: Her name alone is synonymous with a period in time when movie censors would fluster if a woman filled out an angora sweater too proficiently. Along with contemporaries Marilyn Monroe and Jayne Mansfield, Van Doren filled out the unofficial Hollywood blond bombshell sisterhood known as the Three Ms.

The curvaceous actress starred in juvenile delinquent classics like *High School Confidential*, *Sex Kittens Go to College*, *Ain't Misbehavin'*, and *The Beat Generation*. A list of her former boyfriends reads like a who's who in Hollywood history: Johnny Carson, Clark Gable, Elvis Presley, Steve McQueen, Joe Namath, and Burt Reynolds are among a few of her past paramours.

Van Doren is not shy about revealing her age; she was born in 1931 and looks sexier than most women half her age. In 2006, she and fellow sex symbol Pamela Anderson (thirty-six years Van Doren's junior) posed seductively for a *Vanity Fair* photo shoot, and even in her mid-seventies, Van Doren was capable of visually upstaging the much younger Anderson.

It was an absolute honor when this legendary icon agreed to give us a quick interview and share a few of her weird Hollywood recollections with us.

According to Van Doren, Secretary of State Henry Kissinger had pursued her on a number of occasions when he was in Los Angeles. Van Doren politely declined each advance, but when she attended a Washington, DC, dinner function for West German Chancellor Willy Brandt, Kissinger made his play.

Van Doren had been seated next to Kissinger. "As soon as I got there, I found out that Henry was my dinner date. I'm on one side [of Kissinger] and Mrs. Rockefeller is on the other side, he sitting in between us." As the evening wore on, the president got up to speak, and Kissinger worked up his nerve. "I felt his hand on my knee. Here was this guy who was supposed to be figuring out how to get us out of Vietnam, and it seemed to me that all he was thinking about was hanky panky."

Van Doren has always maintained an appreciative and levelheaded attitude toward her sex symbol image. She remains comfortable with her legacy, not ready to rest on her well-shaped laurels.

Kama Kosmic Krusader

It seems that movie and television directors won't even think of shooting a single frame of film in Venice Beach without a cameo by this city's most recognized street performer: Harry Perry, or, as he prefers to call himself, the Kama Kosmic Krusader.

Perry has portrayed himself, often as little more than background ambience, in movies like *Dragnet*, *White Men Can't Jump*, and *Down and Out in Beverly Hills*. But it wasn't acting that lured the Detroit native to the City of Angels in 1974; it was music.

Perry recalls, "I used to work with this dude Tony Newton. Tony played bass for the Four Tops, and Smokey Robinson, lots of big names, and Motown kind of moved to LA in seventy-three or seventy-four, so I moved too. . . . I used say to Tony, 'I wish I could just play guitar all day,' and he'd ask me, 'What's stopping you?' I'd try to tell him I needed to work, and pay rent, and he told me if I really wanted to play guitar all day I'd find a way."

Perry did indeed find a way. It didn't happen overnight, but eventually Perry became an honest-to-goodness LA icon.

Always a bit of a health nut, Perry says he used to take daily walks from lifeguard station twenty-six in Santa Monica up to the pier and back. He'd play the guitar and sing, but, "It used to take me all day."

He recalls, "My friend Alice convinced me to wear skates instead of walking—blue suede skates. This was around 1976, part of the big Venice roller revolution. I didn't want to wear them at first, but some girls have the ability to talk you into anything," Perry conceded with a huge belly laugh.

After donning the four-wheeled footwear, the energetic performer said he suddenly was able to make ten trips a day from the lifeguard shack to the pier. "I started sneaking up skating behind people, catching them by surprise. I'd be all

hunched over Groucho Marx style, and I'd sing in their ear as they walked. It's fun to watch how I startle them sometimes."

When asked if the turban was a religious decision, Perry answers, "I started practicing yoga with Yogi Bhajan. He's passed away now, but in the course of practicing yoga I started wearing a turban. There are all these theories about practicing yoga, and it seems I can feel the energy stay within me if I wear the turban." Perry credits yoga with getting him off of marijuana and alcohol. "I realized I didn't need that stuff; all I need is deep breathing exercises."

Perry also realized the image of the roller skating musician in a giant turban worked to set him apart from the average busker, and he started to enjoy not just the attention but also the additional money he would find in his pocket at the end of the day. He was always talented, but now he had a gimmick, and a good gimmick can go a long way in Los Angeles.

Perry insists it's not about the money. "I've got enough of an education where I could make $100,000 at some corporate job if I wanted. . . . I make an existence doing what I love, and that's better than sitting at a desk."

Combining his two passions, music and fitness, Perry gets only about three hours of sleep a day, but such is the life of a Kama Kosmic Krusader. "My day begins early. I run twenty miles each morning. I work out at Gold's Gym, with the beautiful girls, pump iron with the big muscle guys, then get some juice and skate around. After that, if my band is sober enough I'll rehearse with the band, then I head up to Hollywood at the Rainbow [Room] at night and play until three in the morning, and start all over again."

The roller guitarist says he has gone years of playing 365 days on the Venice Ocean Front Walk. "Oh yeah, I've played Christmas and New Year's, Thanksgiving. If I'm in town, I'm here." Of course now and then a gig will take him away from the beach. He has played Ozzfest and opened for Jane's Addiction. He's happy to share stories of fellow Venice musicians that have made the big time. He is friends with the members of Papa Roach and the Stone Temple Pilots. "I knew them when they were Mighty Joe Young," Perry reflects with a smile.

If you want to catch Harry Perry perform in Venice, don't bother. No one can catch Harry Perry. But don't worry; if you hang around for a few minutes, he'll catch you—probably Groucho Marx style.

Dennis Woodruff

If there were a speck of factory paint showing through Dennis Woodruff's art car, you'd never notice it through the glued-on plastic toys, seashells, and four-foot papier-mâché bust of Woodruff himself mounted to the roof.

Woodruff's mind is exactly like the exterior design of his car. It seems random, cluttered, hard to read, and difficult to follow, but the message is pretty simple when you step back and digest the information. The message is: "Notice me. I want to succeed in this business." It's all the guy ever thinks about.

I follow Woodruff to his home, a tiny rented bungalow a few blocks off Melrose. Not long ago he was living out of a Dennis Woodruff art van. He's grateful to have a bed and daily shower. Woodruff shares, "My biggest frustration [with this town] has been trying to figure out how to survive in a dignified way."

He is a tall, powerfully built man in his mid-fifties, and the years of rejection and dejection are clearly displayed on his weathered face. He offers me a part in his latest movie, *Obsession, Letters to David Lynch.* He's got a strange charisma. He's compelling, and I'm rooting for him to win, but the odds seem stacked high against him. He really is a Hollywood legend—not the feel-good rags-to-riches kind of legend, perhaps more the rags-to-different-kind-of-rags kind of legend. But his tenacity, not to mention his cars, have made him an honest-to-goodness legend in this town nonetheless.

He has written, starred in, produced, and directed close to a dozen films, and he has sold thousands of copies of his films out of his car trunk over the years. Nowadays, thanks to the Internet and the price of gas, he doesn't have to drive around as much as he used to.

"I grew up in Huntington Beach, and knew John Wayne

lived in Newport [Beach]. I always wanted to meet him, so I rode my bike to his place, and painted his address on his sidewalk, knocked on his door, and asked him for some money." Woodruff maintains the Duke wanted to check out the job before parting with any cash, so he moseyed on down to his curb. Wayne was impressed with the job, told the youngster he admired his chutzpah, shelled out a couple bucks, and let young Dennis know he had a future in Hollywood.

It's rare to see a two-person camera shot in a Woodruff film, and that's because Woodruff can't afford a cameraman. In his film *Spaceman*, Woodruff plays the title role of an alien who comes to Earth and announces in a clipped monotone, "I am Spaceman [pause] from outer space." Throughout the entire film, Woodruff wears a reflective astronaut helmet, and the actor opposite him is clearly seen holding a small video camera in the mirrored plastic visor.

My favorite line in the movie comes after a female reporter ascertains that there is only one gender on the planet from which Spaceman hails. Confused, the journalist asks how his race procreates. In what may have been scripted camp, improv brilliance, or lazy writing, Spaceman replies lifelessly, "On my planet people grow on trees [pause] and we pick them [pause] like an egg."

I love it. It's a great line. There's more magic like that, and it's well worth the sawbuck. Like Ed Wood's films, Woodruff's movies are better when enjoyed with a group of people. I guarantee if you watch *Spaceman* with a group of friends, you'll spend the better part of the next month looking for openings to use the "egg tree" line on one another.

Some months later I met up with Woodruff again on the Sunset Strip at a Starbucks. He was cheerful and offered me a shopping bag full of two of his films, *Spaceman* and *Obsession, Letters to David Lynch.* I was pretty excited, because I was in *Obsession.* After chatting over java for about an hour, I said good-bye to Dennis Woodruff and we went our separate ways. I couldn't wait to pop in the DVD.

I am in Woodruff's film for about five seconds. I did some great work, if I do say so myself, all improvised right off the top of my clever little head, but most of it was relegated to the cutting room floor. I have to admit, I was a little disappointed to have such a tiny role, but then I realized I just became part of Hollywood history and consoled myself with this undeniable fact: Dennis Woodruff is a legend.

Melissa Burech, Tattoo Girl

Each day is an exciting new adventure she can't wait to begin, admits Melissa Burech. Sadly, her life did not start out that way; Burech is an incest survivor.

According to Burech, her grandfather abused her from the time she was six months old until he died six years later. The emotional pain and guilt that survivors of childhood sexual abuse carry throughout their life is impossible to measure, and it is little surprise many of them develop self-destructive behaviors. Suicidal thoughts, deep depression, poor self-esteem, self-mutilation, and drug abuse are common in abuse victims.

Burech says she started slicing her arms with knives and razors when she was in second grade. By the time she was nine years old, cutting had become a daily ritual. Medical experts explain that cutting is a coping mechanism very common in abused children. Cutting often makes the person feel alive while also giving them a sense of control over their own body.

At a loss to help their daughter, Melissa's parents hospitalized her at the age of twelve, but that experience didn't have the desired effect. By the time she was fifteen years old, Melissa started using drugs and alcohol and became promiscuous.

It wasn't until a close friend of hers lost custody of her children that Burech realized her own life was spinning out of control, and she wanted to stop it. At twenty-one years old, Burech went cold turkey, got herself sober, and helped raise her

friend's children. It was at that period in her young life that she realized her mission in life.

"I feel I've been put through everything I've been put through so I could help other people out," she humbly declares.

Looking to start life anew, she moved from West Virginia to California, enrolled in college, and began working toward a degree in mental health counseling. Living the life of a struggling student in Los Angeles, Burech searched for inexpensive, fun ways to spend her precious spare time. "I decided, why not go to a couple TV show tapings? And I started bumping into famous people. One day I met [singer-songwriter] Amy Lee from Evanescence. I didn't have anything for her to sign, so I told her, 'sign my arm,' and she was like, 'well if I do that then you have

to turn it into a tattoo.'" Amy Lee's music had been an influence on her, so Burech agreed to do it.

Thus began the quest for the lasting signatures of more than two hundred celebrities Burech has admired throughout her life. In just over a year, this determined young woman has handed a Sharpie and her bare arms to fifty some significant stars. She then heads to a tattoo parlor (which gives her a healthy discount) and has the autographs permanently applied to her flesh.

The list of famous signatories is literally an arm long. Among the names on her right arm (dedicated to actors) are Angelina Jolie, Heather Locklear, Kevin James, Ashton Kutcher, and Christina Applegate. The left arm is her "musicians arm," and it includes the tattooed names of Sheryl Crow, Nelly, and Jennifer Nettles.

On her wish list are the autographs of Meg Ryan, Tim McGraw, and Shirley Temple. Burech smiles sweetly when she recollects how she'd escape into her Shirley Temple video collection as a small child when she'd start to feel sad. "Shirley Temple would always make me laugh and dance when I was a little girl. When things got really bad, I'd always pop her in." She acknowledges that she's not sure how she'll get Temple's autograph, as they don't exactly run in the same circles. "I don't know how to get her, because she doesn't go to Adam Sandler premieres, so it may be difficult, but I'll get her."

Discovering a unique way to overcome her self-destructive tendencies has helped Burech rise above some incredibly difficult hurdles in her life. "I was a self-injurer; I cut myself a lot. Now when I look down at my arms, I'm happy instead of being depressed. Instead of the scars, I see the people who have been a positive influence in my life."

It should be stressed that Burech's list of influential people includes more than just celebrities. She has the names and faces of friends and family on her torso. She is concerned however, that she will run out of space on her arms, and has accepted the fact that she will ultimately have to explore the possibility of other parts of her body. "I guess eventually I'll have to have them sign my legs, but I'm going to have to start working out before I do that." She shyly states, "I don't really want to ask a celebrity to sign my legs, but I guess it's better than asking them to sign my butt." She pauses and with a bashful giggle adds, "But some of them might be into that."

Now that she has her own life under control, this gentle selfless spirit is just as committed to helping others. She implores anyone reading who may have a history of abuse in his or her own life to make the first step. "I suggest that you get help, and start making a difference in your own life. I do it *for* myself, but not *by* myself. Stay clean. Life is so much better clean."

If you're a survivor of childhood sexual abuse and need help, Burech strongly suggests contacting 1-800-4-A-CHILD, or www.childhelp.org.

Butch Patrick Weird Facts

By the tender age of nine, Butch Patrick had more television credits than baby teeth (or fangs, as the case may be). Most TV viewers know Patrick as Herman and Lily's lovable little wolf-boy, Eddie Munster. He is also remembered for his work on the Sid and Marty Krofft cult fave *Lidsville.*

© RD/Kenney/Retna Ltd./Corbis

These days Patrick keeps himself as busy as ever. He is writing a book, makes personal appearances across the country, and also does media promotion work. Having spent a portion of his youth at 1313 Mockingbird Lane, Patrick is no stranger to weirdness. He was kind enough to sit down with us and address all things weird and fascinating in his life.

Patrick's first tale is an experience he had with the "other side." He's never seen an actual ghost, but he doesn't entirely dismiss them out of hand. According to paranormalist Bonnie Vent, Patrick's presence was requested by the ghost of Jesse Shepherd. Shepherd is a long-dead opera singer and one of the current spirits who are believed to haunt the Villa Montezuma in San Diego.

WEIRD HOLLYWOOD: So, Butch, how did this ghost even know about you? Is he a big Munsters fan?

BUTCH PATRICK: (chuckles): Maybe, but apparently he's alive and around in another dimension. What I found interesting is Jesse [through a medium] told me that I was married to Bonnie [Vent] in another life in the 1800s. He told us my name was John and her name was Maria. This was weird, because when I first met Bonnie, I kept calling her Maria for some reason.

WH: Legitimately weird. Anything else that we could classify as weird?

BP: Well, the story goes Jesse Shepherd died on stage, giving a performance. It's funny; he was at the piano, and he bent over, and [the audience] thought he was taking a bow, and they kept applauding, applauding, applauding, until someone finally said, "Hey, I think he's dead."

WH: So are you pursuing a career in ghost hunting?

BP: No, but my sister said she said once she saw our dad, who died twenty-two years ago, in her rearview mirror. I wouldn't consider her a wacko, but she said she was driving, and she checked her mirror, and there's our dad, sitting shotgun in a car behind her. I tend to think it's possible.

WH: I understand your stepdad played professional baseball.

BP: Yes, his name was Ken Hunt. He played for the Angels and the Yankees. I got to spend time with Mickey Mantle because of him, and he's actually buried alongside Roger Maris.

WH: Okay, then, speaking of baseball hats—kind of—any odd anecdotes about your days on *Lidsville*?

BP: I got along very well with Sharon Baird. She was a former Mouseketeer, who played Raunchy Rabbit. She and I got along great. Charles (Nelson Reilly), he liked me very much—maybe a little too much. *(Butch breaks into some good-natured laughter.)* Billie Hayes, who played Weenie the Genie, was very talented. Loved her. You know, at the time, I didn't really like doing the show too much because it seemed silly to me as a teenager, but I look back now and think of *Pee Wee's Playhouse*, and think the Krofft brothers were twenty years ahead of their time.

WH: What about your *Munsters* days? Any recollections of Fred Gwynne?

BP: Fred was a true renaissance man. He was a wonderful illustrator, and he wrote children's books. He had a strange relationship with Hollywood. He always told me not to trust "the suits." He was great. He took me aside one time when I had to play a beatnik, and showed me how to do it. He was like that.

WH: Al "Grandpa" Lewis?

BP: Al and I used to throw the baseball around a lot. Poor Fred was either always in makeup or doing a scene, but Al and I would toss the ball. Al was an athlete when he was younger, and he used to be a scout for the NBA.

WH: Yvonne De Carlo?

BP: Very sweet woman. Called me her TV baby. She was the movie star of the group, but Marilyn—Beverly Owens, the first Marilyn—I had a huge crush on, and she actually took me to see *Mary Poppins* at the Chinese Theater for its premiere. So my first date was with Marilyn Munster. I was eleven and she was probably twenty-two.

WH: Nice score, Butch. What about the second Marilyn, Pat Priest?

BP: A lot of people don't even realize there were two Marilyns. She's got a great home up in Idaho, and you may not know this, but her mother was the treasurer of the United States at one time. Ivy Baker Priest—she served during the Eisenhower administration.

WH: Wow, the mother of Marilyn Munster had her signature on American currency. That is weird.

BP: Yes. We definitely had a very interesting, eclectic group of people on that show.

Bela Lugosi, Ed Wood, and Plan 9 from Outer Space

Already an established actor in his native Hungary, Bela Lugosi emigrated at the age of thirty-eight following the collapse of his political party. The liberal-leaning Old World thespian made his living in the United States primarily as a laborer until he was noticed, at age forty-four, playing the title role on stage in the gothic classic *Dracula*. Three years later, in 1931, he won the part of the malevolent monster again, after months of campaigning for the screen version. It is widely accepted that the job had been promised to fellow horror legend Lon Chaney, but Chaney died of a throat hemorrhage before production started.

Lugosi's thick, exotic Eastern European accent and his penetrating gaze captivated audience members from the utterance of his first on-screen sentence. His enunciation

proved to be both a blessing and a curse, however. Whereas professional rival Boris Karloff was able to leave the monster genre from time to time, Lugosi's voice made it virtually impossible for moviegoers to see him as anything other than a slightly different version of Dracula.

Almost immediately he was typecast as the villain in a slew of B horror films. By the mid-1930s the horror genre had fallen out of favor with the big studios, and Lugosi was forced to accept smaller paychecks from independent producers just to make ends meet. Lugosi's career did get a slight bump playing the hunchback Ygor in 1939's *Son of Frankenstein*, where he teamed up with Karloff and Basil Rathbone. Despite the success of the picture, Lugosi found himself once again in low-budget horrors.

Severe back problems haunted Lugosi throughout his adult life. As the 1950s approached, Lugosi was working sporadically, and his "secret" addiction to painkillers such as morphine and methadone gave studios little reason to take a chance on the former star. Lugosi was poverty stricken and dependent on drugs when he met a young filmmaker named Ed Wood.

Wood had long been an admirer of Lugosi's. His passionate knowledge of Lugosi's career, coupled with Lugosi's own financial concerns, made it relatively easy to strike a deal. For the sum of $1,000 for one day's work, Ed Wood, the man who would years later be awarded the Golden Turkey Award for Worst Director of All Time, had persuaded his boyhood idol to star in his semi-autobiographical docudrama about transvestism, *Glen or Glenda*.

Lugosi played the part of the Scientist. Unaware that the movie was about a man who enjoyed dressing in women's clothes, he sinisterly delivered such incongruent lines as, "Beware . . . beware! Beware of the big green dragon that sits on your doorstep. He eats little boys . . . puppy dog tails, and big, fat snails. Beware, take care . . . beware!"

Two years later, after no calls from a major studio, Lugosi realized that his morphine addiction had grown out of control. He checked himself into a state-run facility to straighten out. Upon release, Lugosi went back to work for Wood, starring as Dr. Eric Vornoff in 1955's *Bride of the Atom*. Once again he gave menacing life to Wood's convoluted dialogue. Comedian Gilbert Gottfried has almost made a second career of quoting Lugosi's lines from this movie on his many appearances on Howard Stern's radio show. "Home? I have no home. Hunted, despised, living like an animal! The jungle is my home. But I will show the world that I can be its master! I will perfect my own race of people. A race of atomic supermen, which will conquer the world! Ha ha ha ha ha ha!"

A year after the release of *Bride of the Atom,* Lugosi died of a heart attack. But even in death it seems Lugosi could not break Wood's hold. Wood possessed a few minutes of footage in which Lugosi spends time walking near the home of fellow horror actor Tor Johnson (see page 226). Adding that to a few frames he owned of Lugosi in his Dracula costume in a cemetery, Wood began filming his most (in)famous movie of all: *Plan 9 from Outer Space.*

The cast included Wood regulars Lyle Talbot, Bunny Breckenridge, the Amazing Criswell (see page 96), Vampira (Maila Nurmi), and Tor Johnson. Although Lugosi earned the posthumous billing as the Ghoul Man, it was Wood family chiropractor Tom Mason who did most of the work, doubling for the late Lugosi. Pulling his cape over the bridge of his nose, the much taller and younger Mason plodded through the entire movie more concerned with concealing his identity than giving a credible performance.

Whatever became of plans one through eight from outer space was never addressed; however, the tombstones that bend in the breeze, flaming hubcaps as destroyed alien spacecrafts, and the inimitable writing style of Ed Wood all contributed to *Plan 9*'s cult following to this day.

The Amazing Criswell

Greetings my friends, and imagine, if you will, a nationally syndicated psychic so extraordinarily and consistently incorrect that his failed predictions still manage to amuse and amaze decades after his death in 1982.

Listen with your mind's ear, if you dare, to the declamatory delivery of a man in a sequined tuxedo, sitting upright in a coffin, the very coffin in which he claimed to spend hours of nocturnal unconsciousness, where his body's natural functions were suspended so that it may be restored during this period of time.

Envision if you can, dear gentle readers, a flamboyant silvery spit curl so spectacularly exceptional that it would make Kryptonian elder Jor-El green with envy.

If you were capable of such remarkable contemplation, then please, without haste, continue reading about the astonishing individual known simply as the Amazing Criswell.

Born Jeron Criswell Konig on August 18, 1907, Criswell gained mild show business fame in the early fifties by purchasing time on a local Los Angeles TV station and huckstering his Criswell Family Vitamins. Thanks in large part to his ostentatious presentation, he quickly became a local celebrity. Soon Criswell claimed that he possessed clairvoyant abilities and started making outlandish prophecies. These eccentric forecasts delighted talk show hosts Jack Paar and, later, Johnny Carson, and Criswell found himself to be a semi-regular guest on their programs.

Criswell was introduced to lightly regarded filmmaker Ed Wood in the mid-fifties, and he lent his talents to three of Wood's projects: *Plan 9 from Outer Space*, *Night of the Ghouls*, and *Orgy of the Dead*. It's interesting to point out that while *Night of the Ghouls* was filmed in 1959, Wood did not have the financial wherewithal to have the film processed. It wasn't released until producer, writer, and Ed Wood fan Wade Williams learned of this lost movie and paid off the bill in 1983. By that time both Criswell and Wood were dead.

Criswell often boasted that his predictions came to fruition 87 percent of the time, but a quick scan of any of the books he wrote will quickly dispel that claim. He is, however, credited for divining, on a March 1963 Jack

"I predict this very book you now hold in your hands, will cure the entire universe of disease, poverty, and male pattern baldness."

Paar appearance, that John F. Kennedy would not seek re-election for the national office in 1964, citing that something "major" was going to happen to the president in November 1963.

And now, if your very eyes can come to grips with the sheer genius that is the Amazing Criswell, we at *Weird Hollywood* bring you some astounding quotes and predictions that proceeded directly from the brain through the mouth of this extraordinary showman.

Criswell Scripted

"Greetings, my friends. We are all interested in the future, for that is where you and I are going to spend the rest of our lives. And remember, my friends . . . future events such as these . . . will affect you, in the future."

"I am Criswell! For years, I have told the almost unbelievable . . . related the unreal, and shown it to be *more* . . . than a fact."

"Perhaps on your way home, someone will pass you in the dark, and you will never know it, for they will be from *outer space*!"

". . . his *dead wife* was watching."

"She pleases me. Permit her to live in the world of the snakes."

"Torture, torture! It pleasures me!"

Criswell's Predictions

"I predict public executions will be shown on television, sponsored by your local gas company!"

"I predict that our local American doctors will go on strike, and will be replaced by African witch doctors!"

"I predict there will be no welfare in the future. And I predict the death penalty for all freeloaders."

"I predict a wealthy San Francisco attorney will announce his marriage to his mother and a Hollywood producer will openly declare his daughter is going to bear his child, and a young man in Arkansas will ask to be legally wed to his pet cat."

"I predict the assassination of Fidel Castro by a woman, on August 9, 1970."

"I predict that man's exploration of space and the building of space stations will be the salvation of the human race. . . By 1999 there will be more than two hundred of these space stations in existence. They will house entire colonies—men, women, and children. . . When the earth is destroyed on August 18, 1999, these space colonists will be the only Earth-humans left in the universe."

Gary Owens: The Voice of Hollywood

A member of the Television Hall of Fame and the Radio Hall of Fame, and a recipient of a star on Hollywood's Walk of Fame, Gary Owens has done it all in this town. Many know Owens as the ear-cupped on-air announcer for the classic counterculture comedy *Rowan and Martin's Laugh-In.* Some know him best for his humorous broadcasting for decades on Los Angeles radio, and others are aware of his work in animation. He has supplied voices for more than three thousand animated cartoon episodes. He has been a television writer, producer, announcer, actor, cartoonist, author, and disc jockey.

Owens is not just a part of Hollywood history; he's also a devotee of the events and people who helped shape this town, and he might very well be the nicest guy in Hollywood. A nice guy in Hollywood? That's weird enough.

"I had my ear placed in cement over at NBC." He recalls in a low somber voice that belies his offbeat sense of humor, "Dan Rowan and Dick Martin pressed my head into the wet cement in the parking lot where Johnny Carson and Ed McMahon used to park. It was a big event, and they had a nurse present, because it's not a good thing to have cement dry in your ear."

Noticing that he had tickled our weird funny bone, Owens then proudly announces, "I started the Girning Society a number of years back." After patiently waiting for the obvious follow-up question, he continues. "Girning was very popular in early England—centuries ago. It was a practice to contort your face, or to make faces. So we ran a contest at the radio station to see who would be the best girner. [T]he winner was Mrs. Frances L. Sayers. She was a lovely lady who could swallow her nose." Honorary Girning Society members include Monty Python members Terry Gilliam and Terry Jones (see facing page).

Radio giveaways were another format for Owens to display his affinity for the unusual. "I used to run a spot urging listeners to send in a self-addressed stamped envelope to receive a free one. So when we'd get a letter, we'd send back a postcard with a big red 'one' printed on it."

Comedy legend Albert Brooks started out as an intern on Owens's radio show at KMPC, and he, along with Arg the Wonder Mutant and a guy named Harvey who played

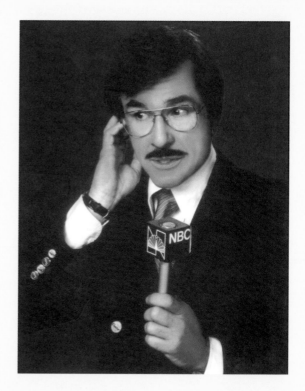

the tuba, joined Owens in his annual World's Shortest Parade. Owens recalls, "We'd have thousands of people show up to these things. I'd blow a whistle, we'd all take one half step backward, and the parade was over."

Another weird project Owens remembers fondly is the Map of Movie Extras' Homes. Owens and actor Jesse White put together a bus tour so visiting sightseers could visit the homes of the people normally relegated to nonspeaking roles in film. "Well, of course we used very hip people, so they were all in on the joke, but it was a lot of fun. We'd drive by a modest house, and I'd say things like, 'This is the home of Harold Minkler. He lives here on Wilcox and Hollywood. Harold, what was your favorite movie extra assignment?' 'Well, I milled at a bus station for a movie once. I'm a pretty good miller.'"

A noted punster, Owens loves to have fun with the English language. The man who introduced a nation to the catch phrase "From beautiful downtown Burbank . . ." almost entered *Funk & Wagnalls Dictionary* for a word he made up with friends over lunch one day. "Insegrevious. It's a totally nonsensical word that purposefully has no meaning. You can use it to mean something is good or bad, but it doesn't really mean good or bad, because the word is intentionally meaningless, but it can also mean whatever you'd like," Owens explained.

He was friendly with silent screen comic Harold Lloyd and knew Moe Howard of Three Stooges fame quite well. It came as a shock to Owens when he realized in the early eighties that the Stooges were not represented on the Hollywood Walk of Fame. Owens used his national radio show to start a letter-writing campaign. "We received over thirty thousand letters from all around the world in a very short time, and they were finally awarded a star. Milton Berle was there. Adam West was there. Moe and Larry had unfortunately passed by that time, but Joe

Besser showed up and said some very nice things." Ever the prankster, Owens tried to get their star tilted slightly, "so people would fall down trying to read it, but they wouldn't let me."

Owens doesn't bring it up, but he paid for the Three Stooges star. He also paid for lunch at Jerry's Deli. I tried to explain to him that I had an expense budget for this kind of thing, but he wouldn't hear of it. He's a very, very nice guy, and that might be weird in Hollywood, but it's also what this town needs: more weirdos like Gary Owens.

My Lunch with Gary Owens

I spoke to Gary Owens a number of times on the phone before we met officially at Jerry's Deli in Encino. His voice is so familiar and deep, that I found myself lowering my own intonation subconsciously.

I mentioned that I admired his work as a voice actor on various classic kids' shows, and without a moment's hesitation Owens became the character Space Ghost. He delivered silly but funny nonsense lines into an imaginary two-way communicator strapped to his wrist. "Jan! Jace! Don't order the tuna salad! I can say no more! Quickly, Blip, get that chopped liver to go—the fate of the world depends on it!" Owens's voice dropped ten decibels. The tables rumbled, and milkshakes spilled onto the laps of patrons throughout the eatery. He's just that good.

Clint Howard

As a second-grader, he matched wits on the set with the formidable and worldly Capt. James T. Kirk. He taught an animated man-cub how to march like a proper elephant, and he's tangled with both Tango and Cash. He's Clint Howard, and if you're a fan of pop culture, you're a fan of Clint Howard.

Howard picked up his first Hollywood gig at the tender age of three, acting opposite his older brother, Ron, on the *Andy Griffith Show.* Since then it's been a steady stream of roles, many of them of the offbeat variety, such as his role as otherworldly Balok, on *Star Trek.* We sat down with Howard at his favorite Cajun restaurant in Burbank (he recommended the spoonbread) to talk about his weird Hollywood experiences. He was kind enough to bring along a coupon for $8 off the meal. (He must have gotten wind of my limited expense budget.)

At first Howard was hesitant to admit his upbringing could be considered weird, but when it was brought to his attention that his annual paycheck at the age of eight was bigger than a college educated executive's income, he reluctantly agreed.

We talked about Howard's fondest Hollywood memories, even though some of them didn't take place in Hollywood.

Working with a Bear

Howard worked opposite a five-hundred-pound bear in the 1967 TV show *Gentle Ben.* The show was shot in Florida, and Howard recalls being taken to "the compound" to meet his costar.

"Oh, yeah, it was scary at first, but . . . they threw this huge steak his way. He sniffed it, didn't like it. And then they threw a box of doughnuts, and he wolfed down this box of doughnuts."

© Paul Mounce/Corbis

The bear was a bit of a carb addict. "What that bear really liked was sweets. [He] ate twenty-four loaves of bread a day, a couple of bags of Monkey Chow, half a dozen heads of lettuce, and doughnuts and . . . big bottles of Coke. They'd put cookies in my pocket, or rub honey on my hand. When they did the famous shot of the bear kissing me, I had a Life Saver in my mouth. He didn't have any front teeth and didn't have any front claws.

"A lot of times . . . it was too hot. So the second season, they built an air-conditioned trailer for the bear. That'll fix everything, right? Well the first day, the bear likes it in the trailer. They couldn't get him out. They literally had to get a bunch of Teamsters to jack up the trailer and slide the bear out, and the next day that trailer went away. After that they put him in the shade."

Meeting Nixon in DC

Howard actually cut his journalistic teeth at ten years old. His first interview was President Richard M. Nixon, for the Art Linkletter special "A Kid's Eye View of Washington." He appeared with Maureen McCormick from the *Brady Bunch*, Darby Hinton from *Daniel Boone*, and a young actor named H. B. Barnum III.

"Nobody could ever figure out what H.B. had done or been in, but ya know, he filled out the roster," he quips.

Howard enjoyed his trip to the nation's capital. He and his castmates reported on DC landmarks and did homework in the basement of the Smithsonian Institution, but he was especially excited about meeting the president.

"I said, 'Mr. President, I'm a young actor, and I pay taxes, yet I don't get to vote. Isn't that taxation without representation?'" Even decades later, Howard is still pleased at himself for coming up with the probing inquiry.

Unfortunately they wouldn't let him ask that question.

Vacant-Lot Variety Show

Catching Fonzie's fastballs is one thing, but pitching show ideas to Steven Spielberg, David Geffen, and Jeffrey Katzenberg is another thing altogether. During the early 2000s Howard was the host of the short-lived cult classic, *The Clint Howard Variety Show*.

"I interviewed people like Adam Sandler and Andy Dick, Sally Kirkland and Judge Reinhold. The celebrity interviews took place in low beach chairs in a corner of a vacant lot. I'd interview someone like Johnny Ramone, for like fifty seconds, and I'd ask two quick questions and by the time the third question came up I'd go, 'Oh, I'm sorry, that's all the time we have for this segment, but as you know each guest on the *Clint Howard Variety Show* receives fifteen dollars and a turkey. Turkey provided by Haaandy Market Restaurant. Handy Market of Burbank, your neighborhood grocer since 1967.' Then my sidekick, my announcer, Big Mike, would come over with this big dripping turkey in a bag and hand it to the celebrity and I'd pull fifteen dollars out of my pocket and give it to the guest."

Happy Days on the Baseball Diamond

"I was a pretty good high school baseball player. I caught a little when I was a junior. Around that time, the *Happy Days* show got a team together. They would play Sunday double headers in Poinsettia Park in Hollywood. We played against guys like Alice Cooper, which was cool.

"Ron must have volunteered me because I was pretty good, and I was a pseudo celebrity. Henry [Winkler] knew nothing about sports. He grew up in Manhattan. But for some reason, he had this innate ability to throw an underhanded strike. He had this little fade . . . but his ball would always go in. I saw this as a catcher and thought, 'This works.' Now, he couldn't field. Henry developed into a really good pitcher, and [since] he was the Fonz, it made sense for Henry to pitch."

The team enjoyed almost as much success in the final box scores as they did in the Nielsen ratings, and executive producer Garry Marshall decided the team should tour the country. "We played in Wrigley Field in Chicago, Milwaukee, Shea Stadium, and Veterans Stadium in Philadelphia in front of sixty thousand people. . . . We won that game. I'd say we won about 70 percent of our games."

Melrose Larry Green

Holding up a sign on a street corner is a great way to get your opinion out there. People love it." So says street corner prophet, O. J. Simpson nemesis, former LA mayoral candidate, and official member of Howard Stern's Wack Pack, Melrose Larry Green.

Melrose, as he prefers to be called, is an accountant by trade. He refers to himself as an old hippie from Brandeis, but he points out that comedian Jackie Mason, whom Melrose considers a pal, prefers to call him a lunatic. "I think he thinks it's too much negative attention."

Making his opinions known to anyone who would listen was never good enough for Melrose. He felt the need to broadcast his beliefs to a wider audience—to those who didn't want to listen to his point of view. The crafty old hippie remembered being stuck in traffic with his father when he was just a boy. He recalled how frustrated his old man would get sitting helplessly in the gridlock, and an idea came to him. He could hold up hand-written posters to a captive audience, knowing full well the vulnerable motorists would be compelled to read his musings.

This is not to say Melrose does what he does just to annoy. That's only part of his charm. Of course annoying people has its price. Melrose has been honked at plenty, been flipped the finger on numerous occasions, and even had a bottle of urine thrown at him. Apparently it's a small price to pay for fame, however tenuous that fame is. Melrose received his first taste of national attention thanks to Howard Stern. Stern's agent

saw Melrose's HOWARD STERN FOR PRESIDENT sign. "He told Howard about me."

Stern, who was mildly amused at Melrose's antics at first, became absolutely fascinated with the sign-wielding CPA during the O. J. Simpson murder trial.

"I would go down to the courthouse and hold up signs, and scream things like, 'Good morning, murderer!' Howard and CNN still play that sound byte to this day." He then added, "I would go down there, and I would be very bold and brazen, screaming at O.J. until the cops left. As soon as the police left, five minutes later [I was] out of there."

Being wacky for Wack Pack sake doesn't interest Melrose as much as it used to. The former 1960s radical has become more conservative with age. He claims to have given a lot of thought to the political process and believes the judicial system would benefit from professional juries. These days he preaches to get involved in local city and state affairs.

"Democracy is what you make of it. You just can't sit back at a cocktail party and say, 'They're all crooks.' If you don't vote, you have no right to complain."

That's not to say he has completely abandoned his silly roots. He can still be seen at various corners when the muse strikes, holding his homemade placards, attracting both negative and positive attention.

"There's a lot of traffic in Hollywood, and a lot of tourists wonder, 'Who is this moron? Who is this lunatic?' Well, it's Melrose Larry Green, and I would rather be a famous lunatic than an unknown accountant."

> "I would go down to the courthouse and hold up signs, and scream things like, 'Good morning, murderer!'"

Skip E. Lowe and the Trilussa

It's a little surreal to be this close to Skip E. Lowe. For years I had been mesmerized by his cable access television program, *Skip E. Lowe Looks at Hollywood*, which is also available at www.youtube.com. We chat; I ask him who is favorite interview was, and he goes on about Marlon Brando, Shelley Winters, and Tony Curtis. We engage in more small talk, and, when the moment is right, I take my chance and shoot the question I'm dying to ask. With fire in his eyes, he responds. "Martin Short is brilliant and funny, he can sing, and dance and act. *And* he's been ripping me off for years."

Lowe is kidding—kind of. He is referring to Short's popular character Jiminy Glick, a fictional creation that Lowe thinks people interpret as him.

Using a voice that sounds like air being slowly bleated out of a particularly effeminate balloon, Glick is a gluttonous, self-important, forgetful crank who longs for the glamorous glory days of a Hollywood long gone.

Aside from the appreciation of Tinseltown's past, the sometimes flappable but always affable Lowe shares nothing in common with Short's fictional creation—except for the voice. Short does nail the voice. Short's Glick may share some mannerisms and quirks with Lowe, but Glick has none of Lowe's warmth and genuine interest in each visitor who sits beside him on the TV screen.

Luminaries such as Orson Welles, Milton Berle, and Bette Davis have all accepted the invitation from this tiny silver-haired pixie of a talk show host. Leaning in with such fascination, Lowe lures his television audience in to an intimate conversation between himself and the performer of a bygone era. The viewer can't help but be drawn in further by each new word.

Similarly I find myself completely mesmerized by whatever comes out of his mouth. He has the dirt on everyone in this town, and he's only too happy to share the gossip, as long as it's off the record.

We drive down to a sandwich place Lowe promises has the best ham and cheese for under five bucks. He's right.

A stand-up comedian and emcee by trade, a teenage Lowe ran numbers for the Mafia in Chicago until one day, overcome by temptation, he lost the mob's money because of his own gambling addiction. Fearful of his fate if he admitted his mistake, he checked himself into the Chicago State Hospital in hopes of avoiding their particular brand of retribution.

"I didn't know I was signing myself in for ninety days," he confesses after borrowing a twenty from me to play the California Pick Three. "I thought I could get out when I felt it would be safe. Well, I was in there for ninety days, and it was like [*One Flew over the*] *Cuckoo's Nest* in there, so to pass the time, I put on shows. I had all the nuts in the Chicago State Hospital singing and dancing and we had a marvelous time."

Lowe eventually flew over the cuckoo's nest and escaped his Neapolitan cronies by flying off to Europe and Vietnam to entertain the troops. He opened for the Everly Brothers, and Diana Ross and the Supremes.

Nowadays Lowe still performs as master of ceremonies to a diverse group of performers every Monday night at Trilussa Ristorante, at 9601 Brighton Way in Beverly Hills. Musicians, painters, comics, belly dancers, Dean Martin and Jerry Lewis impersonators, and folks who just love to croon—it's an eclectic, old-school crowd. Lowe attracts an audience of famous friends as well. Sally Kirkland, Eartha Kitt, Rip Taylor, Jackie Stallone, and any number of actresses who shared an on-screen kiss with Elvis Presley have been known to drop by to say hello. So if old Hollywood is your thing, Skip E. Lowe is not just your man, he's a *Weird Hollywood* treasure.

Just don't bring up Martin Short.

George Barris, the King of Kustomizers

The Batmobile, Greased Lightning, the Munster Koach, the General Lee, KITT the Knight Rider—these are not only some of the bitchinest rides to ever lay rubber on Hollywood Boulevard—they were also all designed by or at the direction of the same man, the legendary King of Kustomizers, George Barris.

Barris is a small ball of energy despite a recent heart attack and even more recent knee surgery, and he becomes quite animated when talking about his passion. Barris's office is a shrine to twentieth-century American pop culture. On display in his workspace are an autographed drawing from Batman creator Bob Kane; photos of himself with the Rat Pack, Bob Hope, the cast of *The A-Team,* and Burt Reynolds; and thousands of miniature movie and TV car models.

His love affair with the automobile began when Barris was a youngster. He remembers his first custom job, sometime in the late 1930s. "Before I could even drive, my parents gave me their hand-me-down 1925 Buick, and I went into the hardware store and got some house paint and went to Woolworth's and put some foxtails on it. Went to another store and bought some pots and pans and made hubcaps out of them, then I took some doorknobs off my mother's cabinets and put them in the grill, and it made the car look great—and when I went to school I had the greatest looking car in the world. I was thirteen, my brother was sixteen, so he'd drive us to school. Of course when we got home, my mother was upset because she couldn't get into any of her cabinets." Barris laughs himself to tears with the memory.

Asked if this was something all the kids in the neighborhood were doing at the time, Barris explodes with pride. "No! I was the first."

His brother Sam and he garnered so much attention with their modified vehicle that it wasn't long before the two sold the souped-up Buick for a tidy profit and reinvested the money into their next project: a 1929 Model A. Soon the Barris boys were hanging out in various mechanic garages in nearby Sacramento, learning the finer points of bodywork.

When Sam joined the armed services during World War II, George moved to Los Angeles and opened up a shop of his own. Sam rejoined his younger sibling after a military discharge in 1945, and the pair began the Barris Brothers Custom Shop. Sam did most of the bodywork, while George designed and painted cars and managed the business.

The boys were beginning to get a name for themselves, and George in particular fell in love with the dangerous and illegal sport of street racing. When asked how many crashes he's been in, Barris rolls his eyes, laughs, and admits he can't count that high.

The Barris boys were starting to get a reputation as top-notch customizers. Racing magazines and car shows took

notice of their skillfully unique work, and soon Hollywood came calling. In 1958, the now cult favorite *High School Confidential*, starring Mamie Van Doren (see page 84), Jerry Lee Lewis, and Michael Landon also starred a number of hotrods built and designed by the Barris boys.

The role the automobile was starting to play on the big screen kept the Barris Brothers Custom Shop hopping. The Michelangelo of motor vehicles worked with Alfred Hitchcock in *North by Northwest* and developed a friendship with James Dean during the filming of *Rebel Without a Cause*. Business was booming, and a need for more creative talent led to the hiring of some of the biggest names in the business. Dick Dean, Dean Jeffries, Von Dutch, Bill De Carr, Jocko Johnson, and Curley Hurlbert all plied their trade under Barris's employ. Eventually Sam retired from the business, but by that time the shop had the best fabricators and craftsmen in the business. The Barris name had become a mark of excellence.

As the fifties gave way to the sixties, the motion picture industry was giving ground to television audiences. The producers of a new show, which showcased the wild misadventures of a dirt poor mountain family suddenly rich and uprooted to Beverly Hills, contacted Barris in 1961. He promptly found an "old jalopy that was sitting on the 10 freeway in San Bernardino" and turned it into the *Beverly Hillbillies* hotrod (see above).

Designing the now world famous Munster Koach was

a snap compared to what Barris had to do to procure some of the "custom" pieces to its counterpart, Grandpa's special vehicle, the Dragula. "The show and the car became so popular that we all decided Al Lewis [Grandpa Munster] should have his own car, too. I decided since he was such a dramatic character, we would put a chemistry lab in the middle of the car. . . . [P]eople still talk about it."

The one car Barris gets asked about more than any other is the Batmobile from the old Adam West and Burt Ward *Batman* series. The Batmobile started out as a 1955 Lincoln Futura concept car that was just sitting around as a part of his personal collection. When ABC Television asked Barris to design a stylish but gimmicky car in three weeks, Barris realized there was no way to build one from scratch, so he decided to modify the Lincoln. According to Barris there were seven Batmobiles created for the show.

By the 1980s, Barris owned more than two hundred cars, and storage was becoming a problem. His own showroom is only so big, and shuffling his collection from car museum to car museum was beginning to become a chore. It was with some sadness that Barris sold off a majority of his collection.

"In the fifties, Hollywood exchanged the cowboy's horse for the hotrod. The sixties was about personality cars, the seventies and eighties were about giant car crashes, and now, even though they can use CGI [computer-generated imagery], it still looks better to the eye if it's a real car, and a real stuntman inside. It's going to be exciting to see where it all goes."

George Barris on Toby Halicki

Henry B. Halicki, known as Toby by his friends, was the maverick producer, director, actor, and stuntman of some of the best-loved, car-smashingest films of all time.

Barris helped Halicki customize a 1971 fastback

Mustang to look like a 1973 Mach 1 Mustang for his first movie, *Gone in Sixty Seconds*. "Toby loved cars. He grew up around them, and just loved them. When he decided he was getting into the movie business, he figured he'd just write what he knew.

"So we had one scene where we're coming down Hawthorne Boulevard, and he wanted to crash into a Cadillac dealership and wreck one of the brand-new Cadillacs. So Toby hits it. He's airborne—and he not only hits the Cadillac, but he also takes out the two Cadillacs next to it, and crashes into the showroom and takes out two more. We had to buy five Cadillacs for that shot." Barris shakes his head, suppressing the laughter. "This was definitely not in the budget."

In *Gone in Sixty Seconds 2*, "We made this car that would 'slice' through a hundred police cars. It was a big press scene. We got cars going this way, crashing that way, catching on fire—real exciting stuff. The cable snapped and hit a telephone pole—and this huge pole came crashing down, hitting [Halicki] in the head. Killed him on the spot." At the gruesome memory Barris rubs his forehead with his index finger and thumb.

In 2000, the remake of *Gone in Sixty Seconds* was released, starring Nicolas Cage and Angelina Jolie. Denice Halicki, Toby's widow, was the executive producer.

George Barris on James Dean

Car designer George Barris met James Dean during the famous "chicken" scene of *Rebel Without a Cause* and remained good friends with the brooding young thespian until his death in a car crash at the age of twenty-four. "I built the forty-nine Mercury that was used in that film," declares Barris.

Barris and Dean both had a love for fast cars; they and stunt racer Bill Hickman would spend hours talking and arguing about cars and racecar drivers. According to Barris, Dean was talented behind the wheel, but was not content to be a recreational driver. "Jimmy got out there, and if he got a [driver] in front of him who didn't move too fast, he just butted him and pushed him right in the hay bale."

On his way to a race in Salinas, Dean drove his customized Porsche 550 Spyder instead of having it transported. At an intersection near Cholame, Dean crashed and spun his car (seen here, Barris with Dean lookalike Casper Van Dien).

"What I think happened," Barris says, "the steering shaft come up and hit [Dean] in the neck, broke his neck." The actor died before an ambulance got him to the hospital.

Marty and Elayne at the Dresden Room

Let's just set the record straight. You haven't really heard "Girl from Ipanema" until you've seen it live at the Dresden Room—over the clattering of half-empty highball glasses, the boozy giggling of the girls at the back table, and the happy drunk guy who is convinced his slurry version is just as good as the staged performance.

Throw in some faux stonewalls, red-cushioned booths, and dark ambient lighting from fixtures you've seen only at old people's yard sales, and now you're getting closer to the optimum pre-Beatles-era American lounge experience. But you're not there yet.

You can't truly appreciate the song's hypnotic bossa nova beat until you've swayed to the lyrics—flowing like a fine old scotch, from the ruby red lips of a piano-playing, raven-haired chanteuse, Elayne, while the smooth but focused drummer, Marty, lays down a sexy Latin backbeat.

Marty and Elayne Roberts met decades ago when Elayne and a bandmate needed to round out their sound. "I needed a drummer. This bass player and I had auditioned for a job, but we were only sixteen years old, and we needed a drummer, and someone who was over twenty-one so he could sign the contracts. My girlfriend told me about Marty, and I called him up on a Sunday, and my first question was, 'Are you over twenty-one?' We met soon after, and he wound up getting me a gig the next day, and we've been together since."

Since then the jazz duo have played all around the world, but since 1980 they've called the Dresden Room their permanent home. Due to their popularity, most nights it's hard to find a seat in the bar—but there were a number of lean years for the couple.

"We've always loved performing the standards," recalls Elayne, "but in the early eighties, we were told we were playing music from an endangered species list." Still, the

musical duo played on, believing in their hearts the old stuff would pay off again. In 1987, it did.

"We got our music played on a big jazz radio station, and suddenly all these people started coming in. Guys from Frank Zappa's band, and guys from the Red Hot Chili Peppers, and Lindsay Buckingham from Fleetwood Mac, would all come in to sit in with us." Elayne then adds, "And then in 1990 we were in a video with Tom Petty called 'Yer So Bad,' and the place started getting overpacked."

Things haven't slowed down for a second since then for the tuneful twosome. They are as comfortable playing "My Funny Valentine" as they are lounging up the disco hit "Stayin' Alive." Their version of *The Flintstones* theme song has been compared to Miles Davis. They may be considered lounge lizards, but they don't play for camp or kitsch value. They're 100 percent genuine, and maybe that's why they've endured.

Not only are Marty and Elayne happy to announce that their music has successfully bridged the generation gap (according to Elayne, kids are bringing their parents, and parents are bringing their kids to their shows) but they also have a good number of well-known fans. Michelle Pfeiffer, Julia Roberts, Brad Pitt, Sandra Bullock, Kiefer Sutherland, and Sean Penn have all been known to drop in, and some of them actually joined the band for a song or two. Elayne fondly remembers an interesting duet she and Marty backed up one night. "Nicolas Cage and David Lynch came in, and sang 'Love Me Tender,' they were having so much fun."

Of course these two don't get star-struck too easily. Elayne played with Count Basie when she was only thirteen years old, but she does confess to being thrown for a loop the first time she encountered the Chairman of the Board himself, Mr. Francis Albert Sinatra.

"First time he walked in I was so scared I couldn't sing, so I just played the piano." Angry with herself for not seizing an opportunity, Elayne only had to wait three weeks for a second chance. "Frank put his hand on this little spinet (piano) and he said, 'Go ahead, kid.' I sang 'Didn't We' and it was the best I ever sounded in my life. He applauded and blew me a kiss."

After the performance, Elayne sought out the leader of the Rat Pack and thanked him for being so gracious to her. "He looked at me with those big blue eyes, and said, so sternly, 'You earned it, kid. I don't fool around about music. It's too important.' Then he gave me a kiss on the cheek. It was easily one of the high points of my career. I said to Marty, 'Where do I go from here?'"

Asked what's among the weirder experiences they've shared in their years in Hollywood, Elayne bursts out laughing, "One night this guy came in with a clown suit, and he started to sing, and we couldn't see who he was. He was an okay singer, but then he just started cursing. Our boss, Carl, ran up to him and said, 'That will be enough of that,' and escorted him offstage. Later a friend of mine who was there that night said she saw him on television, with the same clown outfit, and she said it was Jim Carrey. Apparently, Jim Carrey used to go around singing as Bobo the Clown at all the different cocktail bars in town."

When talk of retirement enters the conversation, the normally subdued but always attentive Marty jumps in, "It's like Milton Berle told me once, 'Retire to what?' We love what we're doing. We love playing music. We have no plans to retire."

As it is, they barely take a night off. Marty and Elayne play Monday through Saturday 9:00 P.M. to 1:15 A.M. Tuesday is open mike night, so if you think you've got the chops to follow the likes of Count Basie or Ol' Blue Eyes, swing on down to the Dresden Room at 1760 North Vermont Avenue in Los Feliz. You're sure to have a weird and kooky ring-a-ding-ding time, baby.

Personalized Properties

"Home is where the heart is."

—Pliny the Elder

"Home is the place where, when you have to go there, they have to take you in."

—Robert Frost

"A man travels the world in search of what he needs and returns home to find it."

—George Edward Moore

"I wish that guy with all the statues of David would just pack up and move far away. He's killing the resale value of my home."

—Anonymous neighbor of Norwood Young, owner of the House of Seventeen Davids

O*ne definition of home describes a dwelling* or shelter that is the usual residence of a person or family. Another definition is the place in which one's domestic affections are centered. Still another classification is any place of refuge.

Los Angelenos have always prided themselves on their distinctiveness, and that brand of thinking often starts at home. So whether you feel that sense of comfort in a house, an apartment, your car, or your place of employment, be it ever so humble (or weird, as the case may be), welcome to this next chapter.

Quality Shoes Inc.
SALES & REPAIR
11427 SANTA MONICA BLVD. WEST L.A.
(310) 479-3012

W itch House

Beverly Hills has its share of witches, to be sure. However, many of them prefer the creature comforts of a posh mansion to an old-fashioned sorceress shack.

Witches of yesteryear preferred the Old World charm of foreboding gnarled trees, the unflinching eyes of impatient vultures, and intricate spiderweb carvings on the doors of their estates. Instead of a security system that alerts the local police force, these enchanting hags of antiquity would throw foolish trespassers into a fiery oven and eat them for lunch if they dared step foot on their property.

Truly, had the Brothers Grimm been buried in the 90210, they would be turning over in their graves if it weren't for a cartoonish, spooky cottage at 516 North Walden Drive: the Witch's House.

Formerly known as the Spadena House, after the family who once occupied the playfully creepy home, the Witch's House was built in 1921. It served as atmospheric scenery in a number of silent pictures and also doubled as offices and dressing rooms for Willat Studios. The movie company uprooted the home in 1926 from Culver City to its current zip code.

According to Beverly Hills legend, real estate agent Michael Libow, who grew up not far from the ensorceled abode, became frustrated that none of his customers wanted the house as-is. Libow decided to take it upon himself not only to buy the home, but also to restore its somewhat faded and chilling charm. For the price of $1.3 million (and perhaps his mortal soul), Michael Libow became the owner of this beloved building.

The Sunset Lawn Statues

Money may not be able to buy you friends, but it can certainly buy you life-sized statues of people you can imagine are your friends. These friends never disappoint, never double cross, and never ask to borrow money.

People intrude upon this tastefully manicured lawn on a daily basis. At the entrance gate in the front yard, they are stopped in their tracks by the statue guard, who might ask for ID if he could. He's a friendly enough fellow, but no matter how much visitors plead, the statue guard—like the sentry who guarded the great Oz—never allows nosy outsiders entrance. No way, no how.

Of course, uninvited callers can peer through the fence and enviously watch the frozen figurines inside the grounds.

They're picking statue apples, playing on the statue swings, or sitting in the shade of a real tree, reading the statue pages of a statue book.

In the circular driveway there are plenty more statues to behold. Why, there's ol' fishin' statue. He's most likely headin' on down to the ol' statue waterin' hole to catch himself a mess o' statue catfish—or at least he would be if he were able to walk.

Oh, and look over there. Why, it's the jogging statue. That statue is so into physical fitness that he's out there in his statue jogging suit all day and all night, regardless of the weather. He's not jogging, you realize, because he's a statue, but he does have his right knee in a position that sure as heck looks like he means business.

And who's that sleeping on the statue bench, covering his unemployed statue head with a copy of the statue classifieds? Well, it's none other than a statue homeless guy. Will that guy ever get off his lazy statue keester and get himself a job? Highly unlikely, but at least he's not like those statue kids, hanging naked in midclimb on the garden wall, trying to spy on their other statue friends. Hey, that's statue-tory exposure!

The Sunset Boulevard lawn statues are located at 10000 Sunset Boulevard in Beverly Hills.

The Poodle Bush

Italian artist Michelangelo once said, "Every block of stone has a statue inside it, and it is the task of the sculptor to discover it." If this is the case, then Brian Welch, a painting contractor from England, must follow the same muse as the great Renaissance master.

A number of years ago, Welch noticed that the tall leafy archway on the sidewalk bordering his home in North Hills had a distinct shape. In no time at all, the creative craftsman envisioned the entrapped image. With the help of a pair of hedge clippers, he was able to liberate the entangled form from within its own bushy confines.

The figure Welch unleashed was that of a twelve-foot poodle named Fido.

Welch is used to traffic stopping by to take pictures, and he's proud to say that Fido has appeared on the

Discovery Channel. He and his giant pet shrubbery have even starred in a television commercial—for which Welch was paid $800 an hour.

Every six weeks you can find Welch on the corner of Plummer and Hayvenhurst lovingly grooming his blooming pooch. During the Christmas season, Welch decorates the colossal canine with a big red bow around its neck. He also has two other (real) dogs: a Short-haired Pointer and a Lab mix. He professes to love them at least as much as Fido.

One thing is certain: for a dog of that size, the cleanup could be worse.

Hollywood Hounds

Hollywood Hounds, located at 8218 West Sunset Boulevard, is in a building that has an interesting pedigree of its own. The doggie day-care establishment is the former home of actor Fess Parker (television's Davy Crockett) and later became the business offices of animator Jay Ward (Rocky, Bullwinkle, Dudley Do-Right).

The Prestons are very respected in the animal-care industry, and a quick glance around the framed photos in the lobby informs potential clients that Hollywood Hounds has been entrusted with the daily care of the dogs of this some of this town's biggest stars. Portia de Rossi, Drew Barrymore, Heather Locklear, and Paula Abdul have all had their pups gently and lovingly looked after here.

Aside from boarding and grooming, Hollywood Hounds also offers specialized social gatherings for your pooch and his pals. Birthday parties are the most popular, but two other events have been recently (perhaps temporarily) discontinued.

"We no longer do Muttrimonies or Bark mitzvahs," says Maya Preston with a palpable sense of relief. "Muttrimonies are always cute, but it's not easy work. Bark mitzvahs can be even tougher to pull off."

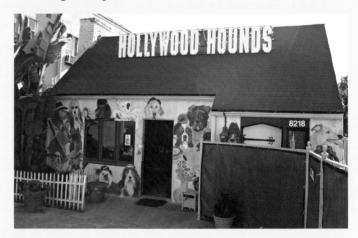

Old Trappers Lodge

The fight. It must have been one doozy of a donnybrook. Pegleg Smith seemed overmatched from the outset—what with his peg leg and all. But there he was, in a battle for his life, going up against the fierce seven-foot Native American warrior chief, Big Bear. It was a gory fracas to be sure, and Pegleg had seen better days. The mighty Big Bear's ax was buried in his upper back, a nasty arrow shot clear through his left shoulder, and his teeth were clenched behind his long gray beard in a breathtaking display of agony and determination.

It's not known who won this bloody hand-to-hand Western-style fight, but it was all faithfully captured in glorious painted cement by the Old Trapper himself, aka John Ehn.

Ehn left his life as a Michigan trapper and wandered west to the Golden State, but he didn't abandon his pioneering spirit. In 1941 he opened up a motel in Woodland Hills, but instinctively he knew something was missing—oddly horrific, giant painted cement sculptures depicting the Old West. He commissioned and then quickly fired an artist, probably when he realized it took not much talent to create these concrete works of art. Luckily Ehn possessed exactly the right amount of not much talent to get the job done himself.

Ehn produced hideous dance hall girls, frighteningly stoic cowboys, and nightmarishly impassive gold miners, made out of concrete. The folk art treasures were declared California state cultural landmarks in 1984, and thus were spared when the lodge was demolished to accommodate new construction.

Luckily the entire collection was transferred to the campus of nearby-Pierce-College, where it is still on display today. Thanks to the tireless research and artistic aptitude of the trapper turned sculptor John Ehn, Early American history majors at Pierce seem to have a (peg) leg up on students at rival colleges.

Joe Oliveri Hair Design

It doesn't officially have a name. Joe Oliveri never thought to call it anything when he placed the fourteen-foot-tall bust in front of his Redondo Beach salon and covered its fiberglass-and-sandstone scalp in flowers in 1972.

"A lot of people call it the Chia Pet, but I had that thing up years before there ever was a Chia Pet," boasts Oliveri, who says the live sculpture was installed in recognition of a dear friend who passed away. Oliveri wanted readers to know that he got the idea from the late sculptor Gemma Taccogna.

Taccogna was an internationally recognized artist who achieved both critical and public acclaim in a variety of media. Her works are and have been in the collections of President Lyndon B. Johnson, Jacqueline Kennedy Onassis, Carol Channing, and Mary Tyler Moore, to name a few. She was also responsible for the street displays for Queen Elizabeth II's coronation.

"I was just staring at this little twelve-inch sculpture she made for me," Oliveri recollected, "and I thought, 'I'd like to put that on my front lawn.'" The flowers were almost an afterthought.

The giant nameless botanical head has gone through many different hairstyles—and flora-styles—in the last four decades. "It's been bobs, and punk rock, pompadours, even geometric. I've had roses, and just all kinds of flowers. I think perennials work the best."

Oliveri admits that he doesn't modify the styles as often as he used to. "I'm getting old," chuckles the solicitous stylist. He does confess that he still changes things up a couple times a season, and he particularly enjoys gussying up the enormous unidentified noggin around Christmastime.

After chatting a bit, Joe seemed to decide that, after all this time, his anonymous gargantuan herbaceous *cabeza* needed a name, and he has issued that challenge to the readers of this book. Oliveri has judiciously appointed me as the final arbitrator.

If you'd like to submit a name for Oliveri's creation, send it to joe@JoeArtistWriter.com Be sure to type "Name Joe Oliveri's Huge Verdant Cranium" in the subject line. The winner will receive a warm flowery feeling and the right to boast about finally naming this doozy of a dendritic dome.

Joe Oliveri's Hair Design is located at 1401 Pacific Coast Highway in Redondo Beach.

The House of the Protective Iconic Statues

A man named Carlos owns the big burgundy structure with gold trim on the corner of St. Charles Place and Crenshaw Boulevard. The color scheme isn't the only thing that sets this building apart from the many other large homes on this stretch of Crenshaw. The residence is also recognizable for its many guardians.

Victorian cherubs battle fierce and deadly snakes just to show they mean business, and lions and tigers patrol the low grounds, while Native American chiefs and winged Renaissance-era archangels tactically position themselves on higher ground in case of an air attack. And if that weren't enough to ward off evildoers, there's a Virgin Mary every fifty feet or so. These guardians are only in sculpture form, but they still give the owner of the manor a bit of comfort.

Carlos speaks limited English, but two of his seven young children, Freddie and Eddie, are happy to translate for their father. Carlos believes his collection brings him good luck. Through his sons, Carlos tells of travels "all over the place" in search of his beloved protective treasures. He purchases a statue only if it "feels right" to him. Even without his army of inanimate sentinels, Carlos is too well liked to fear intruders. He has many friends on his street. From the local merchants to the USC students who live in frat houses on the same thoroughfare, Carlos is recognized and admired throughout the area. His neighbors know Carlos as a loyal friend and a devoted father.

There are close to one hundred protective statues strategically placed on the house and in the yard, but deep down Carlos should know he doesn't need to rely on the three-dimensional modeled images to keep his home safe. He has the love of his family, the trust of good friends—and he also has a pretty elaborate surveillance system and a vigilant huge watchdog named Shadow.

The House of Seventeen Davids

According to his MySpace page, Norwood Young is known as "the Ambassador of Love." According to annoyed neighbors and curious passersby to his Hancock Park mansion, he's the guy with the seventeen David statues lined up along his circular driveway.

Young prefers to call his alabaster estate Youngwood Court, and lists singer, producer, reality show star (*High Maintenance 90210*), and lavish party thrower among his credits. Young is a former *Star Search* contestant and was for a short while a member of the Philadelphia jazz group Pieces of a Dream.

According to the LA Stories blog (www.la-stories. blogspot.com), the entertainer dyes one of his lap dogs purple and the other one blue—it's easier to tell them apart that way. He owns a three-foot-tall marionette of himself, because you never know when you'll want to pull your own strings. Not only does his bathroom come equipped with its own newspaper vending machine, but Young is the front-page headliner on each issue. And the mosaic tile pattern at bottom of the artist's pool supposedly makes up the image of Young's handsome smiling face. It's a narcissist's dream.

Young's choice of outdoor home décor has been a sticking point in this otherwise pleasant suburb since he moved to the manor in the mid-nineties. He has been the subject of numerous television news reports, radio talk show programs, and newspaper and magazine articles. He was even defended by the late Johnnie Cochran against prosecution attorney Leslie Abramson on the short-lived *Judge Judy*–inspired *Roseanne Show*, starring "Judge" Roseanne Barr.

The House of Seventeen Davids, or Youngwood Court, is better known among certain aggravated locals as the blight of this upper-class neighborhood, so if you want to see the eyesore for yourself, take a gander at 304 Muirfield Road. Look at it this way: You can either spend a lot of money for a trip to Florence, Italy, to see the original Michelangelo sculpture, or you can drive to Young's place and see not just one, but seventeen miniature masterpieces for free.

That's sixteen extra statues for nothing, and you don't even have to renew your passport. Seems like a no-brainer to me.

The Hollywood Walk of Fame

It all started back in 1903 when G. W. Hoover (not to be confused with J. Edgar) opened the very first hotel in Hollywood. Initially, the hotel was built as a lodging for land prospectors and miners, but when much of the movie business migrated west to California, it wasn't long before the Hollywood Hotel became *the* resort of the film industry.

There wasn't much competition in the early days, but Hoover made sure that the Hollywood Hotel was the jewel of the West Coast. Stars from the Golden Age of Hollywood would feast in the elegant dining hall, then drink and dance the night away in the grand ballroom. A tradition started when Hoover ordered all his staff to inscribe their favorite celebrity names inside the large gold stars that were painted along the ceiling of his renowned building.

By 1956 the charming two-story hotel was an antiquated relic, and the building was demolished in favor of a high-rise. The painted stars from the ceiling of the building were rescued and placed on the sidewalk in front of the new edifice on the corner of Hollywood and Highland, and the Hollywood Walk of Fame was born.

Footprints in Cement

When Grauman's Chinese Theater first opened in 1927, Sid Grauman was a one-third owner of the palatial movie house. His partners were actors and cofounders of United Artists, Mary Pickford and Douglas Fairbanks, as well as investor Howard Schenk.

In the decades since, many of Hollywood's greats, "kind-of-goods," and "who-the-heck-is-thats" have literally left their impressions outside the main

entrance of the cinema. Traditionally, stars have placed their feet, handprints, and autographs in the wet cement, but some celebrities contributed a little more. Groucho Marx left an imprint of his cigar, Jimmy Durante pressed the profile of his prodigious proboscis, and R2-D2 imprinted his robotic treads. All very cute and entertaining, but how did the tradition start?

Each version of the genesis of the tradition claims the footprints were an accident. According to Grauman, "I walked right into it. While we were building the theater, I accidentally happened to step in some soft concrete. And there it was. So, I went to Mary Pickford immediately. Mary put her foot into it."

Others believe it was silent screen actress Norma Talmadge who accidentally stepped in the drying concrete after an opening night gala. They claim Grauman liked the idea, but preferred to credit his business partner (and bigger showbiz name) Mary Pickford.

The true story may very well rest beneath the drunken feet of Norma's younger sister, comedienne Constance Talmadge. Upon leaving a gala screening at the cinema in an alcohol-induced celebratory haze, the less famous Talmadge sister may have walked through the fresh cement, but the quick-thinking comic planted her handprints, and signed a note of "Best Success" to the theater.

In light of this startling revelation, and in fairness to everyone who has done something stupid while under the influence but never turned that stupid thing into a world-famous institution, I say it's time we give equal time to the drunken little sister version.

To Constance!

The Hollywood High Mural

I'm not sure about the rest of you, but my high school didn't produce a plethora of well-known graduates. The biggest celebrity to come out of Kinnelon High School in Kinnelon, New Jersey, the teenager warehouse I once attended, is probably a guy named Bill Daily. He's now the deputy commissioner of the National Hockey League. (Bill and I actually worked together at the Taco Pit restaurant—we were dishwashers there as teens.) The next famous graduate of my old school played two seasons of football for the then St. Louis Cardinals, and after his brief NFL career was over, he returned to become the assistant football coach for his old high school alma mater. The sad fact is I may be the third most famous graduate. The guy after me has a moderately successful roofing business in the area.

The only reason I bring it up is that Hollywood High School boasts more than five hundred notable graduates or attendees. Not surprisingly, many former students have gone on to become very successful in show business. Among their illustrious alumni are Carol Burnett, Lon Chaney Jr., James Garner, Judy Garland, Mickey Rooney, Ricky Nelson, Laurence Fishburne, Sarah Jessica Parker, Rita Wilson, Brandy, Fay Wray, and Jason Robards.

Among the school's illustrious nonacting former students are Warner Brothers animation legend Chuck Jones, former secretary of state Warren Christopher, attorney Vincent Bugliosi, and *People's Court* judge Joseph Wapner.

To honor not only their gifted grads but also racial diversity in the entertainment industry, the school commissioned artist Eloy Torrez to paint a giant mural titled *Portrait of Hollywood* on the entrance to the academy. The work of art was completed in 2002, and in 2008 the image of another former Hollywood High student was added—the late John Ritter.

During my annual phone call to Kinnelon High School, I was once again informed that there are no plans to hire Torrez to paint a fifty-foot picture of the NHL exec, the assistant football coach, me, and the roofing guy anywhere near that building. I will check back again next year.

Helios House

Helios House is an eco-friendly British Petroleum gas station (is that an oxymoron?) on the corner of Olympic and Robertson in Los Angeles. While the station may dispense the fuel that allows commuters to belch emissions into the stratosphere, in fact it is the first LEED-certified gas station in the country (LEED means Leadership in Energy and Environmental Design). Helios House has gone the extra mile to distinguish itself both functionally and stylistically.

There's no denying the visual uniqueness of the ninety triangular stainless steel panels that make up the canopy for the gas station, but those individual sections are utilitarian too. According to the friendly and knowledgeable Green Team member, who was dressed in a hemp and cotton company uniform, the recyclable solar-powered panels that make up the awning produce enough energy to power the pumps and a house or two. The unfinished exterior also amplifies reflectivity, which decreases the need for lighting, saving about 1,400 kilowatt-hours each year.

The recycled bits of glass that sparkle on the station floor reflect heat away from the underground gas tanks a little cooler and keep the glass out of already overflowing landfills. Recycling is a huge part of the Helios House philosophy. They have recycling bins on the premises for paper, bottles, cans, and even cell phones.

Most people won't use a gas station restroom unless they're extraordinarily desperate, but this one is not just impeccably clean, it's also inviting. A couple minutes in, and you'll find yourself wishing it also included a sunken tub. The materials are again all recycled, and the toilets have two separate flush mechanisms: a small flush for just a little waste, and a bigger flush for the much more obvious waste. There's even a touch-operated monitor that allows you to pick songs to listen to while you're doing your business.

The Garden of Oz

It took a giant twister to transport Dorothy Gale and her house from the family farm in Kansas to the merry old Land of Oz. To residents of the Hollywood Hills, the trip is much easier, but no less magical. The Garden of Oz has been a whimsical neighborhood treasure for years, but access is given only to those who have a key, and a key is bestowed only to children. Those youngsters hoping for a way in are encouraged to leave a letter in the mailbox, and if the Wizard is so inclined, that wish may be granted.

At first glance the garden seems like an eclectic yet quaint little spot of inspired visual reflection, lovingly decorated in brightly painted tiles, colorful marbles, shards of mosaic, and tiny collectible toy figurines. Pressing your head up against the bars of the secured barrier, you notice the same devoted artistic detail on the terraces, sculptures, and stair steps that twist and wind a hundred feet above the street. There is enough real estate devoted to the imagination of children to construct at least two more homes, but it's obvious the owner of this land believes some things are more important than watching a bank account grow.

To assume that this is simply a place for kids to climb and laugh the day away would be to miss the social commentary aimed at the parents by the owner. According to writer Catherine Moye, who has spoken to the proprietor, a wooden statue of Jesus was flown in from the Andes and now resides artistically and respectfully next to a sculpture of the Tin Man. Menorahs from Tel Aviv, mandalas from India, and Buddhas from Japan also find their places beside inhabitants of Oz.

Next to the welcome signs is a placard imploring readers to "Free Tibet." The Dalai Lama is a fan of this flowery childhood paradise, so much so he once dispatched fifteen monks to bless the creatively adorned area.

That said, the message of the Garden of Oz is not one of preachy political views, but rather of embracing the untainted, uncomplicated joys of youth. Even the Wicked Witch of the West herself would come away from this handmade yellow brick road with a smile on her big green face.

Forrest Ackerman and Acker Mansion

"My maternal grandparents were great moviegoers. One year they took me to 356 films; in one particular day we saw seven movies. We started at eleven in the morning [and stayed] until the last one ended at midnight."

And that's how a young Forrest J. Ackerman transformed from a shy little boy into Mr. Science Fiction, the former editor of *Famous Monsters of Filmland* magazine, and the owner of the largest private collection of horror and fantasy film souvenirs. His assortment of more than four hundred thousand items include the original King Kong's hand; a cape and ring belonging to Bela Lugosi; a number of Tribbles, or creatures from the *Star Wars* [*IV: A New Hope*] cantina scene; a golden idol from *Raiders of the Lost Ark*; and Lon Chaney's top hat.

Much of his menagerie of the mystical and macabre used to be on display to the public in his eighteen-room home, Acker Mansion, where visitors such as Vincent Price, Ray Bradbury, Anthony Perkins, Isaac Asimov, and Steven Spielberg signed the guest book.

Ackerman has since moved to a smaller place and has sent a considerable part of his collection to museums in Seattle and Berlin, but his Acker Mini-Mansion is still open to the public. The overseer of all things creepy or otherwordly guesstimates that more than fifty-five thousand people have dropped by to chat and view his treasures since 1951.

Ackerman recalls that one year he received more than 1,300 letters from young admirers of his magazine who were all eager to meet the respected monsterphile. "So my wife and I . . . drove 3,700 miles all over the United States, stopping and meeting many of the fans."

Old age may have caught up to his body, but Ackerman's mind is still sharp. On any given Saturday, between 11 A.M. and noon, you can find him wrapped up in his decorative skeleton blanket, sitting comfortably in his reclining chair and deftly fielding questions from grateful guests, underneath the life masks of Boris Karloff, John Carradine, Peter Lorre, Charles Laughton, and renowned mask sculptor Don Post.

As we left Acker Mini-Mansion, we noticed a sign posted near the front door, which we had somehow overlooked. It was a simple placard, affixed to the left-hand side of the entrance. An uncomplicated two-word admonishment: NO AGENTS. (He was the literary agent for both L. Ron Hubbard and Ed Wood; he refers to himself jokingly as Wood's "illiterary" agent.)

Forrest Ackerman's Mini-Mansion tour at 4511 Russell Avenue is free and open to the public every Saturday between 11 A.M. and noon, but it's always best to call ahead to make sure: 323-666-6326.

El Bordello Alexandra

Compared to some of the residents of Venice Beach, the dragons, man-bats, and centaurs that literally hang out at 20 Westminster Avenue are a tame bunch of creatures. You'd think the liberal-minded citizens of this progressive beach hamlet had seen and accepted it all, but apparently they took an instant dislike to the fantastic statues atop and alongside El Bordello Alexandra.

Bernie Kolb, a handsome man in his late seventies, co-owns and manages the apartment building. "We were just looking to do something to set this building apart from all the others you see on these streets. We got the gargoyles from an Indian reservation, and we painted the building this purplish color with the gold trim."

Next came the Frank Frazetta–inspired paintings on the front of the structure. "Brian [Mylius] did paintings. We found him on the beach. We like his stuff, and we get compliments on his work all the time."

Kolb claims that the neighbors were enraged at the topless vixens and grotesque winged beasts that adorned the rental property. "People thought the gargoyles were evil until we pointed out they're on churches all over Europe. They did make us put brassieres on the women, though."

Kolb smiles when asked about the building's name. "This place [was] a whorehouse in 1911. I always wanted to own a whorehouse, so we named it the Bordello. Alexandra is after my dog [of the same name]. I like to tell people the ghosts of some of the working girls come to visit me"—he pauses—"but they always disappear the moment I wake up."

Kolb, a former actor who studied under Lee Strasberg and performed the lead role in Tennessee Williams's *Orpheus Descending* Off Broadway in New York in the fifties, says the biggest celeb to ever reside here is Leonardo DiCaprio, "a long time ago. Way before he was a big star."

Nowadays, the building is considered a treasured landmark by most of the city, and the waiting list to move into one of the seven units with a glorious rooftop view of the Pacific Ocean is longer than a full-grown demon's wingspan.

The Corkscrew Chimney

As you merrily wind upward along the 8200 block of Hollywood Boulevard in West Hollywood, behind an iron fence you can spot a charming and cozy cottage sitting on a beautifully manicured lawn on a hill just above the street.

This quaint little cabin projects an almost fairy-tale quality, owed to its unusual corkscrew chimney. The winding brick design of the fanciful chimney actually has a practical purpose. It is engineered to prevent fiery sparks from flying from the top of the smokestack onto the rooftop or nearby trees.

According to a neighbor, the inhabitants of this delightful domicile are not seven diminutive friends and a beautiful young princess, but, in fact, the owners of a national pizza chain.

The Coca-Cola Bottling Plant

Ever get the feeling while traveling on South Central Avenue that you've driven right into the Pacific Ocean? Don't panic and drop anchor; steady your course and sail straight through. The high seas are several nautical miles away. You've most likely just passed the Coca-Cola bottling plant.

For those of you who have journeyed by this giant building that looks like an oceanliner, the question has to be: What's the connection between America's best-selling soft drink and this colossal landlocked cruiser?

Bob Phillips, vice president of public relations and communications for the Coca-Cola Bottling Company of Southern California, may not have much room on his business card for anything besides his official title, but he does have plenty of knowledge when it comes to this famous piece of Los Angeles architecture.

Phillips explained that during the early thirties the franchise bottling company was quickly growing bigger and bigger. Thanks to the popularity of the soda, what had been one fairly large industrial building had expanded into three separate bustling facilities. Despite a booming business, employees started to grumble about walking from building to building, especially in inclement weather, so a call went out to architect Robert Derrah.

Derrah had established a name for himself as a pioneer in the Streamline Moderne (or post–Art Deco) school of design. Wikipedia describes Streamline Moderne as "an architectural style emphasizing curving forms, long horizontal lines, and sometimes nautical elements."

Derrah convinced the Barbee family, sailing enthusiasts and owners of the Coke franchise at the time, of his new design. The steamship façade is actually a constructed "wrap" around the three buildings, complete with portholes, planking decks, and cosmetic air horns. Phillips pointed out that much of the interior matches the maritime motif, and that many of the offices are decorated with captain's hats, life preservers, and similarly themed oceangoing items.

To visit this enormous street-faring craft, set course for 1334 South Central Avenue.

The Chemosphere

Perched upon its twenty-nine-foot concrete pedestal high above the Hollywood Hills sits a showpiece of California Modernism. Many local residents aren't aware that this octagonal edifice even has a name. Most who see it call it the spaceship house, and it's a fair nickname.

The glassy futuristic structure is formally known as the Chemosphere. Since its completion in 1960 it has been featured in many television programs and movies.

The Chemosphere is the work of architectural visionary John Lautner. Lautner's daughter Judith, of the John Lautner Foundation, says that it was not her father's intention to design a cool or weird building simply for the sake of coolness or weirdness. Lautner was a protege of Frank Lloyd Wright and was taught by the master to understand and appreciate the canvas an architect has to work upon.

According to Ms. Lautner, "If you understand the reason for its existence and if you understand the benefits of the way [Chemosphere] is designed, you'll see it's anything but weird. Some architects make names for themselves by trying to create buildings just for looks. Mr. Lautner never did that. He was an idealistic Midwesterner [from Michigan] who cared about making living spaces that made life better for the occupants. I realize this is, unfortunately, not the goal of many architects."

In the late fifties, original owner Leonard Malin fell in love with the plot of land. He could not, however, figure out how to build a house on a forty-five-degree slope in a region of the country known for its devastating earthquakes. Malin contracted Lautner, who realized that the home had to be elevated above the property. The 2,500-square-foot Chemosphere rests safely on a supporting column (twenty feet in diameter) buried well beneath the earth.

The current resident, publisher Benedikt Taschen, had this to say about the house in a 2005 *Los Angeles Times* article:

> *"What was great about Lautner is that he had this dualism about nature and the city. On the other side, it's very quiet," he says of the home's northern edge, which contains the bedroom and his office. "It's pure nature, with all kinds of animals: skunks, bobcats, coyotes, deer. They are not shy; you almost have nose prints on the window. And here," Taschen says, walking toward the living room window that faces the Valley's homes and skyscrapers along the 101 freeway, "it's all city."*

Of course there will always be some who see this masterpiece as just a very odd construction, and while that was not the original intent of the designer, its visual uniqueness cannot be denied.

The Charmed House on Carroll Avenue

Well before this Eastlake Victorian became the set for the horror-fantasy-comedy-soap opera *Charmed*, the home belonged to a mere mortal. Murray Burns bought the house in 1977 from a beguiling neighbor, Planaria, and she later became his wife. The Burnses still love it here.

Located high above the 101 freeway, the view of the front of the home suggests late 1800s San Francisco, but from the backyard there's a spectacular view of Los Angeles.

Nope, it's not witchcraft. As faithful viewers of the show know, the Halliwell women on *Charmed* use their supernatural powers every week to fight the forces of evil in the City by the Bay. What many of those viewers do not know is that the purple building the good witches call home is actually located on Carroll Avenue in Los Angeles—a street that proudly claims to have the highest concentration of Victorian homes in one of the oldest neighborhoods in the city.

It also may be one of the most popular sets for movies and TV. For example, did you know that the movie *Big Trouble in Little China* was not shot in Little China but on Carroll Avenue? Were you aware that the television remake of *East of Eden* was filmed nowhere near Eden but instead on Carroll Avenue? And director John Landis shot Michael Jackson's groundbreaking "Thriller" video—you guessed it—right here on Carroll Avenue.

Murray Burns says that many of the homes on the quaint thoroughfare have made appearances on both the big and small screen, but even years after the series ended, the *Charmed* house still seems to get a lot of attention.

"One day I saw a taxi cab pull up, and two young women got out of the cab, so I approached them, and realized they didn't speak English. They were Japanese," said Burns. "I asked the cab driver, 'Where did you pick these

two up?' he said 'The airport—they came directly from the airport,' so I asked 'Where are you going take them after this?' and he said, 'Back to the airport.'"

Planaria Burns added that the couple still gets flooded with fan mail for the house. Sometimes it's kids writing in asking for the floor plans of the house for a school project. Many of the letters come from people from foreign countries, explaining how they're learning English by watching the show.

"Most of the letters we got when the show was on the air was invariably the same thing," Murray says. "Young girls would write, telling us how much they love the house, and then they let it slip that they've written a script for the show," he continues, barely suppressing his smile. "In this particular script they have introduced a new younger female character, and oh, by the way, here's my headshot, do you think you could pass it along to the producers?"

The couple accepts all the attentions aimed at their famous abode with good nature, and generally they are happy to answer any questions that visitors have.

California Graceland

The Elvis impersonator has left the building, and the building has left its mark on this unassuming North Hills community.

The front gate, aside from needing some minor repair work, is a dead ringer for the barrier still standing on Elvis Presley Boulevard in Memphis. The manor itself is not an exact replica, but the four white Corinthian columns flanked by two lion statues on either side of the front porch make for more than a passing facsimile of Graceland.

The current owners were not available for questions, but neighborhood rumor says the home was originally built by an Elvis impersonator who not only emulated Presley's onstage persona, but also attempted to model his offstage life after the hip-swiveling troubadour. The imitator so loved the legend that much of the architecture of the North Hills mansion mirrors that of Presley's own estate. From the jungle room, to the famous wall of television sets, to the long-mirrored hallways, the California Graceland allegedly attempts to pay homage to the eastward original.

It seems when this Elvis impersonator crooned, "Baby Let's Play House," he wasn't just paying lip (twitching) service.

The Bunny Museum

Nestled inside a quiet and tranquil Pasadena neighborhood is a charming 1928 Spanish hacienda with a distinctive fifteen-foot-tall bush trimmed into the shape of a giant bunny. Surrounding the bunny bush are dozens of white wire-frame bunny silhouettes. Near the front entrance is a six-foot bunny wearing purple suspenders, carrying a basket of carrots. The people who live here like bunnies and I'm about to find out how much.

Candace Frazee and Steve Lubanki are the curators of the Bunny Museum. Frazee greets me at the door and invites me to "Hop on in." The museum is also their home, with every space taken up by collectibles: bunny blankets, beds, hairbrushes, toothbrushes, and bath towels. The Bunny Museum boasts twenty-four thousand bunnies and bunny-related bric-a-brac, and, like bunnies in the wild, they multiply rapidly around here.

The bunny that started the whole thing is a stuffed smiling hare, holding in his outstretched arms an oversized red heart, with the inscription I LOVE YOU THIS MUCH. "My husband, Steve, bought this for me [in 1992] on Valentine's Day, because we call each other 'Honey Bunny.' Then I gave him this one at Easter," she says, gesturing to a tasteful white rabbit made of china. "And then before you know it, we're giving each other a bunny every day as a love token."

At the Bunny Museum there is the bride-and-groom bunny section, the angel bunny section, music box bunny section, and there's even a section called the pretenders. Behind the museum glass you can see Tweety Bird with bunny ears on his head and the M&M's guys with bunny ears, and it's a good bet that Garfield the cat doesn't have a deeper affection for Mondays just because he's wearing those bunny ears. There are bunnies in sombreros strumming guitars, bunnies in straw hats smoking corncob pipes. There are king and queen bunnies, rodeo bunnies, conservative bunnies and hippie bunnies, and Santa bunnies.

The bunnies are made of wood, crystal, ceramics, brass, wicker, and plastic, and they also have four freeze-dried bunnies made of flesh, fur, and bone. These deceased bunnies were at one time the couple's domesticated pets, but they hopped off to the great carrot garden in the sky. "They seem pretty lifelike, except for the glass eyes," says Frazee.

If it sounds like Frazee does all the legwork around here, that's only partly true. Lubanki, who is known as a Zen master of bicycles, operates the Open Road Bicycle Shop in Pasadena. Now, he is a successful businessman, and he realizes that sometimes in business you have to diversify. This is why Lubanki opened up Bicycles and Bunnies in the back of his already thriving business. Because sometimes bicycle enthusiasts enter the store wanting a sweet set of twenty-seven-inch forks, but they leave with a terra-cotta figurine of Thumper, too.

The couple has plans to move their home-museum to a bigger location eventually. Until then, like a pair of Energizer bunnies, Frazee and Lubanki will keep their labor of love going, and going, and going . . .

The Bunny Museum is located at 1933 Jefferson Drive in Pasadena. Admission is free, but they do accept bunnies (not real ones, though). The museum is open 365 days a year, but you need to call ahead for an appointment: 626-798-8848.

The Brady Bunch House

It's the story of a lovely North Hollywood middle-class neighborhood and a humble abode that—in reality—does not have a maid's quarters, a teeter-totter, an Astroturf backyard, or a converted hipster hangout in the attic, complete with swinging psychedelic seventies beads in the doorway. It's the story of one of television's most recognizable dwellings: the Brady Bunch house. In real life, the residence is owned by a woman who is as charming and delightful as any character on the wholesome seventies sitcom: Violet McCallister.

McCallister, now widowed, moved into the cozy cottage with her husband, George, during the height of *The Brady Bunch*'s first-run popularity in 1972. She confides that camera crews were never a bother to her because all of the stock exterior shots of the home were taken for the pilot episode in 1969, and the interiors were all shot at Paramount Studios (Stage 5). The house was not used for the two popular satirical Brady Bunch movies.

Over the years, McCallister has seen the occasional Brady fan drive by or stop to take pictures, and for the most part she says the visitors have always been pleasant and respectful. Even the Brady boys, clean-cut and well behaved, stopped by on separate occasions.

Barry Williams (Greg) had dated the beauty pageant–winning daughter of one of McCallister's good friends and had been a visitor to the house a number of times during that courtship. Christopher Knight (Peter) drove up in a classic car and introduced himself as the host of a television special featuring famous TV homes. Naturally the producers selected the Brady place as one of the homes to include in the show.

Mike Lookinland (Bobby) surprised her one day with a little freckle-faced tyke. Lookinland politely explained that he had never seen the house in person before and his son—McCallister guessed the child to be about eight years old—had turned into quite a *Brady Bunch* fan and wanted to see the house in real life. McCallister happily obliged with a quick tour.

The grown-up Brady men impressed McCallister, who has heard the sad tales of former child stars gone wrong, but each one of these boys turned out to become fine young gentlemen, the kindly woman asserts.

Glimpsing the front yard of this celebrated building can send chills down the spine of even the casual *Brady Bunch* viewer, but it's fair to say that it would warm Mike and Carol Brady's hearts to know that McCallister is herself very nice, very welcoming, and, quite naturally, very Brady-like.

Bootmobiles

If you're anything like me, you feel a little more professional and a bit more cosmopolitan after a fresh shoeshine. There's an extra confidence in your step, and you feel just a tad better about yourself, especially if you've had your boots repaired by Quality Shoes in Santa Monica—home of the Bootmobiles.

Owner Rouben Papikian tells me that the Bootmobiles have been great promotional vehicles for years. The original Bootmobile—or, as Papikian calls it, his "baby"—is a red 1971 Honda 600 built to look like an oversized European hiking boot. This customized car was the brainchild of an uncle of Papikian's who has since moved to Henderson, Nevada, and built a brand-new Bootmobile out there.

"I love this little car," Papikian said of the small Honda, "but it's getting old, and isn't running well at the moment." He also went on to explain that the engine is just a tiny V2, and that there's no air-conditioning in the auto. But there's no hiding his affection for the shoe-car. "It's been in that show *Curb Your Enthusiasm* and a couple movies," boasted the coupe's owner.

His other four-wheeled piece of footwear is a Mercury Villager minivan in the shape of a large black cowboy boot. When asked what kind of mileage he gets, he laughed and offered, "Probably not as much as it would be if it didn't have all this steel and fiberglass on it."

It was not an uncommon sight to see the Bootmobiles cruising up and down Santa Monica Boulevard a few years ago, but nowadays the cars are usually parked in front of the store. "They're good advertising."

Like a classic pair of wingtips or the perfect black pumps, these Bootmobiles will never go out of style.

Visit them at Quality Shoes, 11427 Santa Monica Boulevard.

Alexander, Ruler of the World

When it comes to the Alexander, Ruler of the World Apartment Complex—yes that's the name of the place—most people seem to fall into one of two camps: One side hates the building and finds the decor to be a gaudy and overwhelmingly tasteless assault on their senses. The other side loves it and finds it to be a gaudy and overwhelmingly tasteless assault on their senses.

Owner George Panousis belongs to neither of the aforementioned schools of thought. Panousis, born in Greece, is fiercely proud of the face-lift he's given the place since he purchased it in the mid-nineties.

According to one of the workers at Alexander, Ruler of the World, the exterior is faithful to traditional Greek style in both color choice and design. The building contains sixty single units, but no parking, and utilities are included in the monthly bill. Most of the residents are students, actors, and acting students. Rudolph Valentino is rumored to have been a midnight visitor on many an evening, having kept a paramour in one of the rooms during his reign as Hollywood's biggest heartthrob. Divine, the transgendered star of numerous John Waters films, is also suspected of keeping an apartment here for similarly romantic reasons.

People who ordinarily just drove by the estate are now pulling over and taking pictures, and it has been added to the itineraries a number of Hollywood guided bus tours. It has been the talk of the mostly beige neighborhood since Panousis decided to fund the controversial renovation. Love it or hate it, you can't miss the Alexander, Ruler of the World Apartment Complex. (I happen to be in the "love it" camp, but look at the title of the book you're reading.)

Alexander, Ruler of the World is located at 830 Van Ness Street, right across the street from Paramount Studios.

The Neff Airform House

California architect Wallace Neff established a name for himself designing opulent mansions and romantic haciendas for Hollywood's rich and fashionable. Charlie Chaplin, Mary Pickford, and Cary Grant were among Neff's famous and wealthy clients.

He was the grandson of the founder of Rand-McNally (publisher of maps, atlases, and globes) and grew up in the lap of luxury. After years of being architect to the stars, it was an artistically uncharacteristic and financially less rewarding decision to design what he termed "airform houses."

Neff saw a need for affordable housing during World War II. Soldiers were coming home from the war, and other families were trying to get by on a military salary, so Neff came up with the idea to construct modest homes out of cheap but durable materials. He also invented a way to erect these buildings in a relatively quick manner. The airform houses were also known as igloos, dome houses, and, perhaps most descriptively, balloon homes.

An oversized thick rubber balloon (about twelve feet high) would be half inflated with air. The balloon was fastened on top of a concrete base, and then fully inflated. Once it reached the proper curved form, a layer of concrete would be poured over the elastic material. On top of that a covering of insulation would be laid down, and finally another layer of concrete. When the concrete set, the balloon would be deflated and used again for the next airform house.

Pasadena artist Steve Roden and his wife are the current residents of the only remaining Neff airform home, where Neff lived with his brother before he passed away in 1982. Roden loves the one-thousand-square-foot two-bedroom house despite the lack of sufficient closet space.

The Neff Airform House is located at 1087 South Los Robles Avenue in Pasadena.

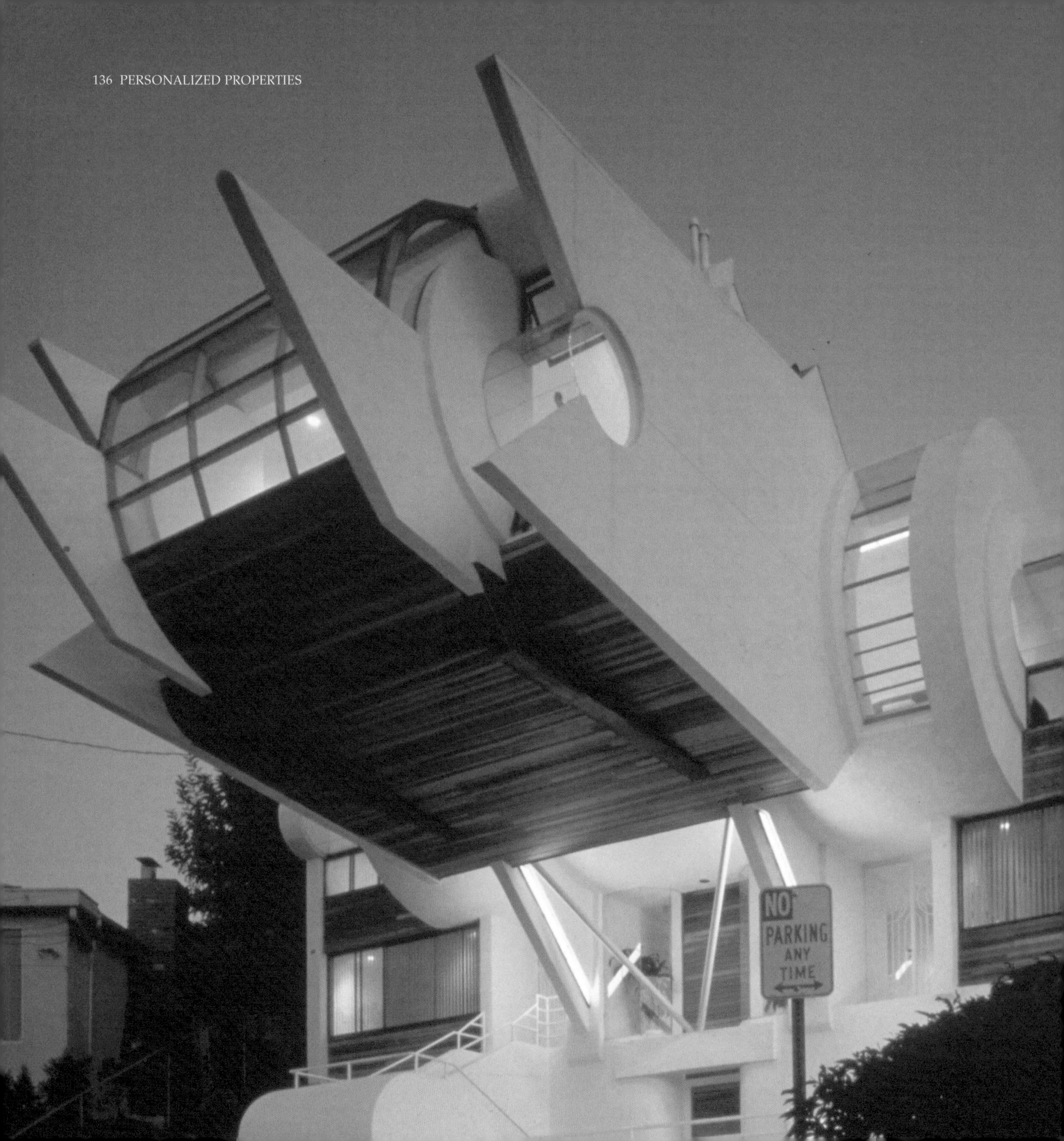
NO
PARKING
ANY
TIME

Harnell House

High above the San Fernando Valley,

Harnell lives in a house that some think looks like a spacecraft and others compare to a Transformer. It's the tricked-out place he retires to when he's not working as a voice artist as the Crash Bandicoot, Captain Hero, and Wakko Warner cartoon characters.

Harnell recalls the first day he laid eyes on what would become his dream house. "I was walking down Ventura Boulevard, and there was a real estate office, and in the window, they had pictures of houses, and I saw this one, and said, 'Oh my God, I have to have this'—because it looks like a toy. I love cool stuff, I thought it was unique, and it was a nice representation of my tastes."

Respected architect Robert Harvey Oshatz (www.oshatz.com) built the futuristic domicile, and while Oshatz is known for building some whimsical structures, he takes each project very seriously.

"An architect is an artist, creator, logician of evolving aesthetic structures; a designer of not only the visual, but the internal space," says the master builder. "Every site I design has its own sense of poetry. I respond to the environment and tailor the property to the personality and the land it sits on. I make rational design decisions based on the surroundings."

Oshatz describes how the "wings" of the building block the view of the necessary but ugly power lines. He adds, "The living room is supported by a cantilever, which makes it feel as if you're floating above the city."

With the breathtaking backdrop of the street lights of the Valley below, Harnell treats us to impersonations of a dead-on Adam West——both the sixties crime-fighting version and the *Family Guy* mayor. Next he's doing Captain Kirk—William Shatner happens to live in the neighborhood—followed by Shatner's *Boston Legal* character. The guy is good.

And the place is cool, not only for the architecture, which is unquestionably cool, but also for the impressive collection of pop culture autographs that adorns the walls. Among his favorites are the Walt Disney autograph, the Beatles' signatures on an album cover, and the entire cast of the *Wizard of Oz* on a movie poster.

However, the animation cell of his alter ego, Wakko, has to get top billing because it's signed by creator Steven Spielberg, just for Harnell. "I just think it's cool the guy knows my name, let alone signed this to me."

So if you ever find yourself in the hills of Studio City, and you happen across a building that looks for all the world like a Transformers sanctuary, do not interfere—the fate of the universe may hang in the balance. The building may very well uproot and turn into the giant robotic Transformer known as Ironhide (who happens to be voiced by Harnell).

Fellowship Shrine

Somehow, hidden close to where the mountains meet the sea at Pacific Palisades, is a scenic and spiritual sanctuary that simply has to be experienced to be believed. This nonfictional Shangri-La consists of ten acres of the most awe-inspiring and little known landscape Southern California has to offer, and is identified as The Self-Realization Fellowship Shrine.

A giant spring-fed lake is the centerpiece of the property. Oversized koi, graceful swans, and the ever-present turtles seem to coexist in such Disneyesque bliss it would come as little surprise to any guest if the aquatic creatures suddenly broke into a perfectly choreographed, peppy little three-minute song-and-dance number and then went back to the business of just hanging out in the water.

Surrounding the seemingly enchanted lagoon are an amazing collection of gorgeous flowers of every conceivable color. Add that to the lush greenery, cascading waterfalls, an authentic looking Dutch windmill, and the massive Golden Lotus Archway. Underneath the alabaster cloisters rests a thousand-year-old Chinese stone sarcophagus, which reputedly contains a portion of the ashes of Indian political and spiritual leader Mahatma Gandhi.

How this picturesque park has remained such an open-aired secret so close to the busy Pacific Coast Highway remains as mysterious as it is tranquil. Created in 1950 by Yogi Paramahansa Yogananda, the memorial is a physical extension of the humanitarian teachings Yogananda brought to America from his native India in 1920. The Fellowship declares itself to be a society. It seeks to foster greater harmony and understanding

among those of all races, religions, and nationalities by introducing Yogananda's universal teachings on the ancient science of yoga. If your jaded inner voice is concerned this awe-inspiring oasis is simply a front to convert simple-minded followers to any specific religion,

Underneath rests a thousand-year-old Chinese stone sarcophagus.

fear not. All of the world's major religions are well represented here, and there is a perceivable atmosphere of acceptance and respect for each faith. That is not to say there are no religious services on the grounds; the windmill serves as a chapel on Sunday mornings, but there is no pious or preachy hard sell here. It seems no one, grounds employees or fellow visitors, intrudes upon your reflective space except to offer a tranquil smile or a peaceful nod.

Over the years the shrine has attracted some famous visitors, including Elvis Presley, someone who had seen his share of worshipful devotion during his lifetime. It is said Elvis was so impressed with both the atmosphere of the shrine and the teachings of Yogananda that he once approached a monk who gave up a promising acting career and said, "Man, you made the right choice."

Visit the Self-Realization Fellowship Shrine yourself at 17190 Sunset Boulevard in Pacific Palisades.

Roadside Oddities

Americans *have had a love affair* with roadside attractions since
the advent of reasonably priced automobiles. Before cars, families
that ate out were limited to whatever local restaurants were within walking distance.

With a motor car, however, suddenly families had choices. They didn't have to eat at Joe's. They could have a meal at Ron's down the road a ways, or only a couple of more miles up the pike, they could sup at Phil's, Luigi's, Pedro's, or Wong's.

Now there was competition for the family's dollar.

It's a proven scientific fact that if you're driving by two seemingly equal but previously unexplored luncheonettes, nine out of ten Americans will choose the café with the eatery with a super-sized statue—for instance, the chubby kid in suspenders holding a hamburger above his impossibly wavy hair.

The same tried-and-true principles apply if you're selling mufflers, furniture, or legal advice. Make it big, make it memorable, and if it isn't too much trouble, make it tacky.

There was a time in this country when kitsch was considered a threat to American culture. Now of course it has *become* American culture, and no single city has embraced the kitsch movement quite like Los Angeles. So let's all jump into our reasonably priced automobiles. Together we'll cruise past gigantic clown ballerinas, oversized buckets of chicken, and massive onion-shaped houses of worship, our iPods queued up to Randy Newman's "I Love L.A." We love it!

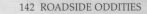

Hiking to the Hollywood Sign

In one of our many weekend "weird" explorations from Orange County to L.A., my friends Jonathan and Logan and I decided to see if we could walk up to the famous Hollywood sign. After some exploring of the nearby mental hospital, we used my GPS to drive as close to the sign as we could. We parked in a neighborhood high up in the hills and started walking. It took us a long time to figure out the correct starting point and path to the top.

Once we did, we made our way up a steep hill full of bushes and weeds toward the sign. At about what seemed like halfway there, we passed a barbed-wire cage filled with security cameras and motion sensors, but we didn't think anything of it and continued. As we hiked toward the sign, it never seemed like it was getting any closer. Finally, after about an hour of hiking and only one NO TRESPASSING sign, we made it to the top.

I was amazed by the gigantic fifty-foot letters that towered over us. The whole word was constructed out of steel with ladders going up the sides of all the letters. I made my way to the top of an *O* to take in the amazing view of Southern California. On the letters were more security camera and motion sensors. We thought that every tourist helicopter flying by to observe the sign was going to send down a SWAT team to arrest us. It never happened though. I think that as long as we didn't hurt anything, no one should care. After spending some time at the sign we made our way back down the hills to our car with no problems.—*Jonathan Crellin, www.adventure.tk*

Hollywood Sign Timeline

The world-famous sign was initially constructed in 1923 as a giant ad for the Hollywoodland Real Estate Group to publicize premier properties in the wooded hills that overlooked downtown Hollywood.

- The cost of the construction: $21,000. It read hollywoodland, meant to stand for only a year and a half.
- Each forty-five-foot letter is made up of three-by-nine-foot metal squares.
- Four thousand twenty-watt bulbs spaced eight inches apart blinked throughout the night, visible from twenty-five miles away.
- In 1932 actress Peg Entwistle became the first person to commit suicide at the sign by jumping off the H.
- By 1945 the sign was an eyesore. Residents lobbied for its removal.
- In 1949, the Hollywood Chamber of Commerce removed LAND from the sign and restored the rest.
- In the mid-1970s, the sign once again in disrepair, *PLAYBOY* founder Hugh Hefner hosted a star-studded fund-raising party and auctioned off letters, replacing them with new letters made of Australian steel.
- Among the buyers, at the cost of $27,777 per letter, were Gene Autry, Alice Cooper, Hefner, Warner Brothers, and Andy Williams.
- The sign was lit up for the first time in decades on January 1, 2000, in celebration of the new millennium.
- In 2005 the sign was stripped and repainted white. That same year, the original 1923 sign was bought via an eBay sale by producer Dan Bliss.

Over the years, the sign has been unofficially altered. Here's a list of some of the more creative modifications:

- HOLLYWEED: 1976, after the passage of a state law decriminalizing marijuana.
- GO NAVY: 1983, before the annual Army-Navy game (played at the Rose Bowl).
- FOX: 1987, in promotion of the new television network.
- OLLYWOOD: 1987, a political comment regarding Oliver North and the Iran-Contra hearings.
- HOLYWOOD: 1987, to commemorate the arrival of Pope John Paul II.
- OIL WAR: 1991, another political comment, this time on the Gulf War.

(Author's note to self: Figure out a way to construct a forty-five-foot-tall weird sign. Place next to Hollywood sign. Sell lots of Weird Hollywood books. Get rich off royalties.)

Kindle's Donuts

It's as true in the donut game as it is in the real estate business. The key to success is in the location. The better-known Randy's Donuts undoubtedly owes much of its accomplishment to its plum spot right off the 405 freeway. Thousands of cars pass the eatery daily, traveling to and from nearby Los Angeles International Airport. Kindle's Donuts, meanwhile, sits in relative obscurity just a few miles away. How else can you explain the fame and status bestowed upon Randy's Donuts while, mere miles away, Kindle's Donuts is comparatively unknown?

Hollywood has made a star of Randy's; the snack shack has shared silver screen billing with Hollywood legends such as Jack Nicholson, Richard Gere, and Eddie Murphy. The geographically challenged Kindle's, on the other hand, would be lucky to rate a guest appearance in a Dustin Diamond infomercial.

The buildings are nearly identical—not much of a surprise, since they were both originally part of the Big Donut Drive-In chain that sprang up in the Los Angeles area in the early fifties. The menus are fairly similar, and if there ever was an all-out donut menu battle, the nod would likely go Kindle's, if only for the sheer size of their Texas-style donut.

Kindle's isn't the only giant donut doppelgänger in the Los Angeles area that fails to achieve the notoriety of Randy's. A few of the other former Big Donut shops still exist (Dale's Donuts in Compton, Donut King II in Gardena, and Bellflower Bagels in Bellflower), but, like Kindle's, they also live in the giant circular shadow cast by their more popular rival.

If you're the type who likes to root for the underdog while consuming the sweet sugary deliciousness of a jelly-filled pastry, then Kindle's Donuts is the place for you.

Kindle's Donuts is located at 10003 South Normandie Avenue in Los Angeles.

Randy's Donuts

Just a few miles up the 405 freeway, north of Los Angeles International Airport, stands possibly the most famous donut shop in the world.

Built in 1952, Randy's Donuts in Inglewood has become almost moviemaker shorthand for "this story takes place in Los Angeles."

In much the same way a glimpse of the Eiffel Tower suggests the elegance of Paris, or the Coliseum cues the viewer to the antiquity of Rome, the twenty-three-foot-diameter cement pastry that sits atop the roof of the donuttery implies all that is kitschy about the City of Angels.

Movies that have filmed this storefront include *Earth Girls Are Easy*, *Stripped to Kill*, and *Problem Child 2*. While these films are less than extraordinary pieces of cinematographic genius, the doughnuts themselves are pretty tasty.

Randy's Donuts is located at 805 West Manchester Avenue. Do yourself a favor and grab a bear claw, or perhaps a honey glazed. If nothing else, it promises to be much more palatable than *Problem Child 3*.

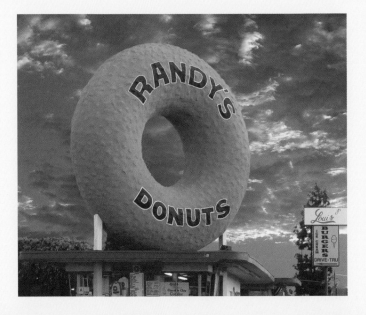

The Donut Hole

Have you ever dreamed of a magical place where you didn't have to lift your rump from your well-worn chair cushion to partake of a sweet ring-shaped cake made of rich, deep-fried dough? If so, then momentarily remove yourself from your favorite recliner, lumber out to your car, and head to 15300 East Amar Road in La Puente. Once inside your automobile, you won't even have to shift your butt cheeks from the comfort of your front seat until you've picked the last morsel of donut from your lap and put it into your hungry mouth, where it belongs.

How could such a sweet experience be tangible, and not just the stuff of fanciful legend? Because, my éclair eating friend, you've just driven through the Donut Hole.

The drive-thru window is certainly not a novelty in Southern California, but it's hard for even the most experienced fast-food connoisseurs not to get a little giddy as they enter the roughly thirty-foot-long giant "chocolate-covered" tunnel that is the Donut Hole.

The Donut Hole was built in 1968, and it is the sole survivor in a chain of five. What kind of unspeakable inhumanity would cause the other four to fold, I dare not say. Let us just be thankful that this marvel of architecture still stands.

You Are the Star Mural

It's quite a gathering, and it's not hard to imagine, based upon the attendees, that trouble is going to break out any minute.

A leather-jacketed hoodlum rubs shoulders with the Queen of the Nile, who is rebelliously ignoring her date. The burly all-American cowboy drapes his arm around the gun-toting but dapper gangster, and behind them a charming man, all dressed in green, is careful not to poke the crazed samurai warrior with his bow and arrow. If all that doesn't sound like it has the makings to ignite the grandest donnybrook of all, Richard Pryor looks none too pleased to see a black-faced white jazz singer sitting just one row in front of him.

Luckily, if things do get out of hand, there's a mighty being in the crowd with powers and abilities far beyond those of mortal men, and if push comes to shove he could fly counterclockwise around the planet really fast and turn back time.

This scene can be viewed any day of the week at the corner of Wilcox and Hollywood Boulevard. *You Are the Star* is the name of this popular piece of wall art, painted by artist Thomas Suriya in 1983. Suriya claims that he had never painted a mural, let alone a portrait, before undertaking this twenty-by-thirty-foot homage to the icons of film.

There are seventy-one familiar faces in this tour de force of street painting. The artist's vision was to create the ultimate movie theater environment but in reverse, "with the stars looking out at the world, which is a projection—the opposite of what we do when we go to the movies."

Be careful when viewing the huge work of art, though. The way Godzilla is giving King Kong the stink eye, it seems like only a matter of time before things get ugly.

Walt Disney Concert Hall

For years, Walt Disney and his company have prided themselves on traditional themes, but there is nothing staid about the Walt Disney Concert Hall, located at 111 South Grand Avenue. Passing by the shiny metallic building, one might swear that the entire structure has come alive, bowing and buckling as if it were an animated edifice in an unreleased *Fantasia* sequence.

Founded in 1987 with a donation of $50 million from Lillian Disney (Walt's widow), the auditorium, which might look like a giant origami project run amok, has given downtown Los Angeles a sorely lacking cultural landmark. But before the first nail was even hammered, bickering began on everything from the shape, the building materials, the budget, and the parking lot. The public outcry was so strong that Los Angeles architect Frank Gehry was required to make more than sixty design revisions on the project—an inconvenience that interfered with the construction of the unique building for more than ten years.

Some of the complaints continue. One report stated that because of the nature of the materials used in the construction of the building, the sidewalk would heat up to 140°F, which was hot enough to "melt plastic and cause serious sunburn to people standing on the street." Another concern was that reflections off parts of the mirrorlike facade were so intense that the glare was causing a problem for passing motorists as well as employees in nearby offices.

Occupying three and a half acres, the Walt Disney Concert Hall has become the home to the Los Angeles Philharmonic. The final price tag for the project was $274 million (including $110 million just for the underground parking garage). Response to the innovative architecture has been overwhelmingly positive.

Watto's Junkyard

Don't you hate it when your ion thruster is expelling large amounts of positive ions, but not quite enough of the electrically stimulated atoms to equal the negative charge being forced out? If your spacecraft is running up a negative voltage, you probably need a new electron emitter. And if you're at a loss as to where to locate one of those, you might try Norton Sales, at 7429 Laurel Canyon Boulevard in North Hollywood.

Norton Sales is a veritable gold mine of discarded machinery and outer space spare parts. Owner Carlos Guzman says the twelve-thousand-square-foot shop and warehouse have been supplying rocket parts to aerospace companies, filmmakers, and collectors since 1962. Everything from simple nuts and bolts to Apollo X-15 XLR99 engines can be found in this modern-day space age junkyard.

Some of Guzman's geekier customers have even taken to calling the store Watto's Junkyard after the fictional secondhand shop where a young Anakin Skywalker worked as a slave for the cunning Toydarian storeowner Watto. The friendly Guzman is amused at the comparisons made to the cantankerous winged *Star Wars* junk dealer, and he is currently looking into buying a few Watto's Junkyard–related URLs to redirect to his existing Web site (www.nortonsalesinc.com).

While Guzman does not claim to have any parts to fix fey droids with English accents, he does have the equipment to launch a craft out of this planet's atmosphere, as well as the parts to totally pimp your ride. "Yes," Guzman offers with a smile. "We don't just sell parts from the Gemini mission; we also sell parts that can be used on a Cadillac."

And while spare parts for a Caddy can be an expensive undertaking, some of the equipment in Norton Sales can orbit into seven figures. "Some of what we have here are really museum pieces and pieces for collectors. They've been on lunar missions, so they are valuable as history, too."

Guzman has set up an eBay business for collectors who don't live in the Los Angeles area, but he says Norton Sales gets a good amount of foot traffic, too, including retired astronaut Buzz Aldrin, the second person to set foot on the moon.

So whether you're thinking of tricking out your Escalade or building a multimillion-dollar rocket ship, visit the good folks at Norton Sales, but save your Jedi mind tricks for some other junkyard caretaker.

Venice Beach Freakshow

The Venice Beach Freakshow is a throwback to old-time carnival attractions. For the very low price of just $3, owner Todd Ray allows you to enter a mysterious world of four-legged chickens and Sri Lankan sea monsters.

Ever since childhood, Ray has been fascinated with the bizarre. "When I was a kid, I loved carnivals. I saw a man perform who was called The Human Cigarette Factory. He was a small man who couldn't use his ossified arms and legs. He could take a cigarette paper and tobacco, and, using only his chin, shoulder, and tongue, roll a cigarette and light it! [H]e told me that if he could do this in his condition, then I could do anything. At the time, this meant a *lot* to me. His name was Otis Jordan, and the Freakshow is dedicated to his memory."

Before opening his homage to nature's oddities, Ray was a music producer for twenty-five years, and he has collected

TWO HEADED RACCOON

RAISED IN HUNTERSVILLE, N.C. NAMED SMOKEY AND THE BANDIT!

Ray, who claims he will pay top dollar for a cyclops cat or a six-legged frog, is on constant lookout for new additions to his fantastic menagerie, and he has recently added a live two-headed kingsnake to the collection and plans to expand the business. There are more than sixty strange creatures at the Venice Beach Freakshow, but that isn't even a tenth of Ray's collection, which still takes up residence in various rooms in his home.

"I do this to remind people about the wonders and curiosities of the universe and our world." Ray says. "As children, we never had a problem seeing the mysteries of life, but as adults we often forget that we are living on a rock floating in outer space. We are freaks in the universe—an anomaly of enormous magnitude. Come into the Venice Beach Freakshow and you will be reminded of the weird world that we live in."

The Venice Beach Freakshow is located at 909 Ocean Front Walk.

three Grammy Awards for his efforts. He has worked with some fairly freakish performers, including Mick Jagger, the Beastie Boys, Cypress Hill, and Audioslave. It was during this period in his life that he started seriously collecting the creatures and rarities.

Ray's wife, Danielle, acts as ticket taker and answers all the inquiries about the abnormal attractions. Daughter Asia does her part by lying on a bed of nails and performing contortions outside the shop. Son Phoenix helps his dad draw onlookers with the assistance of Myrtle and Squirtle, the Two-Headed Turtle.

When asked why he chose Venice Beach as his business locale, the colorful curator to the curious countered, "When Venice was first created in the early 1900s, it was more like a carnival. It was called the Coney Island of the Pacific! There were piers with roller coasters, Ferris wheels. Today people have forgotten that part of Venice's history, but not us. We represent the original vibe of Venice every day!"

Tony's Transmissions

Tall, dark, and handsome, an imposing statue stands stoically watching over his place of business. His steely gaze invites potential customers yet acts as a warning to potential troublemakers. Above his lips sits a perfectly manicured mustache. It is a noble mustache that harkens back to a more romantic period in the City of Angels. Valentino would have killed for such a 'stache.

Enrique Caldo has worked for Tony's Transmissions (4327 East Cesar Chavez Avenue) since 1991, and he remembers a time when the robust figure was not part of Tony's landscape. "He wasn't here when we originally opened. He's been here since about 1997, but he doesn't really have a name. Before he was here, he was at a mechanic shop on Third and Eastern. People come by and take pictures all the time. . . . Everybody loves him."

Caldo feels that the handsome, unnamed mascot has been good business for the successful automotive repair garage and adds, "He is very popular around here. He's even been in the *LA Times.*"

A random sampling of people walking by on the street seem to back up Caldo's claims. "Oh yeah, that dude has been around since I was a kid. He's cool," stated one impressed onlooker. A group of teenage girls giggled when asked to share their thoughts. "He's cuter than your boyfriend," laughed one of the young ladies, pointing to her friend, who didn't offer an objection. "It's true. He is," the friend confessed.

An enormous icon in this East Los Angeles neighborhood, he is part security guard, part friend, part Latin lover, all molded into one twenty-foot advertisement for Tony's Transmissions. Like many colorful men of mystery, his name may not be known, but his presence is surely felt.

The Onion Church

The Sepulveda Unitarian Universalist Society may be better known in its community by its less formal name: the Onion Church. Situated in North Hills at 9550 Haskell Avenue, this uniquely formed house of worship has been an iconic and spiritual landmark in the San Fernando Valley since it was first erected in 1964.

The onion-shaped cathedral was intentionally designed to resemble a giant onion. Thanks to the fine drafting skills of architect Frank Ehrenthal, the building does indeed look like a forty-foot onion.

The Museum of Jurassic Technology

Museums are traditionally institutions where one would expect to find objects of historical, scientific, or artistic value. If that's the case, then the Museum of Jurassic Technology is an anomaly across the board.

This "museum" and its exhibits blur the line between what is real and what is a ruse. They mix inconsequential truths with outlandish fabrications, and the observer is left to wonder at what point he is being had.

For starters, the museum hides itself in wide-open Venice Boulevard in Culver City. The museum masquerades quite convincingly as an abandoned storefront, a squatter's lodging, or possibly a crack house. That, as it turns out, was my first clue that everything about this place was not above suspicion.

Why would anyone in his or her right mind shell out the money it takes to operate such an elaborate con job? It would certainly be truly bizarre if someone designed this sham just to mess with their clientele's minds. Wouldn't it?

According to UCLA professor Randy Fallows, "The museum's mission is placed within a historical context. On closer inspection, the video contains oblique expressions and historical inaccuracies; however, because its style and narration has a 'measured voice of unassailable institutional authority,' as Lawrence Weschler put it, and because there are truths mixed with the fiction, the video seems reasonable enough on first examination."

So Fallows, a professor at a major university, had to buy a book, written by Lawrence Weschler, to help him understand the hoax.

There is a wing dedicated to old wives' tales. Represented here are yarns such as eating a mouse pie can cure whooping cough, or inhaling duck's breath will help to heal a child of throat disorders. Yes, those are easy deceptions to spot. Those I know are gags. Even if they didn't tell me, I'm bright enough to figure out the mouse pie one.

Elsewhere sits a tiny sculpture of Napoleon inside the eye of a needle. That one is real, and it's impressive. Near that is a diorama depicting the life cycle of the Cameroonian stink ant. Why would anyone make that up? They wouldn't. A skeleton of a European mole is displayed right next to a horn that grew from the head of Mary Davis. Now I'm mad again! Just when I thought I could tell the difference from deception and certainty, they went and threw in a horn that supposedly protruded out of some woman's head, a woman with a name so plain that it has to be false, and now I find myself doubting that they even have moles in Europe. Brain hurts. Feeling enraged.

Curse you, Museum of Jurassic Technology!

I took a deep breath and told myself not to let this museum get the best of me. Suddenly I recalled a little quotation from eighteenth-century German philosopher Johann Kasper Dipplinger that I think sums up my entire encounter at this so-called museum: "Reality reveals itself only to those who have the ability to see the genuine as the false, and the counterfeit as truth."

Psych! There is no Johann Kasper Dipplinger. I just made it up.

And therein lies the message in the Museum of Jurassic Technology: It feels good to make people feel stupid.

The Big Chair

When I first laid eyes on the really big chair outside the L.A. Mart in downtown LA (at 1933 South Broadway), I have to confess, my eyes welled up with tears, and I was proud to be an American. Some adore travel, others are addicted to exercise; I am pleased to admit I belong to that great but silent majority: people who love to sit down. I viewed the beautifully massive chair from the comfort of the fully reclinable, heated front seat (complete with lumbar support) of my SUV. I almost couldn't wait to get home and sit, relaxed, in front of my computer to learn more.

Thanks to Google, I learned that this nearly sixty-foot homage to the seated position was created by an Italian-based company named Promosedia, which graciously donated the colossal chair to the city of Los Angeles. I was overcome by a feeling of love for the nation that gave civilization Michelangelo, the Tarantella, and spicy meatballs, for the same Italian furniture producer had constructed a similar chair that is displayed on its own native soil. A wave of solidarity washed over my very soul, and I felt a warm kinship to my Neapolitan brethren. There was a definite sense that this really big chair, lovingly placed in a parking lot just outside a preeminent shopping mall, and its twin shared a connection akin to France's donation of the Statue of Liberty to New York City.

You may laugh at the comparison at first, but the Statue of Liberty is pretty cool too. It's no giant chair, but I don't feel the need to hold that against Alexandre Gustave Eiffel or the country of France. If you recall your history lessons, you are aware the brilliant engineer Eiffel also designed a smaller scale version of Lady Liberty, but presented the United States with the larger model, keeping the smaller scale version in Paris at the Jardin du Luxembourg.

Though the giant chair in Italy is slightly taller than the one in Los Angeles, I can cut them some slack. Here in America we can also proudly boast of the world's largest rubber band ball, the world's longest single strand of leg hair, and the entire cast of MTV's *Jackass*. We don't need the world's largest chair, too.

Thai Dogs

It's huge, it's filthy, and it's inedible. If that sounds like every hot dog you've ever seen in the big city, this one is unique because it's made of papier-mâché, and it sits on top of an abandoned Thai restaurant named Thai Town Express.

The fifteen-foot frankfurter has called the roof of this tiny eatery home for decades now. Originally the oversized wienie sat appropriately enough on top of Red's Hot Dog Stand, but according to a former employee of Thai Town Express, there is a condition in the lease that stipulated the big hot dog has to remain balanced atop the building, regardless of the establishment. And darn it, that condition is going to be followed to the letter.

We at *Weird Hollywood* staged an impromptu and very "scientific" hot dog poll. We stood near the plaster pup and asked randomly selected people their thoughts.

Ron from Burbank said, "Yes, I want the hot dog to stay. This town needs more landmarks like that. They got rid of the Tail o' the Pup; we need to keep the Thai food hot dog."

Carol from Santa Monica replied, "I like it. It's dirty and it belongs here."

Arturo from North Hollywood voted, "Keep the hot dog! Even if they tear down the building, they have to keep the hot dog."

Michael from Kingston, Massachusetts, added, "I'll tell you whatever you want to hear if you can tell me how to get to the Chinese Theater." On second thought he added, "I love the giant hot dog, and I will no longer spend my hard-earned tourist dollar anywhere in Los Angeles County if they ever remove [it]."

And finally, David from East Los Angeles weighed in. "Oh yeah, they got to keep the big dog. I love the big dog."

So there you have it. In a random sampling of passersby, all agree they love the big dog. Smart money says it'll be torn down within the year.

The Television Hall of Fame

Ralph Kramden and Ed Norton are together again. So are George Burns and Gracie Allen, and Jim Henson and Rowlf the Dog—and they've all been bronzed to assure everyone they'll be around for a long time. Where is this wonderful small-screen reunion taking place? In the Valley, that's where. Well, to be more specific, in the courtyard of the Academy of Television Arts and Sciences building—the organization that annually awards the Emmys.

The statues, busts, and bas-reliefs that decorate Hall of Fame Plaza were envisioned and supervised fittingly enough by production designer Jan Scott, winner of eleven prime-time Emmy awards, more than any other woman in the history of television.

The honor of being cast in three dimensions does not belong only to the on-screen talent. Writers Paddy Chayefsky and Rod Serling are on display here, as are TV animation pioneers William Hanna and Joe Barbera and CBS executive William Paley. It's not likely many people are posing for pictures next to top-tier management though, especially since Lucille Ball is striking a camera-ready pose so close by. Other notable talent includes Johnny Carson, Milton Berle, Walter Cronkite, Oprah Winfrey, and Walt Disney.

It's a little difficult find this spectacular visual tribute to the talent that has kept America glued to the boob tube for decades on end, but the address is 5220 Lankershim Boulevard. You can't really see the statues from the street, but just park and walk in. If you see a big pink building and a twenty-seven-foot Emmy, you're in the right place.

In the words of the selection committee, the Hall of Fame is for "persons who have made outstanding contributions in the arts, sciences, or management of television, based upon either cumulative contributions and achievements or a singular contribution or achievement."

The Singing Beach Chairs

What's most amazing about the Singing Beach Chairs of Santa Monica is that they aren't constantly occupied.

The Singing Beach Chairs provide an outdoor audio-visual experience by San Francisco artist Douglas Hollis, whose public art works are found all over California, and all over the country in cities like Seattle, Oklahoma City, and Tampa.

The almost surreal pastel-colored chairs are made of stainless steel, but the five backing anodized aluminum tubes are fifteen-foot-tall musical pipes.

As you near the installation that appears to be part lifeguard towers, part giant baby high chairs, your ears detect sorrowful, almost religious notes. Don't get freaked out, free spirits. Nobody is messing with your mind. It's simply the ocean breeze playing a sad melodic tune through the lyrical cylinders.

Scoops Gelato

Thanks to Tai Kim, owner and culinary mastermind of Scoops at 712 North Heliotrope Drive, now you can have your ice cream and smoke it, too. Kind of.

Kim is reputed to be a mastermind when it comes to mixing up batches of his eclectic gelato combinations, and among his more famous recipes is his original Nicotine Peppermint concoction. Naturally, he offers some obviously tasty blends like Orange Chocolate and Mango Lemon. He even submits other exotic tastes, such as Pistachio and Figs, but it's his bizarre yet delicious creations that keep the mostly college-aged customers lined up out the door.

Some of his more popular menu items include Hemp Oil and Honey and the Elvis—a mingling of bacon, banana, and peanut butter. On Saturdays Kim's party-themed combinations have garnered a loyal following: Beer Sorbet, Pabst and Avocado, Vanilla and Jack Daniels, and Mint and Jim Beam.

If you find yourself wishing for a unique and tasty treat but don't see it on display, fear not, intrepid epicurean explorer. Scoops has a dry erase board for you to make your requests, and Kim often creates from those desires. Care for a kimchi and cheese sugar cone, anyone, or Hawaiian Punch and liverwurst in a cup?

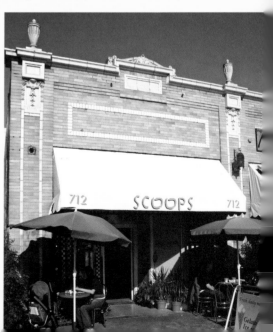

Bronze Dino Battle

The staged battle in bronze is a life-sized homage to the actual skeletal reconstruction of the same titanic clash inside the nearby Natural History Museum of Los Angeles. The outdoor statues of *Tyrannosaurus rex* and *Triceratops* were made possible by S. Jerome Tamkin and Judith D. Tamkin and the Tamkin Foundation, in honor of their grandchildren and the future grandchildren of Los Angeles.

My dino geeky friend James says, "Recent studies have shown *T. rex* were probably wussies who most likely scavenged for their own food rather than hunted for it. I wouldn't mess with a *Triceratops*."

Beverly Gardens Park

The pock-faced French hunter skillfully prepares his shell-shocked hellhounds. Cupping his ear, he is alerted to the clanging gong, courtesy of the jelly-legged jackrabbit. Off in the distance, brightly colored flowers coyly beckon onlookers to come into the garden for a closer look.

This is not the stuff of Lewis Carroll, or even characters from the long-awaited sequel to *Army of Darkness*. These are just a few of the statues in the Beverly Gardens Park in beautiful Beverly Hills.

A plaque beneath the *Hunter and Hounds* sculpture explains that the blemishes on the face of the male figure and his canine companions were caused by bullet holes and shrapnel during a bombardment of Chatteau Thierry in the "second battle of the Marne" in 1918.

Created in 1911, the park is roughly two miles long and runs along the northwest side of Santa Monica Boulevard, covering the entire city limit of Beverly Hills. While you're here, stop and see the rose and cactus gardens, ornate stone park benches, lily pond, and fountains.

DIMEBAG DARRELL
INDUCTED MAY 17, 2007

DEF LEPPARD
SEPTEMBER 5, 2000

The Hollywood Rockwalk

When most people think of Hollywood, they conjure up images of movies and television stars, but the music industry has been a thriving part of Hollywood since the Capitol Records Tower was erected in 1956. Sunset Boulevard in particular has been a vital and vibrant backdrop of undiscovered musicians' struggle to the top. From sixties acts like the Byrds and Frank Zappa, to David Bowie and Iggy Pop in the seventies, to Mötley Crüe and Guns N' Roses in the eighties, the Sunset Strip inspires musical creativity.

The Who's drummer Keith Moon threw a television set out of a hotel window onto this famous street. Keith Richards of the Rolling Stones did the same thing. Led Zeppelin drummer John Bonham drove his motorcycle off of this renowned thoroughfare and into the lobby of his hotel, and Jim Morrison of the Doors hung, perilously by his fingertips, off of numerous balconies high above the Sunset Strip. Oh, and by the way, these guys also contributed to some of the greatest music of the twentieth century.

In keeping with the rock-and-roll history associated with this famously infamous street, the Hollywood Rockwalk was dedicated to honor the bands and solo acts who not only have made significant contributions to the music business, but also have worked overtime to give debauchery and hedonism a good name.

Since 1985, the pavement in front of the huge Guitar Center has immortalized the handprints (and footprint, in the case of one-armed Def Leppard drummer Rick Allen) of rock's most melodious pleasure seekers. Ozzy Osbourne, James Brown, and Little Richard are among the dozens of notables. The members of Aerosmith, KISS, and Van Halen have all slammed their hands into worse than Rockwalk's wet cement, and not only did heavy metalists Iron Maiden imprint their digits, but zombified group mascot Eddie lost one of his skeletal hands in the cement celebration.

Along the wall are rows of three-dimensional bronze plaques dedicated posthumously to performers who burned out before their cement impressions ever had a chance to fade away. Names as diverse as Elvis Presley, Muddy Waters, Dimebag Darrell, Jimi Hendrix, Stevie Ray Vaughn, John Lennon, and Miles Davis are all reverently represented.

You can also find names like Beatles producer George Martin and entertainment magnate Dick Clark's autographed hand impressions on the Rockwalk.

Roscoe's House of Chicken and Waffles

It's a mouthful just to say the name, but it's a mouthful you won't regret when the plate arrives at your table. You may have second thoughts down the road when your cardiologist asks you why you thought a daily diet of deep fried chicken, batter-cooked waffles slathered in butter and maple syrup, and refillable Coke was a good idea, but when that savory aroma hits your anticipating nostrils, no doctor in the world could keep that fork from entering your mouth.

According to Roscoe's Web site, owner Herb Hudson and his friend Roscoe decided in 1975 to leave the cold Harlem winters behind and venture west to sunny LA. Hudson enrolled at Pepperdine University and studied theology with an emphasis on business. Apparently the good Lord blessed Hudson with the realization that there were very few affordable all-night eateries in Hollywood. Working his trademarked

mysterious ways, the Lord also blessed Hudson with the divine knowledge there were absolutely no restaurants in the area that specialized in chicken and waffles. Roscoe's House of Chicken and Waffles opened at the Hollywood address in 1976. Since then they have opened up four other dining establishments in Southern California.

Jessica Simpson, Oprah Winfrey, Bruce Willis, Snoop Dogg, and Larry King have all stood in line to partake of the inimitable taste treat combo of fried domestic fowl and the thick, crisp pancakelike breakfast favorite. One thing Roscoe's prides itself on (aside from its unique menu) is treating every customer equally. Employee J. J. Keno tells a favorite story to illustrate the point. "Someone came in last year and said, 'Hey, you got LeBron James standing out there on the sidewalk waiting in line.' But that's just how it is. I said, 'When he gets in here, we'll treat him real nice.'"

That philosophy has kept Roscoe's griddles sizzling since this nation's bicentennial—that way of thinking is just fine to the thousands of loyal patrons who must believe angioplasty is an Italian appetizer they haven't ordered yet.

Monster Park

Monster Park in San Gabriel, a playground built entirely of brightly painted concrete beasts, is a bastion of creative kid play, a kind of "homestead holdout" in pint-size play. Tucked neatly within Vincent Lugo Park, locals dubbed it Monster Park (or Dinosaur Park, or sometimes even Dragon Park) long ago, and now the unique animals in this playground are considered endangered species.

Artist Benjamin Dominguez, a Mexican immigrant, specialized in concrete play structures and built the animals here in 1965. Dominguez's, who passed on to a more heavenly playground in 1974, contributed concrete art to the Chapultepec Zoo in Mexico City; Washington Park in El Paso, Texas; and Atlantis Play Center in Garden Grove, California. Sadly, some of his creations have been torn down for lack of maintenance.

It's nice to see the concerned community members of

San Gabriel pull together and fight to keep this wonderfully imaginative if imperiled park from being demolished too. Yes, not surprisingly, there was talk of destroying Minnie the Whale, Stella the Starfish, and all of their extraordinary cement pals. But thanks to the Friends of La Laguna, a nonprofit organization comprised of parents, lovers of folk art, and people who have fond memories of this place as children themselves, it looks like the park may just survive.

Saving this beloved landmark wasn't easy. They held rallies, knocked on doors, collected signatures, and got the story in newspapers and magazines and on television and radio. And the battle isn't over; they still need to raise funds for upkeep and maintenance.

Monster Park is located at the corner of Wells and Ramona in San Gabriel. To help preserve the park, visit www.friendsoflalaguna.com.

La Salsa Man

Americans love big things that aren't supposed to be that big. There's no real rational explanation as to why parents will shove four antsy children into the Ford Explorer and travel three hundred miles to see a two-story limestone cow, but it happens daily. How else could you explain the love affair this country has with the country's largest ball of twine, or the world's largest cell phone, or the guy who played Bull on *Night Court*?

Muffler Men are a perfect example of our affection of all things large that have no right being as large as they are. The term "Muffler Man" is shorthand for basically any large fiberglass statue, usually with arms outstretched to hold whatever a particular retail store is selling. Traditionally these have been mufflers, but Muffler Men have been known to hold golf clubs, axes, and space helmets in their meatier-than-they-ought-to-be paws.

La Salsa Man (also known as Malibu Man) in Malibu is one such mammoth. He most likely started out as a Muffler Man, but had dropped his muffler for a huge hamburger by the time he arrived in the affluent beach community sometime in the seventies. It's fair to say that he was not immediately welcomed into the neighborhood with jumbo-sized open arms. A number of residents felt that a humongous man in a colossal chef's hat holding a behemoth burger was a bit gauche.

Fast forward to today. He now sports a suave *bandito* mustache, a serape, and a sombrero, and the feast he's holding is now Mexican cuisine, but there's no denying his Muffler Man roots. And local residents couldn't think of their city landscape without him.

That's the thing about Muffler Men: They grow on you.

Visit him at 22800 Pacific Coast Highway on top of the La Salsa restaurant.

Kentucky Fried Restaurant

If you're anything like me, nothing makes your hunger kick into overdrive more than a big building in the shape of the food you're craving. Imagine how many more times you'd dine at Morton's on Figueroa if the steakhouse were built in the shape of giant cow. Gladstone's restaurant in Malibu could easily do twice as much business were the eatery constructed to resemble an oversized monkfish.

I dream of a glorious day when a ravenous motorist doesn't have to go to all the trouble of reading signs and menus to decide which eatery he'd like to patronize.

Do I want Chinese? No problem, I'll simply drive to the structure that looks like a huge piece of sweet-and-sour pork. Do I have an appetite for Italian? If so, it's easy enough to spot the gargantuan pizza slice tower, complete with anchovy windows.

Luckily the good people at Kentucky Fried Chicken share my vision of a cityscape dotted with enormous flapjacks and burritos. Located at 340 North Western Avenue is a brilliantly designed postmodern piece of architecture. From the front, the edifice is a study of interplay between angles and curves, simulating a three-story bucket of deep-fried deliciousness.

The genius of this design, however, is that from behind, the fast-food establishment appears to be an immense (albeit angular) concrete chicken (sincere compliments to Jeffrey Daniels and Associates).

Will my fanciful reverie of food-shaped skyscrapers ever become a reality? Maybe, maybe not. But thanks to the imagination of a brilliant architectural firm, the financing of one colossal chicken conglomerate, and the hopes and prayers of one slightly demented author who probably needs to get outside a little more and not skip his medication so often, maybe one day this dream will come true. Maybe one day.

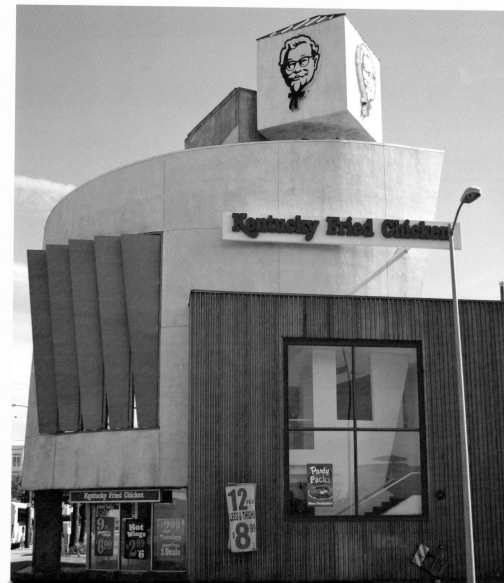

The Giant Hand Car Wash

I have often thought that if I had hands bigger than my car, I'd wash that automobile of mine a lot more often. Why, it would be no more trouble than brushing my teeth, or scrubbing behind my ears, so what's the bother in giving my precious vehicle the solid buffing and polishing it deserves?

It takes about five more minutes to realize that if my hands were bigger than my car, I couldn't even get in the thing, and I would have bigger concerns than the cleanliness of my car. That's why I go the Hand Car Wash in Studio City. It's the best car wash by enormous free-floating hands.

Veteran car washers at the Hand Car Wash in Studio City are very protective of around their five-digited chief nowadays. It seems that the hand, the sponge in its gigantic palm, and the life-sized replica 1957 fiery red Corvette that sits atop the sponge, originally exceeded the city ordinance for giant hands holding big sponges and regular-sized Corvette facsimiles. The hand had to be amputated at the wrist by a few feet. Ouch!

Go on down and have that dirty car of yours washed at the Hand Car Wash in Studio City at 11514 Ventura Boulevard. But I recommend keeping an arm's distance.

The Giant Binoculars

A pair of giant binoculars might seem out of place on Main Street in Venice Beach, but out of place is just business as usual for Swedish-born artist Claes Oldenburg. If you run across something huge that is supposed to be much much smaller, there's a good chance the object in question will also bear the exaggerated fingerprints of Oldenburg.

Oldenburg, the child of a Swedish diplomat who first came to America as a child, is world renowned for his prodigious sculpture portrayals of ordinary objects as king-sized wonders. In Philadelphia, just steps from city hall, Oldenburg is responsible for a forty-five-foot-high clothespin. Barcelona is home to a sixty-eight-foot-tall book of matches, complete with lit matchstick. Smack dab in the middle of Tokyo's International Exhibition is a fifty-foot handsaw, shoved about a quarter of the way into the ground.

Apparently, the binoculars were not originally intended to stand at the entryway of the Chiat/Day/Mojo advertising agency at 340 Main Street, but as legendary adman Jay Chiat was going over the building plans with architect Frank Gehry, they both felt something was missing at the foyer. Gehry was a fan of Oldenburg's work, and knew the Pop Art legend (along with his artist wife, Coosje van Bruggen) was preparing a pair of behemoth binoculars for a work in Venice, Italy. The two agreed that both Venices should share more than just watery thoroughfares, and so the mammoth monument to this optical device was born.

The steel framed binoculars take up a space measuring forty-five feet by forty-four feet by eighteen feet. The exterior is composed of concrete and cement plaster.

The Flying Pig

It doesn't have to be a cold day in Hell, and it makes no matter if the moon is or isn't blue, but if you venture passed 1960 North Topanga Canyon Road, you will most definitely see a pig fly.

Okay, maybe he's not flying—it's more like he's impaled on a twelve-foot iron pole, and, truth be told, the pig is made of two thousand pounds of concrete, plaster, and rebar. But he does have wings—concrete, plaster, and rebar wings.

The hefty hovering hog stops traffic regularly, according to Peter Norwood, who, along with artist-sculptor Chris Budzig, placed the pretty pink plaster porcine precariously upon the pole back in 2003.

"Chris is a lunatic friend of mine, and one day we were drinking some beers, and he turned to me and said, 'Let's make a flying pig,'" said Norwood. "We started out sculpting him on the ground, but knew we wanted him to fly. Then we realized he was getting pretty heavy, so instead of renting a crane after we were finished, we built a scaffold, hoisted him on top, and finished sculpting him in the air."

Budzig is no stranger to creating fanciful beasts for his own amusement. He became locally notorious for constructing concrete floats of the Republican elephant and the Democratic mule for the annual Will Gear Memorial Day Parade. As a commentary on the two-party system, Budzig designed the animals to blow smoke out of their concrete hindquarters as the inanimate animals were waltzed on through the procession. The gaseous political icons caught the attention of certain city council members who didn't appreciate Budzig's editorial on civic bureaucracy, and they have since taken more of an interest in which floats will "float" during the annual ceremony and which will not.

Currently the three-acre plot of land the flying pig soars over is used as part of Norwood's excavation business, Topanga Hauling. Norwood's wife, Victoria, enjoys the family business but dreams of starting her own nursery on the picturesque property. Maybe she will—when pigs fly.

The Cinerama Dome

Each one of the 316 hexagonal concrete panels that make up the geodesic dome of the Cinerama Dome's roof weighs an incredible 3,200 pounds. The construction of the entire building was completed in sixteen weeks, just in time to premiere the 1963 epic comedy classic *It's a Mad, Mad, Mad, Mad World*. The movie boasts a litany of Hollywood's comic geniuses and features quick cameos from some of the most brilliant funnymen to ever grace the big screen. Taking advantage of big screens is precisely why this hemispheric theater was designed in the first place.

Cinerama is the trademarked name for a widescreen process that works by simultaneously projecting images from three synchronized thirty-five millimeter projectors onto a huge, deeply curved screen, and for the corporation that was formed to market it.

In February 1963, Cinerama revealed a new design of movie theaters that would best show off their widescreen capabilities. Based on the geodesic architectural principles of R. Buckminster Fuller, these movie houses would be half as expensive and take half the time to build as their traditional counterparts, and they promised a more visually rewarding theatrical experience.

During April of the same year, Pacific Theaters declared its plans to erect the very first theater based on Cinerama's model. Pacific Theaters promised that Hollywood's first new major theater in thirty-three years would be complete before the exclusive premiere of *It's a Mad, Mad, Mad, Mad World*. Existing buildings were demolished, and construction began in late June.

Despite the tight schedule, the theater was indeed finished by the November 2 deadline, and both the Cinerama Dome and the three-hour film were proclaimed instant successes. The dome is a separate part of the Arclight multiplex and has recently received state-of-the-art stereophonic upgrades. It is still considered one of the most prominent theaters in the entire world.

hicken Boy

Amy Inouye was a young woman all alone in a big city when she moved to Los Angeles in the early eighties. Far from the comfort of her family and friends, one lonely soul in a vast metropolis, Amy was concerned she would lose her connection to humanity itself. Enter Chicken Boy.

Decades later Amy recounts how she and Chicken Boy met. "I was cruising around in my car, trying to make

a connection with this city. I looked up, and there he was. I thought he was the welcoming committee."

Chicken Boy was gainfully employed at the time and was quite well known. He was the face (and grandiose human body) of a popular eatery whose specialty was its deep-fried garlic chicken dinner. No wonder he captivated the impressionable art student.

"As the years rolled by, he remained an oddly comforting constant in my life. I would tour out-of-towners past him late at night. I would look up and greet him on my way to Grand Central Market. People were starting to ask me how he was."

But of course nothing good lasts forever, even the innocent friendship of a blossoming artist and a twenty-three-foot tall fiberglass statue with the body of a Greek god and the head of a delicious meal. "One evening I drove by and the restaurant was boarded up. I took down the number of the Realtors and called them to find out what would be the statue's fate."

This was the beginning of a twenty-three-year odyssey for the pair. For a while the once proud capon lad stayed at his location, but it was clear he felt abandoned. His former employers had flown the coop.

After a dozen or so phone calls to the appropriate people, Amy was able to rescue Chicken Boy. At a cost of $3,000, a team of highly experienced chicken removers were brought in. Enjoying his newfound freedom, Chicken Boy bounced around from "several outdoor storage facilities, friends' backyards, and the back parking lot of my work building," states Amy, who, after all they've been through together, considers herself to be Chicken Boy's mom.

Today, Chicken Boy is once again a proud member of the California workforce. You can visit him at his new location atop Amy's new place of work, Future Studio. Like the Chicken Boy, it's an amalgamation. Part art gallery, part trendy novelty store, it's located at 5558 North Figueroa Street in Highland Park, along historic Route 66.

The fact that Amy was there for her fowl-feathered friend in good times and bad times speaks a lot to the character of this unique and caring woman. And the fact that this unique and caring woman developed such a strong emotional tie to a gigantic inanimate half man, half chicken speaks a lot to the city of Los Angeles in the eighties.

To inquire more about their special affinity, write Amy and Chicken Boy online at www.chickenboy.com.

Ripley's Believe it or Not Odditorium

At first we thought it might be weird to include the Ripley's Believe it or Not Odditorium at 6780 Hollywood Boulevard in our book of weird. It is, after all, commercially weird, and we were concerned the weird purists might call some sort of weird foul if we were to skip a story on something so obviously and commercially weird.

We feared classic followers of the bizarre, as you might very well know, since you might very well be one, could come to the conclusion that we took the easy way out since Ripley's is a well-known museum chain that celebrates the strange.

Well, we here at *Weird Hollywood* are sticklers for keeping it real—real weird, that is, and we contend that it would just be plain weird to not include a building devoted entirely to all things weird, which happens to be located right in the heart of downtown Hollywood. Mind you, this building has a giant *T. rex* busting out of the roof, eating a clock . . . right smack dab on Hollywood Boulevard.

This idiosyncratic edifice also contains shrunken heads, three-headed babies, a statue of Marilyn Monroe made out of a quarter of a million shredded dollar bills and a human hair bikini. That's some bona fide weirdness right there.

So after weighing the pros and cons, it became a no-brainer. We would be derelict in our duty to bring you the finest weirdness Hollywood and its surrounding areas had to offer if we didn't mention the museum that also contains "proof" of a Chinese man who lived his entire life with a candle growing out of the top of his skull.

It was either that or we'd have to write a story on how weird it was that we didn't include a story on a building devoted to such weirdness as a paintings made up of butterfly wings, or a portrait of John Wayne created entirely of lint—and writing something like that would have just been weird.

We'll tell you one thing we won't do. We won't even mention the obviously commercially weird Guinness World of Records Museum, located right next door to Ripley's, at 6764 Hollywood Boulevard. It's a veritable pantheon of weirdness.

Capitol Tower

The Capitol Records Building, also known as the Capitol Records Tower, has been one of the most recognized landmarks in Hollywood since 1956. At 150 feet high, the tower was as tall as Los Angeles ordinances permitted at the time. Artists as diverse as Frank Sinatra, Pink Floyd, Snoop Dogg, and Radiohead have all recorded at the distinctive thirteen-story earthquake-resistant tower.

Nicknamed "The House That Nat Built" because of the vast amount of revenue brought in by singer Nat King Cole during the fifties, the building was designed by world-famous architect Welton Becket. While many believe the structure was designed to resemble a stack of records on a turntable, that was evidently not Becket's plan. The edifice is nevertheless the world's first circular office building. Becket, a pioneer in the post–World War II Futurism movement, is responsible for much of the overall look of Los Angeles and Hollywood, including the Dorothy Chandler Pavilion, the Cinerama Dome, UCLA Medical Center, and the 176-acre commercial and residential district known as Century City.

Atop the "needle," a red blinking light has been spelling out the word "Hollywood" in Morse code since Lyla Morse, granddaughter of Samuel Morse, activated the switch at the building's grand opening. The message was changed out for an entire year in 1992 to read "Capitol 50" in honor of the fiftieth anniversary of the record label.

Capitol Records does not conduct tours of its historic building, but you are allowed to venture into the lobby and peek at the framed gold records of the Beatles, David Bowie, and Coldplay, to name a few.

The Camera Obscura

You know what Santa Monica's got? A little bit of everything, that's what. Great beaches, of course, and the world-famous Santa Monica Pier, which houses the world-famous Santa Monica Carousel and the world-famous Santa Monica Ferris Wheel. Santa Monica has a wonderful library, great restaurants, tons of shopping, and an impressive array of live entertainment venues.

You know what else Santa Monica's got? Long lines of people waiting to park near the beach, or eat at a great restaurant, or ride on a world-famous amusement ride.

Now, here's the way I see it: If you don't like long lines, you've got one choice. You can go to the Camera Obscura. Camera Obscura, at 1450 Ocean Avenue, is located on the second floor of the Senior Recreation Center building. A camera obscura is a pitch-black boxlike device or room in which images of objects outside are received through an aperture and projected in their natural colors on a surface inside. It is used for sketching, exhibition, and other purposes. If that sounds fun on paper, just wait until you experience it in person.

Imagine a dark ten-foot-square room with a four-foot in diameter white "plate" in the middle. On the plate, projected from an opening in the ceiling, is a live nonreversed mirror image of the Santa Monica beach. It's a lot like looking at a real-time video feed, but it's all done with gears and reflective glass, and there's no rewind button.

To the side of the plate, there's a nautical wheel that turns 360 degrees. Spin the wheel a little bit and see the pier. Spin a bit more and check out the hotels across the street, the palm trees right outside, or the current gridlock on Ocean Avenue—all reflected on this very white plate. If you're feeling particularly brazen, you can tilt the plate upward to look at the Santa Monica sky, or downward to view Santa Monica dirt, grass, pavement, or sand.

I suppose you could go outside and look at all these things with the naked eye, but that would be defeating the purpose. If you go inside the Camera Obscura and look at Santa Monica, you're doing something you didn't have to stand in line for.

So next time you're in San Mo (as the local hipsters call it), swing on over to the Camera Obscura. It's a guaranteed ten minutes of pleasantly mediocre time passing.

Bullwinkle and Rocky Statue

Dudley Do-Right, George of the Jungle,

Super Chicken, Tom Slick, and Hoppity Hopper—mention those names even now to certain discerning baby boomers, and their eyes glisten with fondness.

Those characters all sprang from the brilliant and somewhat eccentric mind of the late great Jay Ward. A real estate agent by trade, Ward, with the help of innovative partners Alexander Anderson and Bill Scott, created some of the hippest, quirkiest, and subtly subversive cartoons that ever graced the television screen.

Perhaps the most popular of all of his creations, though, were the plucky pair of heroes from Frostbite Falls, Minnesota: Bullwinkle J. Moose and Rocket "Rocky" J. Squirrel. Week in and week out, Bullwinkle and Rocky helped save this great nation of ours from the nefarious likes of animated Cold War adversaries Boris Badenov, Natasha Fatale, and Fearless Leader. Although it was never a huge commercial success, the show managed to stay on the air for fourteen years owing to fierce loyalty from the viewers it did have. Originally called *Rocky and His Friends*, the program debuted in 1959.

In an effort to kick off the new 1961 television season, Ward erected a fifteen-foot likeness of his beloved moose and squirrel in front of his studio, renamed the failing program *The Bullwinkle Show*, and threw a party. The festivity was an all-out success. Blond bombshell Jayne Mansfield performed as mistress of ceremonies. Walt Disney was among the animators and celebrities who were asked to dip their drinking elbows and sign their names in the cement base of the large iconic figures in a winking nod to the Grauman's Chinese Theater footprint tradition.

Originally Bullwinkle was dressed in a one-piece men's turn-of-the-century swimsuit, in an attempt to lampoon the statue of a bikini-clad cowgirl advertising the Sahara Hotel and Casino in Las Vegas that stood directly across the street. He now sports a sweater with the letter *W* (for "Ward") emblazoned upon it.

Sadly, the Jay Ward Studios are no longer on Sunset, but Ward's influence is felt in such shows as *The Simpsons*, *Family Guy*, and *SpongeBob SquarePants*. Luckily, the likeness of one dim-witted but good-hearted moose and his earnest and loyal flying rodent pal still stand in testament to the all that's good, pure, and slightly offbeat in Tinseltown.

Ballerina Clown

Most enjoy it, some tolerate it, and there are still those who really despise the thirty-foot-tall Ballerina Clown that stands on pointed toe atop the entrance of Long's Pharmacy in Venice Beach.

Part sad hobo buffoon, complete with five o'clock shadow and a lonely teardrop running down its cheek, and part graceful *danseuse*, artist Jonathan Borofsky sees this piece as a logical synthesis of the spirit of Venice Beach itself. In an interview he gave to *Carnegie Mellon Magazine* in 2002, Borofsky explains his work: "That image is a lot tougher than most of the images that I put out in the world. I thought it was acceptable [because] it was right along the beach there, a block away, where people are dressed in all kinds of costumes and outfits. There's a lot of street performers. It seemed like a very appropriate place to put an image that deals with the duality within all of us. It's a male and a female mixed together—the male clown and the female ballerina, and the duality of performance: the street performer and the ballerina, the traditional, classical performer. A mixing of opposites [in a] splashy, showy kind of way. Now it's accepted pretty much as an icon in the city. But for the first few years, it had its detractors."

The Ballerina Clown is located in Venice Beach on the corner of Main and Rose. Judge it for yourself.

Ascent

A total of thirty-one bronze men's shoes (roughly size twenty) corkscrew around the glass elevator of the four-story Cherokee Whitley Parking Garage at 1710 North Cherokee Avenue in Hollywood. Artist Kim Yasuda was commissioned to create the illusion of an invisible, weightless dancing giant in 1994.

The piece is titled *Ascent*, and, according to the placard affixed to a nearby wall, the sculpture was inspired by the exploration of sequential imaging done by photographer Eadweard Muybridge in the late 1880s. Muybridge performed studies of human and animal motion by means of timed remote-activated cameras. His work was the precursor to motion pictures.

The figureless performance of shoes is reminiscent of the Hollywood musical extravaganzas of the 1940s, in which entertainers like Fred Astaire and Ginger Rogers appeared to "dance on air."

Santa Monica Art Tool

Weighing in at more than 28,000 pounds, the Santa Monica Art Tool was designed to be, like many of artist's Carl Cheng's creations, an interactive public experience. The obvious problem is that at fourteen tons it requires the interactivity of a dozen or so well-muscled participants to get this concrete cylinder to budge from its resting spot alongside the famous pier. The inscription alongside the piece suggests that the Art Tool is to be pulled by a city tractor, but where's the interactive public experience in that?

While it doesn't happen often, after the cumbersome beach toy is rolled, a twelve-foot-wide topographical map of the city of Los Angeles is created in the sand. Two-inch-tall traffic-jammed freeways result as they wind around suburban neighborhoods and industrial parks.

Hollywood Ghosts

Hollywood has been enamored with the shadowy spirits of the dead even before the studios started rolling film. Some celluloid ghosts have been frightening; see *13 Ghosts* or *The Blair Witch Project*. Some have been funny; see *Abbott and Costello's Hold That Ghost* or *Ghostbusters*.

If ghosts truly do remain on this earthly plane, Hollywood is as good a haunt as they could ask for: warm weather, beautiful people, fine dining. Plus, if they want to go to some trendy hotspot, they don't have to wait in line—they just do that cool "walk through walls" ghost trick, and bam, they've got the sweetest seat in the joint.

Like their theatrical counterparts, the phantoms of Tinseltown come in all types of personalities. In this chapter you will read about the spectral visions of schoolchildren burned in a fire—too concerned with their eternal recess to report for their heavenly rewards; the ever-vigilant sitcom uncle who, even in death, takes his duties as legal guardian solemnly; and the grisly ghouls whose lives were ended in gruesome fashion, and in turn have terrified those who dare to tip-toe too close to where they expired.

So now, dear reader, turn out all the lights, grab a flashlight, and curl up under your covers as you read the startling, spooky, sometimes humorous, and oftentimes sad tales of the ghosts of Hollywood.

Ghosts of the Hollywood Roosevelt

Recently Hollywood's young and idle rich have turned the Roosevelt Hotel into a trendy after-hours spot, but it's also become very popular with the afterlife crowd as well. Claiming up to thirty-five individual resident ghosts, including some very famous, very dead celebrities, the Roosevelt is believed to be the most haunted building in this town.

Undoubtedly the most famous of all the phantoms is Tinseltown's favorite blond bombshell herself, Marilyn Monroe. The movie star beauty posed poolside on the diving board of this famous hotel for her first print ad before she was famous, and she was a frequent guest of the hotel, often staying in her favorite room, 246, during the 1950s. The full-length mirror, which was once part of the décor of Monroe's cabana, was relocated to the second-floor mezzanine after her suicide in 1962. A ghost of a glamorous blonde fitting Monroe's description has been spotted in the reflection—only to vanish when the viewer turns around.

Montgomery Clift was a friend of Monroe's in life, and apparently in death they still keep in touch. Clift spent three months in room 928, preparing for his role as Private Prewitt in the 1953 film *From Here to Eternity*. The handsome actor spent many nights rehearsing his lines and learning how to play the bugle for his part, but maybe Clift was unsatisfied with his onscreen performance, because the perfectionist poltergeist has been heard blowing his brass instrument and running his dialogue over and over in the wee hours of the night. He's even been known to get physical with select guests and employees.

Then there's the story of the young brother and sister whose father excused himself from the room momentarily to run an errand. When dad returned, he discovered both young children had left their suite to play in the pool.

Tragically, they both drowned. On occasion the two have been spotted giggling and running through the lobby, only to evaporate a moment later.

One woman who has worked for the Roosevelt claims that she was in a room, filling up the minibar, when she heard the voice of a young boy teasing her. "He was saying 'Minibar! Minibar!' He just kept saying it. Like he was making fun of me. I looked around—it's not a big room—and there was no one there." She also claims that lights have a habit of switching themselves off and on in certain rooms, "and hair dryers too! I was in a room, and as I was walking out the hair dryer went on. I walked over to turn it off, but it went off by itself—then it turned on again and off again."

Some members of maintenance have reported mopping the floors only to see walking footprints appear before their very eyes on the still-damp tile, and the ghost of a man in a white suit has been known to tickle the ivories at odd hours of the evening.

Another mysterious happening is the cold spot in the Blossom Ballroom, the location of the very first Academy Awards ceremony, where it is regularly 10 degrees colder than anywhere else in the room.

The most gruesome sighting is the headless man, who, according the lore of this lodging establishment, was violently decapitated in the building many years ago. In 2008, a young woman who had been working at the front desk for only six months let herself into room 213 to make sure the previous visitors had vacated. The guests had checked out, but the bloody headless body of a decades-old murder victim had, in the meantime, checked in. The poor rookie was so shaken up by the incident that she fell to the ground, rocked herself in the fetal position, and remained there until she was found by security. She quit the next day.

Janis Sang Here, Drank Here, Died Here—Her Ghost Still Haunts Here

The renowned Sunset Sound Studios, located on the corner of Sunset and Highland, has been the setting of such popular yet musically diverse albums as the soundtrack to Disney's *Bambi* and the Rolling Stones' gritty yet decadent *Exile on Main Street*. On October 4, 1970, Janis Joplin left the famous studios after putting the finishing touches on her final album, Pearl, and traveled two and a half miles to her favorite chili-serving dive bar, Barney's Beanery on Santa Monica Boulevard.

The gravelly voiced rock vocalist was a regular at the restaurant whenever she was in town, and rock-and-roll legend has it that it was at this cozy eatery that the bluesy gypsy thundered a right fist into the intoxicated face of fellow patron Jim Morrison. Joplin also carved her name in her favorite table just months before she passed on. The table now hangs on the ceiling above the first booth in the left aisle. It reads '70 JANIS LYN.

On the night of her death, Joplin threw back a couple screwdrivers at Barney's and retired to her hotel room (number 105) just three and a half miles away at the Landmark Hotel, now called Highland Gardens. Joplin changed into her pajamas, shot some heroin into her vein, and sauntered to the front desk to grab a pack of cigarettes. Upon returning to her room, the singer collapsed and ultimately died from the fatal injection. According to Hollywood historian Scott Michaels, the dose was too pure for her system to handle, and it's said that a number of Los Angeles junkies died that week from that particular batch of the drug.

If you're hoping to encounter the ghost of Janis, you can request her room (they charge you extra), but some say it's not necessary. All you have to do is go down to the lobby and mention Joplin's name. Those who have worked at the hotel swear doors will open and slam shut by themselves at the very mention. Pictures have been known to fly off the wall, and the phones start to ring incessantly, but no one is ever on the other end.

The Vogue Theater's Ghosts

Going to the movies can be a hassle. After a half-mile schlep and waiting in line, it's time to empty your wallet for admission and snacks. Add to that the uncomfortable chairs, unidentified goo on the floor, and noisy children acting like little monsters, well, it's enough to make you want to stay home.

But if you're at the Vogue Theater in Hollywood, the noisy children aren't monsters—they're ghosts.

Apparently this old movie house is loaded with things that go bump in the night. The International Society for Paranormal Research claims to have documented more than four thousand paranormal experiences since 1997 alone. The ghost-hunting guild has declared the Vogue Theater, located at 6675 Hollywood Boulevard, as the most actively haunted property in the history of Hollywood.

As for the supernatural squirts, give them a break; they died years ago along with their teacher, Miss Elizabeth. The 1901 fire burned to the ground the four-room schoolhouse that previously stood here. Since then the kiddie ghosts been calling the Vogue their personal playground.

The eerie urchins aren't the only residents of this shadowy cinema. Two of the theater's more famous phantoms worked together for years in this building. Even in death the former employees continue to haunt their old haunt. Danny was the loveable but gruff maintenance man who died of a drug overdose, and Fritz was the German-born house projectionist who plied his trade at the Vogue for more than forty years. He was said to have lived for his job, and then he proved it by dying of a heart attack in the projection booth. Legend has it that even after his death, the workaholic ghost of Fritz handled the projection changeover during a film festival while the very much living and salaried projectionist took a nap.

The Vogue no longer operates as a full-time movie theater, and, according to parapsychologist Larry Montz, the spirits no longer inhabit the structure. After years of communicating and learning from the incorporeal beings, Montz claims to have released them "from the earthbound plane."

Tipping Clifton

Clifton Webb performed on both Broadway and the London stage during his illustrious career, but it was Hollywood where he truly felt at home. He died of a heart attack in 1966, but some say he still resides in Tinseltown.

Although the stylish actor didn't achieve silver screen stardom until his mid-fifties, Webb more than made up for lost time after receiving the nomination for Best Actor in a Supporting Role in Otto Preminger's film noir classic *Laura*.

Suddenly the dapper performer became known for attending each and every soirée thrown by the glamorous social set, and he also garnered a reputation as the sophisticated host of many a lavish late-night gala at his own mansion on Rexford Drive. Everyone who was anyone in the forties and fifties enjoyed the perpetual celebration at Clifton's place— including his constant companion and confidante, his devoted and doting mother, Mabelle (pictured here).

Insiders believed the middle-aged star had a bit of an Oedipal complex, so when his darling *mater* passed away in 1960, Webb was said to have become inconsolable, and he withdrew from the Hollywood party scene. After filming a few more pictures, Webb died at the age of seventy-six. Death, however, could not evict the cosmopolitan thespian from his beloved Beverly Hills address. He was said to have haunted his old estate for years until it was torn down and rebuilt. No longer comfortable in his new setting, the urbane apparition packed up his ghostly belongings and moved back in with his mother, who is buried beside him at the Hollywood Forever Cemetery.

Steve Goldstein, renowned Los Angeles grave hunter, cemetery tour guide, and owner of the Web site BeneathLosAngeles.com, believes he may have encountered the late entertainer's spirit one day while leading a group of visitors to the famous funerary grounds. "My friends and I used to do this thing we called 'tipping Clifton,'" explained the graveyard guru. "The seal to his crypt was broken, so you could push, or tip, the marble stone about two inches into the wall. We'd always do it to anyone who was there for the first time. It would freak people out a little. No one expects a crypt to have any give. One day I had a large group of first-timers with me, and as soon as they touched it, a nearby flowerpot fell to the ground. The pot shattered and a bird flew out of it and over our heads. We've always assumed that was Clifton out to get us back for scaring all those unsuspecting people."

Goldstein has no doubt Webb's spirit is still contained within the charnel confines of Hollywood Forever, though his crypt is no longer tippable. Goldstein claims with an air of certainty, "As long as Mabelle stays here, Clifton will be right beside her."

Peg Entwistle's Suicide

Peg Entwistle enjoyed a modicum of success on Broadway, performing in eight plays between the years 1926 and 1932. In May 1932 she was brought out to Los Angeles to perform in a short run of Romney Brent's *The Mad Hopes.* Starring Billie Burke (*The Wizard of Oz*'s Good Witch of the North), the theatrical production received both critical and commercial success, selling out the 1,600-seat theater in its scheduled two-week stint. Entwistle and fellow costar Humphrey Bogart were specifically praised for their fine acting.

The youthful entertainer was already packed and ready to head back to the Great White Way when movie studio Radio Pictures called her in for a screen test. The striking flaxen-haired ingenue signed a one-picture contract, started work in July, and dreamed of becoming Hollywood's next big star.

But the studio deleted most of Entwistle's scenes. Much of her screen time was left on the cutting room floor, and, to make matters worse, the studio refused to pick up her option. Despondent, Entwistle moved in with her uncle Harold, just above her uncle's house on Beachwood Drive.

Informing Uncle Harold that she was heading to a local drugstore, Entwistle instead hiked the slope of Mount Lee and traveled straight to the iconic Hollywoodland sign. Removing her shoes and coat, she placed them neatly at the base of the sign, alongside her purse, which contained a suicide note. Awash in a deep depression, the beautiful blue-eyed twenty-four-year-old climbed the maintenance ladder behind the letter *H* and leaped to her demise. Sadly, even the immediate release of death she'd hoped for eluded her for a time. According to the coroner's report, Entwistle suffered "multiple fractures of the pelvis and probably did not die quickly."

Her broken body was found two days later by a hiker, who reported the incident to local police. The suicide note read: "I am afraid, I am a coward. I am sorry for everything. If I had done this a long time ago, it would have saved a lot of pain. P.E."

In the kind of irony considered too unbelievable for fiction, two days after her remains were discovered, Entwistle's uncle opened a letter addressed to his niece from the Beverly Hills Playhouse. It offered the young actress the lead role in their latest production. Her character was to commit suicide in the play's final act.

To this day there are sightings of Peg Entwistle's ghost on and around the Hollywood sign. Reports are usually the same. A woman dressed in thirties-era clothing leaps off the *H* and vanishes before she hits the ground.

El Compadre Restaurant Hauntings

El Compadre Restaurant at 7408 Sunset Boulevard attracts all types. On any given night you can run into struggling musicians, accomplished actors, retired producers, and the ghosts of two men who were killed in the Mexican eatery back in the fifties.

According to legend, an armed robber held up the cantina back when the establishment was operating under the name Don Pepe's. Two loyal customers charged the thief, and the trigger-happy outlaw shot them both dead. The spectral pair of would-be crime stoppers is often reported hanging out near the piano after hours, and they have supposedly made their presence known to the wait staff on more than just a few occasions.

Ask any El Compadre employee about the ghosts, and you will get a mixture of reactions, but all are aware—as are many customers—of the chilling stories. Some will tell tales of plates crashing, cold spots in the room, and, most famously, the haunted mirror, which sometimes reflects shadowy figures that dissolve as soon as they are spotted. David Castro, son of the owner, knows many of the stories, but has never seen a ghost himself. Other employees turn pale and decline to speak of their experiences.

The trigger-happy outlaw shot them dead.

Johnny Whitaker and the Ghost of Uncle Bill

As a child actor in the sixties and seventies, Johnny Whitaker seemed to star in every other family-friendly film or TV show Hollywood produced. Before he was thirteen years old, the adorable redhead had played alongside such notable personalities as Tony Randall, Mary Wickes, E. G. Marshall, Fred Gwynne, and Jodie Foster.

In 1973, Whitaker portrayed Johnny Stuart in the Sid and Marty Krofft Saturday morning favorite *Sigmund and the Sea Monsters* and played the lead in the movie *Tom Sawyer*, but it was probably his role as the six-year-old orphan in the hit sitcom *Family Affair* that Whitaker is best remembered. According to the series pilot, after the untimely death of his parents, Jody Davis, along with his sisters Sissy and Buffy moved into the Manhattan high-rise of their confirmed bachelor uncle (played by Brian Keith) and his English butler, Mr. French (played by Sebastian Cabot).

Whitaker got along with the entire cast, and he recalls his relationship with Keith as being similar to that of an actual uncle-nephew relationship. "He looked out for me, and my career to a certain extent . . . there was a definitive affection between the two of us," recalls Whitaker, now in middle age.

Keith was already a successful movie actor who prided himself on doing his own stunts when called upon. When the ruggedly handsome actor decided to make the move to smaller screen and take on the role of Uncle Bill Davis, it was bit of a career gamble in those days. But Whitaker chalks it up to a combination of Keith always marching to his own drummer and a very lucrative contract.

Whitaker's and Keith's paths crossed a few times after the show went off the air in 1971, but it had been years since the two had spoken when in 1997 Whitaker found out Keith had been diagnosed with inoperable cancer. "I gave him a call, and said 'Brian, it's Johnny Whitaker,' and in his typical charming but grumpy way he shot back, 'Who gave you this number?!'" Whitaker laughingly recalls.

Immediately Keith apologized and confided that his daughter had only days earlier fatally overdosed on cocaine, and the doctor had just given the seventy-five-year-old thespian a mere five days to live. Just two days after the fond telephone reunion, Keith placed a gun to his temple and shot himself dead in his Malibu home.

Whitaker suddenly found himself getting calls from news organizations around the world, looking for quotes and memories.

"I got a call on my way home and I dropped the phone [while] going sixty miles per hour on the freeway. I took my eyes off the road . . . to pick it up and . . . all the cars in front of me had immediately stopped." Whitaker says he instinctively jumped on the brakes, but that only made his car slide at a forty-five-degree angle into the path of a big rig. "I started to panic, because I think I'm about to be decapitated, and I hear Brian Keith's voice saying [Whitaker does a dead-on imitation of the familiar gruff voice] 'Take your hands off the wheel. Cover! Duck! Roll!'

"Now, Brian had just passed on Tuesday and this is Thursday. I believe Brian was there with me. . . . 'Cover, duck, roll' is a mantra for any stuntman."

The car was demolished, but miraculously Whitaker escaped with only a few minor bruises and cuts. Soon after the accident, Whitaker made his way to the junkyard to claim some personal items from the wreckage. Upon arrival he was greeted by an attendant, who inquired, "Do you mind me asking what happened to the man who drove the car?" Whitaker responded, "I'm the man who was driving." Astonished, the custodian confessed that he had seldom seen such destruction to an automobile, let alone ever met anyone who could walk away from such an ordeal. "You must have someone looking out for you," he whispered in disbelief.

Whitaker chokes up a bit as he recounts, "It was then that I had this warm wonderful feeling, and I said Brian was looking out after me. He saved my life."

Thanks to that spiritual intervention, Whitaker lives each day as if it were a gift, and he made it his life's work to help others view life that way as well. In 2003, Whitaker, a recovering drug addict, founded Paso por Paso (Step by Step), a twelve-step recovery program targeted to the Latino community. The Web site is www. pasoporpaso.org.

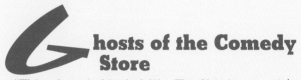hosts of the Comedy Store

"This place is kind of like The Shining. . . . A lot of things have happened here," confides an employee of the Comedy Store who does not wish to be identified. "The Belly Room gives me the heebie-jeebies. They say there's a couple of different spirits that haunt this place."

During the forties and fifties the establishment was known as Ciro's, the most glamorous nightclub in Hollywood. For a time, Ciro's was *the* frolic pad for Tinseltown's rich and famous. Top-tier talent like Dean Martin and Jerry Lewis and the Desi Arnaz Orchestra would swing out to equally well-known hep cats and kittens such as Bette Davis, Frank Sinatra, and Marilyn Monroe.

It wasn't all laughter and riffs at Ciro's, however. While the club may have officially been owned by *Hollywood Reporter* publisher Billy Wilkerson, it was a poorly kept secret that L.A. crime boss Mickey Cohen was running more than a few illicit activities out of the back room at Ciro's.

The anonymous tipster knows the deal: "There's a stairwell in the back, and people don't realize it, but there's a machine gun port there. People have been whacked walking up the stairs. . . . That whole area is creepy."

Modern-day stand-ups at the Comedy Store may be more concerned with tickling a funny bone, but Cohen's boys were more likely to fracture a femur bone, bust a kneecap, or, if mob justice decreed, encourage a dirt nap. Much of this rough business was done in the basement and back room. It is rumored that there are still bodies buried under the floors.

Gus, possibly the most famous ghost of the Comedy Store, worked as a part-time doorman at Ciro's and a

part-time hit man for Cohen's gang. It's unknown whether he was whacked by a goodfella or he was simply a bad doorman, but Gus was murdered, and his ghost still hangs out. Other tales of playful poltergeists and angry spirits of mobsters include candles relighting themselves and chairs moving, despite having been neatly stacked.

Comedian Blake Clark refused to believe in paranormal manifestations until he started working at the Comedy Store. Clark was there when fellow comedian Joey Gaynor taunted the apparitions one night after the club had closed. After Gaynor goaded the ghosts to show themselves, an ashtray levitated off the table and hurled itself at the comic's head. Gaynor ducked just in time, and the projectile exploded against the wall behind him.

In the Comedy Store's lower level, there's the furious ghost of a woman who performed illegal abortions for many of Ciro's dancing girls is said to be violent and frightening—and she's the sweet one by comparison. Another ghoul is described in *Haunted Hollywood* as a hulking, amorphous seven-foot figure of pure malevolence. Still another is capable of chilling the air to the point you can see your own breath, while simultaneously heating your skin until it burns.

The Comedy Store is located on 8433 West Sunset Boulevard and is owned by the legendary surrogate mother of stand-up comics, Mitzi Shore, and her son, comedian-actor Pauly Shore. The 2003 R-rated *Pauly Shore Is Dead* includes a Comedy Store ghost who convinces Pauly to fake his own death—which may or may not be an allusion to the suicide of comedian Steve Lubetkin, whose suicide note said, "My name is Steve Lubetkin. I used to work at the Comedy Store" and whose ghost may just be lurking in the dark corners in and around the building.

Ghost of the Silent Movie Theater

On the evening of January 17, 1997, F. W. Murnau's 1927 classic, *Sunset,* was billed as the marquee movie at the Silent Movie Theater. It was during the showing of Larry Semon's comedy short preceding the film, however, that the night took a very real turn toward murder mystery. A customer walked back to the ticket booth and fired three shots at close range into seventy-four-year-old owner Laurence Austin. The gunman then fired two shots into the chest of theater employee Mary Giles (she survived) and then ran down the aisle, shooting randomly behind him.

Austin was the second owner of the theater. He bought it from the original owners, John and Dorothy Hampton. The Hamptons opened the movie house devoted only to silent films in 1942, years after they had already gone out of fashion. While it was never a huge moneymaker for the couple, who together pulled projectionist duties, ran the snack bar, sold tickets, spliced and repaired old films, and did general upkeep, the Hamptons were able to eke out a living for forty years thanks to repeat business from devoted local lovers of film craft. It is even rumored that during the forties Charlie Chaplin would discreetly visit and watch visions of himself and former colleagues on the soundless screen.

Over the years, the theater developed a loyal following. Sadly, after John Hampton took ill in 1981 and was unable to tend to the business, the theater became abandoned and run down.

Enter film aficionado Austin. In 1991, Fairfax residents noticed that the old theater was receiving a much-needed face-lift. Like the Hamptons before him, refurbishing the old cinema was not done for financial gain—it was clearly a labor of love. Austin became as well known as the previous owners, greeting each and every patron with a handshake and a smile.

News of his murder shocked and saddened the entire movie-going community. Police investigated, and in a case that contains all the classic elements of a disturbing film noir, it was determined that Austin's younger lover and part-time projectionist, James Van Sickle, had hired nineteen-year-old Christian Rodriguez to kill his mature paramour.

Van Sickle apparently found himself in quite a bit of debt, and he was also the sole beneficiary of Austin's will. Not being a very patient man—or, as it turns out, a very loving one, either—he hired Rodriguez to knock off Austin for the inheritance and paid him $25,000 to do so. Van Sickle also kicked in an extra five grand to kill Giles—to make sure it looked like a robbery gone wrong. The police were not thrown off the track.

Austin has been dead for years now, but, according to some, that hasn't stopped him from still showing up on a nightly basis. Silent Movie Theater employee Matt Cornell says there are many reported incidents of spooky occurrences. Customers have reported weird electrical problems, someone brushing against them the dark when there's no one in the room, and feeling cold in certain places. Cornell, who remains skeptical, doesn't completely dismiss those experiences, but adds that theaters themselves have an inherent spookiness to them. "Every picture on the walls of this place is of someone who's been dead for a long time staring down at you. That can definitely give off a haunted vibe."

Whether you're a fan of classic film, or a ghost hunter in search of a phantom movie companion, you can visit at 611 North Fairfax Avenue, or on the Web at www.cinefamily.org.

Bela's Ghost

The name Bela Lugosi conjures up images of bats and coffins, creepy castles and ominous thunderclaps. The distinctively charismatic Hungarian performer, best known for his portrayal of the aristocratic lord of the undead—Dracula—was born mere miles from the dark and fabled vampiric Transylvania, but it was shiny parasitic Hollywood that Lugosi loved—so much so that it has been rumored that he may still be a resident, even decades after his death.

Crucifixes and garlic cloves may have been Dracula's weakness, but the allure of a good cigar was Lugosi's. Most every day, whether he was working or not, the dramatic performer could be found strolling Hollywood Boulevard, exchanging pleasantries with fans on his way to the Hollywood Smoke Shop at the intersection with Vine Street. There he would make small talk with the shopkeeper and purchase a couple of finely rolled stogies. It was at this very store where it is said that Lugosi first met Ed Wood.

UNSPEAKABLE HORRORS FROM OUTER SPACE PARALYZE THE LIVING AND RESURRECT THE DEAD!

PLAN 9 FROM OUTER SPACE

with BELA LUGOSI VAMPIRA LYLE TALBOT

A J. Edward Reynolds Production

Produced and Directed by Edward D. Wood, Jr.

When the impoverished Lugosi passed away in 1959, hundreds of fans lined up outside the mortuary to mourn the man who had given them all such delightful terrors. Lugosi's corpse was dressed in his famous cape and wearing the Dracula family crest ring. His coffin was placed in the hearse, and the driver led the motorcade to Holy Cross Cemetery in Culver City.

No funeral processions were allowed down busy Hollywood Boulevard, a fact the driver of the hearse knew well. As he started to head north toward the graveyard, across Hollywood Boulevard, the driver felt an irresistible tug at his steering wheel. Try as he might, he was unable to correct the course of his vehicle until he and his deceased passenger had crossed the intersection of Hollywood and Vine.

Did the driver experience inexplicable car failure, or was he under the potent vampiric enchantment of the late Lugosi, who wanted just one more whiff of aromatic tobacco before he passed on to the other side?

Suicide Bridge

Her movement is unsettlingly smooth; her demeanor, serene. Barefoot, she glides along the cold concrete—emotionless. Long flowing robes dance behind the woman in silent rhythm as the cool night breeze commands her silky garments to gambol and frolic in a spirited frenzy. Approaching the parapet, she climbs effortlessly to the top. Without uttering a sound, the midnight maiden plunges off the 150-foot-high bridge, only to vanish before reaching the unforgiving pavement below.

This is but one of the many ghost stories of Pasadena's infamous Colorado Street Bridge, better known by locals as Suicide Bridge. Although there is no official count, it is said that close to two hundred people have committed suicide from the 1,486-foot-long overpass since its erection in 1913. Less than two decades after the completion of the bridge, ninety-five people were reported to have plummeted to their deaths.

Why are so many despondent souls drawn to this spot? Some blame the ghost of an original construction crew member who accidentally fell over the side of the bridge, landing in a deep vat of wet cement below. To this day, his haunting cries for help are whispered to have the power to compel the hopeless to join him in the afterlife.

Of all the tales of self-destruction the bridge has to offer, none is as well known as the story of the woman who, in a fit of Depression-era melancholy, tossed her infant girl over the railing, then immediately leaped toward her untimely departure. The mother died on impact, but her child cheated death. The newly motherless youngster was found hours later, crying, scratched, and bruised, in the dense branches of the nearby trees. Legend has it that the baby girl's mother still roams under the bridge, painfully searching in vain for the innocent life she hoped to reconnect with in the hereafter.

Architecturally known for its antique street lamps and Beaux Arts arches, the landmark bridge was part of the celebrated Route 66 until 1940, when the Arroyo Seco Parkway opened. Repairs were made to the bridge after the 1989 Loma Prieta earthquake in faraway Oakland, California, forced city council members to consider the stability of the then seventy-year-old structure. The bridge was closed for a $27 million renovation and reopened again in 1993. Included was the addition of a tall "suicide prevention" rail, complete with spiky deterrents.

The Ghosts of Gravity Hill

One of the greatest urban legends in all of America is the supernatural force often referred to as a gravity hill. Gravity hills are, by folkloric definition, a mystical incline of road in which cars placed in neutral gear appear to roll uphill. There are dozens of these roadside miracle spots in California alone, and practically all high school kids who have been in a car will tell you that either they or their friends have experienced the seemingly inexplicable sensation of this phenomenon.

The loss of young life is often used as a reason for why gravity hills exist. One typical tale is that of the new mother pushing her baby carriage. Out of nowhere, she finds herself confronted by a preoccupied or speeding motorist. The frightened parent makes a desperate attempt to thrust herself and her newborn out of harm's way, but it's too late for them, as the car slams into both mother and child, killing them instantly.

Another story goes like this: A busload of schoolchildren breaks down at the side of the hilly road. While waiting for the driver to repair the vehicle, the children, who were warned by the bus driver not to play in the street, disregard his admonition while his head is buried under the engine's hood. Suddenly the man looks up and sees a car careening down the slope, heading directly for the blissfully unaware kids. He springs into action, but he is too late. He and the children are run down and killed.

These accounts go on to explain that the cars in neutral gear are not rolling up the hill, but are rather being pushed by the spirits of the victims trying to outrun death. Furthermore, if you sprinkle baby powder on the hood of your car, you will find the eerie handprints of the dead.

The cities of Altadena and Moorpark each claim one of these mystery spots as their own. If you decide to explore, it's not uncommon to run into other weird adventure enthusiasts in their own cars trying to experience the abnormality firsthand.

In Altadena, take Lake Avenue until it turns into Loma Alta and travel about another quarter mile. In Moorpark, the approximate address of the gravity hill is 12772 Kagel Canyon Road.

Of course there are those who will tell you that gravity hills are merely optical illusions. But these are often the same fuddy-duddies who go to bed at a sensible hour and get their taxes done in January.

For the rest of you, happy uphill rolling.

★ FIRST INTERCONTINENTAL BALLISTIC MISSILE
   OF THE UNITED STATES
★ FIRST TO FLY 5500 NAUTICAL MILES
   NOVEMBER 28, 1958
★ FIRST TO LIFT A UNITED STATES CAPSULE
   INTO SPACE
★ FIRST SATELLITE TO BROADCAST A MESSAGE
   TO "THE FREE WORLD"
★ FIRST TO RECORD A MESSAGE IN SPACE
   AND BROADCAST IT TO EARTH

Gay's Lion Farm
El Monte Calif.

Gone But Not Forgotten

They say *nothing good lasts forever*, and that adage seems particularly true in Hollywood. On any given day in any given studio, teams of men can be found tearing apart entire "cities" and building up wholly new environments, only to rip those down once that project is wrapped. Restaurants that were once the most happening eateries in town disappear seemingly overnight, and last year's A-list entertainer can sometimes find it hard to book a guest spot on the latest celebrity drug rehab reality show.

If Hollywood has given the world anything of substance, it would be the shared memories of all the people, places, and things it has captured through its lens over the decades.

Folks remember where they were and who they were with when they watched the last episode of *M*A*S*H*. Americans who have never traveled west of West Virginia recognize certain sections of Pacific Coast Highway as well as they do streets in their own town, thanks to movies like *It's a Mad, Mad, Mad, Mad World* and *The Karate Kid*.

And why do tourists from all over the world ask locals how to get to the Hollywood sign? Because they've seen it on film, it somehow struck a chord with them, they realize the transitory nature of this town, and they want to make the physical connection while they have the opportunity.

This chapter is dedicated to the people, places, and things that have given us some measure of joy—whether we ever experienced these encounters in person, or know them only through the magic of film. Hollywood, thanks for the memories.

Rudolph Valentino and the Lady in Black

When Rudolph Valentino died of peritonitis in 1926 at the age of thirty-one, a nation of stunned fans—mostly women—mourned the passing of the silent screen's romantic leading man. Hysterical devotees went into a deep depression upon hearing the news, and it's reported that some actually committed suicide. Valentino was one of the most popular stars of the silent era, and his smoldering good looks and portrayals of passionate romantics earned him the nickname "the Latin Lover."

There has only been one Rudolph Valentino. Since his death, however, there have been dozens of women who have tried to claim the mantle as the original Lady in Black. The legend of the Lady in Black goes all the way back to the first anniversary of the handsome Italian actor's death. On the anniversary of his death each year, the mysterious Lady in Black, dressed in black from head to toe, a long dark veil pulled over her face, walks solemnly to Valentino's grave, places a single red rose, kneels momentarily in silent prayer, then turns and disappears without saying a word.

Some initially believed the Lady in Black might be Pola Negri, Valentino's grieving girlfriend, but Negri never laid claim to the rumor. Press agent Russell Birdwell alleges that the first Lady in Black was a publicity stunt he hatched to keep Valentino's name in the press. Over the years many different women would dress in black and venture to his grave, each professing she was the original. Other opportunists would boast that they were engaged to or had a child by the brooding star, but, upon closer inspection, these assertions never held up.

It is common belief among Valentino enthusiasts that the original Lady in Black was a woman named Ditra Flame. Sickened by all the pretenders, Flame finally made her identity known decades after the death of her idol. Flame recalls being very ill as a child and spending long periods of time in a hospital. Her mother was a good friend of the dashing star, and he visited the ailing child, bringing with him a single red rose.

"You're not going to die at all," the matinee icon assured

her. "You are going to outlive me by many years. But one thing is for sure—if I die before you do, please come and stay by me because I don't want to be alone either."

Flame says she felt better after Valentino's bedside visit, and, heartbroken upon hearing the news of his death, she kept her end of the pact and continued her pilgrimage until

1954, when she decided there was too much commotion and far too many imposters looking to bask in a piece of reflective glory.

Of course Flame's story didn't deter Anna Marie De Carrascosa from maintaining that she was the original Lady in Black. De Carrascosa made her own annual journey until she was struck dead by an oncoming bus in 1973. Her daughter, Estrillita Di Regil, took over the role. Di Regil also had her mother disinterred from a different cemetery and moved to Hollywood Forever so she could visit her mom and Rudy in one convenient trip. De Carrascosa's headstone labels her as the Lady in Black.

According to the officially recognized modern-day Lady in Black, Karie Bible, Di Regil seemed like just another crazy lady more interested in making a spectacle of herself than paying respects to the deceased celebrity. Bible, who gives tours of Hollywood Forever Cemetery (www.cemeterytour.com), claims, "I heard Estrillita Di Regil was a wacky lady. She carved her name into the marble of [Valentino's] crypt." She was also known to show up at the sepulcher on a daily basis, convulsing and wailing like a banshee."

Bible wants it known that she is not one of the crazy ones. She is aware of the assumption, but insists that she's doing this for the love of silent film and her affection for history, not to mention that she's a Valentino fan. "I think society is so focused on what's now and what's hot, and we lose sight of the past and how interesting and vibrant the past can be." She adds, "I'm just keeping the tradition going."

Every August 23, Bible steps out of her hearse limo, dressed in period clothing and the obligatory long black veil, walks into the mausoleum, and places a rose at Valentino's crypt. Sometimes she's asked to speak by the Valentino committee; sometimes she remains a silent guest. Bible insists she's not a jealous Lady in Black, and she encourages others to help celebrate the past. Bible is eager to point out that there is an African American woman named Diane Whitmore who also commemorates the date of Valentino's passing. She dresses in the color of fresh fallen snow and calls herself the Black Lady in White.

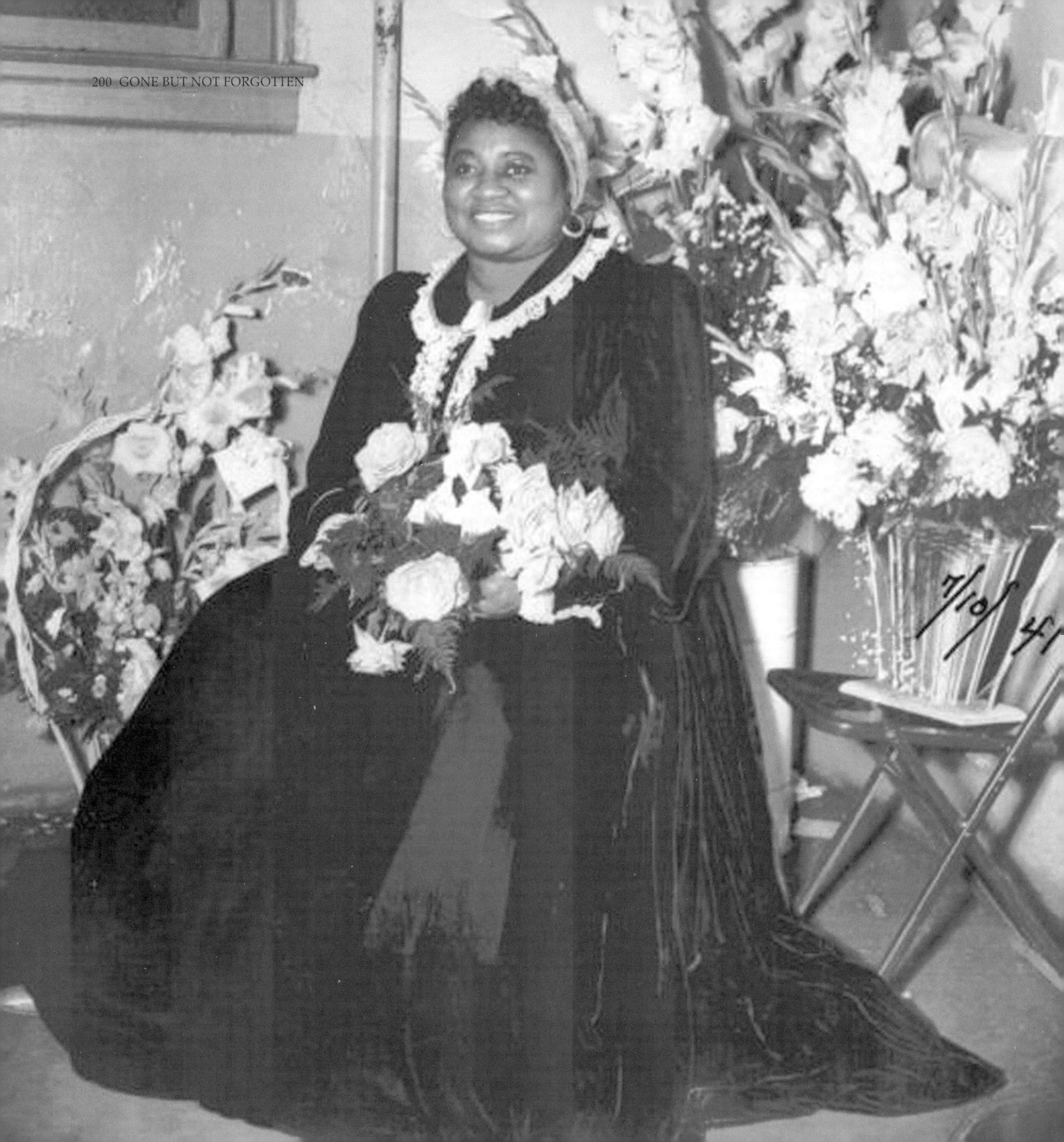
7/10/41

Hattie McDaniel

She was the first black woman to sing on American radio. She was the first black entertainer to win an Academy Award. And her dying wish was to be the first black person laid to rest in Hollywood Memorial Park. Sadly, Hattie McDaniel's last desire remained unfulfilled.

McDaniel's hope was to be interred with the professional peers of her day. Tyrone Power, Douglas Fairbanks, and Rudolph Valentino were all entombed at this mortuary, but the racist "whites only" rule was not lifted for the beloved African American performer, so she was instead buried at Rosedale Cemetery, where she lies today. (A small number of white Angelenos protested the decision to let the deceased actress into Rosedale, but thankfully management ignored their disapproval and allowed her a befitting funeral.)

Her funeral procession, in 1952, was one of the most lavish in the history of Hollywood. The motorcade included 125 limousines, and nearly twenty-five vans were needed to transport the thousands of mostly red roses and white gardenias that adorned her casket.

McDaniel is said to have appeared in more than three hundred films, though she received screen credits for only roughly eighty of them. Times being what they were, she was usually cast in the role of the maid. It was her portrayal of the character Mammy in the epic *Gone with the Wind* that brought the plump, charming actress her greatest acclaim.

The segregated cemetery changed hands in 1998, and in a goodwill effort to right the wrongs of the past, new owner Tyler Cassity extended an offer to move McDaniel's remains to the now renamed Hollywood Forever Cemetery. While the star's family decided against the move, they did accept Cassity's symbolic gesture to erect a memorial tombstone in honor of the talented artist. The inscription includes: "To Honor Her Last Wish . . . Aunt Hattie, You Are a Credit to Your Craft, Your Race, and to Your Family."

The unveiling ceremony took on the tone of an actual funeral. Guests were seated and listened to the stirring words of a minister and the uplifting music of a gospel choir. *Gone with the Wind* costar Olivia DeHavilland summed up the tribute nicely in a letter she sent from France, which read: "This monument will not only respect Hattie's deep desire, but will also give to us who admired her work a place where we can express our regard for her artistry with a flower, a prayer, a thank you."

W. C. Fields Would Rather Be in Forest Lawn

Rumors swirl about what is written on Fields's gravesite. People say he used a fake name, or he couldn't afford to pay for the grave, and others. The most famous story: Fields's will instructed that his memorial would bear the inscription, "All things considered, I'd rather be in Philadelphia." The rumor stems from a 1925 article in Vanity Fair in which Fields proposed the epitaph for himself. The pun is a play on his oft-uttered quote, "I'd rather be dead than in Philadelphia!" (Philadelphia was Fields's birthplace.)

Fields occupies an honored place in the massive Great Mausoleum in the Forest Lawn Memorial Park in Glendale. The location may in fact do more to impress the living with its million-dollar view. It's not clear whether there actually

are spirits here or if the publicity department is just good at quashing rumors. The security staff was surprised that pictures and locations of celebrity graves were common on the Internet. "Those are supposed to be private" is an oft-repeated phrase when the visitor arrives with pictures and locations fresh off of some Web site.

Fields's propensity for pseudonyms apparently spilled over into questions about his birthdate. He was born on April 9, 1879, then again on January 29, 1880. Most historians (and Fields's own son) have settled on the latter date, which is what appears on the brass plaque on the front of his crypt.

The Great Mausoleum is open from 9 A.M. to 4:30 P.M., but only for twenty-minute periods every half-hour, and no peeking at the graves on the way in.

Forest Lawn Memorial Parks

The award for the most impressive collection of dead celebrities has to go to the Forest Lawn Memorial Parks in Glendale and Hollywood Hills. Take a look at this roll call if you will: Spencer Tracy, Humphrey Bogart, Walt Disney, Sammy Davis Jr., Bette Davis, Larry Fine, Clark Gable, and W. C. Fields. That's an impressive Hollywood gathering.

With five complexes in different areas of the county, Forest Lawn Memorial Parks covers more than 1,200 acres in total. The cream of the crop is definitely the park in Glendale. The grounds look as if someone took every painting of heaven that has been produced since the Middle Ages and used them as production drawings. Periodic billboard campaigns dot the Southland, asking motorists to "celebrate a life" with "pre-planning" courtesy of Forest Lawn.

The 1965 film *The Loved One*, written by Terry Southern, was supposed to have been a parody of the uniquely Southern California–Forest Lawn philosophy of overweeningly pastoral resting places for the dead, but a walk through the grounds reveals that it was not far from the truth. The Freedom Mausoleum is a flag-wavers paradise, with a massive and romantic brass statue of George Washington and busts of founding fathers like Benjamin Franklin installed tastefully throughout the buildings. During the cemetery scenes in *The Loved One*, actor Robert Morse courts a lovely mortuary assistant to the strains of soft harp music. All around the mausoleum complex, 101 Strings–inspired versions of old favorites like "Suwannee River" and "Greensleeves" play on a continuous loop through sometimes static-laced outdoor speakers and echo through the crypts. Is it comforting or just strange? Does everyone in the graveyard like this music? Can't they at least install an iPod and leave it on shuffle?

The biggest problem when visiting the real Forest Lawn is that, unlike Hollywood Forever Cemetery, where they will literally sell you a map to the gravesites of the late-and-greats, you are almost entirely on your own navigating through this more traditional burial ground. We advise a printout from any one of the many Web sites that specialize in this sort of thing.

It's quite amazing how many nobodies you will run across in your search to say you visited the grave of Scatman Crothers, who was featured in *The Shining* and was the voice of Hong Kong Phooey, but Forest Lawn silently dissuades tourists and fans.

If you ever wished you could be in the same place as flamboyant pianist Liberace, and funnyman Fred "Rerun" Berry, and the creator of Batman, Bob Kane, then run—do not walk—to Forest Lawn. But walk with a dignified grace once you enter, because I'm serious about them being sticklers for decency. Getting eighty-sixed from a swinging Hollywood shindig carries with it a certain caché; being

bounced from a cemetery, no matter how cool the cemetery, is pretty lame.

Some celebrities had the common courtesy of customizing their commemorative plaques and markers, so as to stand out from the regular noncelebrity dead, like circus legend Clyde Beatty (cool engraving of a lion) or Western clothing designer and original rhinestone cowboy Nudie Cohn (her fashion company's logo; see previous page). Unfortunately, it seems that the more famous the person, the more unassuming the site tends to be.

Local celebrities like longtime LA newscaster Jerry Dunphy and over-the-top right-wing talk show host (and father of actress Rebecca DeMornay) Wally George are completely at home next to a veritable who's who of classic television stars, including Morey Amsterdam, Freddie Prinze, McLean Stevenson, and Isabelle "Weezy Jefferson" Sanford (see below).

Again let me stress that etiquette and restraint are expected and required at this particular graveyard. Don't test them; they will toss you.

BELOVED MOTHER, GRANDMOTHER, GREAT GRANDMOTHER AND FRIEND
PASSED JULY 9, 2004

DEAN MARTIN
JUNE 7, 1917 – DECEMBER 25, 1995
EVERYBODY LOVES SOMEBODY SOMETIME

Westwood Village Memorial

A scant few miles from the hallowed halls of UCLA is the Westwood Village Memorial Park. It is easily the smallest of the celebrity graveyards, but it also offers the most bang for your buck.

Whereas Forest Lawn in Glendale alone consists of more than three hundred acres of peaceful rolling hills, and Hollywood Forever Cemetery is big enough to cause you to become disorientated if you're not paying attention, Westwood Village is about the size of the clothing section in your average department store.

Jack Lemmon and Walter Matthau are once again teamed up for great dramatic effect. Tough guys George C. Scott and Burt Lancaster hang out comfortably with a man's man of a different sort: Truman Capote.

Music legends? Yeah, they got 'em. Beach Boy Carl Wilson is here, as is solo artist and Traveling Wilbury Roy Orbison. Frank Zappa is said to occupy the unmarked grave just eight feet west of Orbison's.

Television stars Carroll O'Connor (Archie Bunker on *All in the Family*), Jim Backus (Thurston Howell III on *Gilligan's Island*), Jonathan Harris (Dr. Smith on *Lost in Space*), and Sebastian Cabot (Giles French on *Family Affair*) all now make Westwood Memorial their eternal TV Land.

Looking for beauties? It's going to be hard to beat this collection of exquisite cadavers: Natalie Wood, Dorothy Stratten, Donna Reed, and the one and only candle in the wind, Norma Jeane Mortenson, aka Marilyn Monroe.

Westwood is even the final resting place of two young stars of the movie *Poltergeist* who were taken way before their time: the adorable Heather O'Rourke, who died on the operating table at the tender age of twelve, and the beautiful Dominique Dunne, who played the older sister

JACK LEMMON

in

to O'Rourke's Carol Anne and, at age twenty-two, was strangled by an estranged boyfriend.

If death seems to be an unfair yet certain eventuality for everyone, consider the very much alive and breathing (at least as of this writing) comedian Jerry Lewis. Lewis's longtime partner, handsome crooner and former Rat Pack member Dean Martin, is entombed in a crypt here at Westwood Memorial. Most days Martin's marble stone is covered in lip prints of every size, shape, and color, proving that even in death, Dino gets more attention than his wacky former sidekick.

RODNEY DANGERFIELD

THERE GOES THE NEIGHBORHOOD

Lucky Stiff

The Pierce Brothers Westwood Village

Memorial Park Cemetery is the final resting place for some of the biggest names in the entire storied history of Hollywood. Included among the graveyard's deceased A-listers are legendary giants like Billy Wilder, Merv Griffin, George C. Scott, and Richard "Freddy" Poncher.

You read that correctly: Freddy Poncher. You see, Poncher had a dream, but what differentiates Poncher from every other schlub with a vision is that Poncher acted on his dream and made that dream an everlasting reality.

According to legend, Poncher spoke of his funeral plans often and with great delight for more than a quarter of a century. Not that he was a morbid man obsessed with death—quite the contrary. Poncher was known to friends and family alike as an outgoing and generous fellow. His grave marker reads, RICHARD F. PONCHER—1905–1986—TO THE MAN WHO GAVE US EVERYTHING AND MORE. YOU'RE ONE IN A MILLION, 'FREDDY.'

On the night Poncher was to be entombed, his trusted pallbearers waited for the grieving guests to leave. The loyal companions and confidants remained huddled around the hearse until the final attendee had left the grounds. Finally, away from the eyes of the public and under the cloak of night, each man grabbed his section of the casket and hoisted it to his shoulder, and, at the count of three, they flipped the earthly remains of their dearly departed friend upside down and shoved his coffin into its burial vault. Poncher's lifetime dream of spending eternity above the sexy star was finally a reality.

When Marilyn Monroe died, Joe DiMaggio, a fiercely private man and former husband of the blonde bombshell, was responsible for the funeral arrangements. It was said that DiMaggio picked the small cemetery for its obscurity. Joltin' Joe could have never imagined that by choosing that seemingly inconsequential location he would not only change the tiny Westwood park into one of the one of the most elite mortuaries in Los Angeles, but he had also unwittingly decided the final resting place of a man who had never even met the beautiful but troubled starlet.

A spokesperson for the Pierce Brothers Westwood Village Memorial Park admits to having heard the story on a number of occasions, but responds that she can neither confirm nor deny the authenticity of this often told tale.

Valhalla Cemetery

Many Angelenos don't even know about Pierce Brothers Valhalla Cemetery, and those graveyard ghouls who do usually just sigh when it's brought up in conversation. It could be the location—North Hollywood, close enough to Burbank airport that you can see the passengers in airplane windows—or, to break it down, its precise location: dangerously close to the pylons and power lines that criss-cross the region, smack up against an industrial red-brick wall, and no fancy gates or mausoleums to greet you.

You can't blame anyone for being surprised that this is the resting place for the Hollywood elite, as well as explorers and aviation pioneers, especially when you see the explosion of Christmas decorations and Santas with SQUEEZE ME HERE! stickers that ho-ho-ho on the crypts long past holiday season. Could Charles King, aka the Amazing Criswell, have predicted that his final resting place would be just a few yards from Bea Benederet—the voice of Betty Rubble and the in-the-flesh Pearl Bodine—both marked by tiny, barely legible, corroded nameplates?

Amelia Earhart has a cenotaph in the Portal of Folded Wings, which houses many early aviators.

Other notables planted at Valhalla include Curly Joe DeRita, Gladys George, Mae Clarke, Mantan Moreland, Oliver Hardy, Madame Sul-Te-Wan, and one of the Sons of the Pioneers . . . but the greatest one of all is Mae Murray, the first movie superstar.

Another resident of Valhalla Memorial Park is "Gorgeous" George Wagner—a famous and flamboyant entertainer who reigned as the King of Pro Wrestling from the late 1940s until his retirement in 1960. Wagner was an unsuccessful wrestler until he came up with the idea for his famous persona. He grew his hair long, bleached it blond, and had it permed into flowing curls. For every match, he entered to the strains of "Pomp and Circumstance." The train of his satin cape was carried by a male assistant, who

nostalgia performances at Billy Rose's Horseshoe Theater. A long twenty-four years later, the former Miss Itsy-Poo of 1922 embarked on a self-promotion tour by bus and made it as far as St. Louis, where she was found wandering penniless, either taken in by the Salvation Army (who sent her back to Hollywood) or arrested for vagrancy, depending on what you read. Foreshadowing celebrity rehab shows, she reenacted this in press photos. Luckily, the Motion Picture and Television Fund—of which Murray had been a founding trustee—and George Hamilton's mother took care of her in her last days; Hamilton once related to me how he danced the tango with her. I like to bring flowers to her grave.—*Donna Lethal*

would disinfect and perfume his master's corner of the ring before George would even think of entering it. He would also do the same for (or to) the opponent's corner. Wagner would use every opportunity to cheat, which delighted or infuriated fans, in many cases causing riots to break out. In many ways, Wagner is the father of modern pro wrestling. He apparently had his name legally changed to Gorgeous George sometime in the 1950s, although his grave marker bears his given name. He is buried in block J, section 9370, lot 4, northeast of the main fountain.

Mae Murray was the *real* Norma Desmond—arguably the first superstar of the silent age, known today for her performance in Erich Von Stroheim's *The Merry Widow*, although Murray got her start on Broadway and was an adept dancer and comedienne as well. She was also one of the first female actresses to have her own production company. Setting the precedent for movie star living, she married one "Prince" David Mdivani, who promptly became her manager and swindled her out of her fortune, and she lost custody of her only son in the process. By the 1940s she was reduced to parodying *Merry Widow* waltz

Hillside Cemetery Fun Facts

It is rumored that only one-third of Dinah Shore is resting at Hillside Memorial. Her husband is buried with a third of her ashes in Palm Springs and the other third is in the custody of a female friend.

Steve Goldstein, author of *Beneath Los Angeles Graves*, was in attendance for Milton Berle's funeral. According to Steve, comedian Jan Murray's tribute to Berle included one of Uncle Miltie's favorite jokes. Berle divorced his original bride, Broadway showgirl Joyce Matthews, only to walk down the aisle with her again some months later. When asked why he decided to remarry, Berle quipped, "Because she reminds me so much of my first wife."

Hillside Memorial is apparently the final resting place of Frankenstein. We were pleasantly surprised to find out he wasn't really a monster after all. The frightened villagers must have mistaken his silence for malice. His grave marker plainly reads he was always caring for others.

The award for most unique grave marker goes to legendary Warner Brothers animator Friz Freleng. We have to admit, it is a little unnerving to see Tweety, Daffy, Porky, and Bugs literally dancing on Freleng's grave. However, there is no evidence to suggest that his marble crypt was built by the Acme Funeral Needs and Bird Seed Supply Company.

Hillside Cemetery

Such a solemn location for so many funny people. If the previous sentence sounds like the punch line from the act of an old Borscht Belt comedian, it is appropriate. Within the tranquil grounds of this cemetery lie the remains of some of the most beloved funnymen of all time. The roll call reads like a Murderers Row of old-school humorists: Milton Berle, Moe Howard, Selma Diamond, Jack Benny, Louie Nye, and Allan Sherman are just some of the all-time greats who are interred at this famous burial ground.

This is not to say that all the spirits at Hillside are practicing their slapstick and spraying each other with seltzer water; this place has its share of strong serious men as well. Detroit slugger Hank Greenberg is safe at home here, but if the ghost of gangster Meyer "Mickey" Cohen wants to start any trouble, he'll have to get through the good guys of the Ponderosa Ranch: Lorne Greene and Michael Landon. Hmm . . . an epic battle between big-city mobsters and frontier cowboys. Sounds like the plot of a particularly bad episode of *Fantasy Island*, which, not coincidentally, was produced by Aaron Spelling, who is entombed here.

And who's going to cater the wrap party of this heavenly production? It would have to be the late Paul Pink, the original owner of Hollywood's most famous hot dog stand: Pink's.

Al Jolson Monument at Hillside

Al Jolson billed himself as the "World's Greatest Entertainer," and artists from Bob Hope to Mick Jagger are said to have agreed with that proclamation. Nowadays Jolson is probably best remembered for performing in blackface, but in his day he conquered Broadway, movies, and radio. At the time of his passing in 1950 at age sixty-four, Jolson was one of the most recognizable people on the planet and was loved by audiences and revered by his peers.

Twenty thousand fans came to pay their last respects at Hollywood's Beth Olam Cemetery. His mortal remains stayed there until a year later, when his widow, Erle, was persuaded to move Jolson's body to the more serene and stately surroundings of Hillside Memorial Park. Mrs. Jolson confided that her husband had always wanted to be buried next to a waterfall, so management at Hillside spared no expense creating a man-made 120-foot cascade. The Widow Jolson paid close to $10,000 for the plot and commissioned architect Paul Williams an additional $75,000 to design the three-story, domed, six-pillar marble structure that occupies it. A bronze statue of the vocalist is perched nearby on one knee, arms theatrically extended as if he were to belt out the final words to his immortal hit "Mammy."

Thanks to the grandeur of the commemorative, not to mention the nature of Los Angeles traffic, the memorial can be easily viewed from the comfort of your car on the 405 freeway in Culver City.

The Spider Pool

In the early 2000s, a group of people assembled in an imaginary space to collect and trade "cheesecake" photos taken from the late 1940s to the early 1960s. This is not pornography; it is "young ladies in various modest states of undress." (My grandparents would have considered these girls to be fallen and trashy. Still, compared to today's tide of starlets who "accidentally" leak their amateur porn and nude photographs to the press, these pictures seem charming and innocent.)

Taken by amateur photographers spurred to join clubs by the invention of the Stereo Realist camera, some ended up in magazines, others in private collections. Bettie Page did this kind of modeling (although she is not in any of the pictures that concern us). These clubs liked to photograph outside, in interesting locations.

Our intrepid Internet collectors found themselves intrigued by these places, many of which had distinctive features. One in particular captivated them. It was a pool, secured into a hillside with a view of the San Fernando Valley in the background. The pool was surrounded by strange loop-de-loops of white cement and extravagantly colored tiles, but its most distinctive feature was the mosaic that adorned a retaining wall above the pool. It depicted a large spider in its web, a tiny blip of a hornet caught off to the side. They began comparing photos, especially their backgrounds, to pick out the features that would help them to figure out where the photos were taken.

By November 2004, they had come up with a triangle of likely territory and a couple of locals to confirm the location. Using a telescope, these explorers saw the spider on the retaining wall. It was on some vacant land, wedged between properties. They hiked up an empty lot to get to it.

What they found was very different from the glorious pictures they had seen. The pool had been removed entirely, because of instability, leaving only a grassy bowl of land near the spider mosaic. Although the white background had been washed away, there was enough contrast to see that the spider, the web, and most of the tiles surrounding it were still whole. It was cause for celebration.

But what is the Spider Pool? We know about its afterlife as a ruin and photography club location, but where did it come from?

Jack McDermott's family records in Los Angeles date back to 1914. His family sold dry goods from the East. Jack, like any young man in a boomtown, looked to the new movie industry to find his destiny. He started as an actor, but eventually moved behind the camera, with a company of actors of his own. He made several silent films, including *Sky Pilot*, *Dinty*, and *Midnight Madness*. He later eschewed directing for writing; his credits include *Blonde or Brunette*, *Stranded in Paris*, and *The Fifty-Fifty Girl*.

As his career blossomed, he wanted more than living in a downtown boarding house with other movie types. Eventually he decided that the place for him to build was the bucolic Hollywood Hills. By 1923, he had settled on a pre-1900 foundation. He conscripted set pieces, most notably from the Norma Talmadge flick *Song of Love*, which he hauled up into the hills with donkeys and put the house together himself. It is believed that the swimming pool area (swimming pools were the height of fashion in post–World War I LA) was developed at this time. It was built on the crest of the ridge, up several stairs (and possibly a secret passage) from the house itself.

Beyond the Algerian-style pieces, he pilfered from other sets, including the sets of *The Thief of Baghdad* and *The Phantom of the Opera*. The result was a long, ramshackle dwelling that combined many different styles, not only Algerian, but also Navajo, Moroccan, and Egyptian. The Spider House turned up in numerous magazines, often described as a "crazy house," a place of debauchery and wonder, full of secret passages, fishponds, and even a fake cemetery complete with skulls made of chalk.

In 1929, McDermott's career wound down. Talkies were all the rage, and it seemed that he couldn't gain any purchase as the industry changed. He wrote some minor plays, had some things optioned for features, and traveled the world. None of it seemed to make him very happy. He was living in the house in 1946 when he accidentally overdosed on pills. He was dead at fifty-three. He'd left scores of movies and a wonder of a house behind him.

In short order, the house burned, though there are records of people living there after that time. The photographers came and went. Kids moved in to squat and throw parties—much to the consternation of the surrounding neighborhood. In 1958, a man bought the property to try to restore it, but he couldn't get it up to code and was prohibited from having a driveway. The property was abandoned in 1962 and dismantled by the city.

I found out about the Spider Pool while roaming the Internet one day. There was just a line about its discovery. I wanted to see what it looked like, so I followed a link down the rabbit hole. Not only is the iconography—the spider, the wasp, the gorgeous tiles—arresting, but also it's very close to the house my parents were living in when I was born. I had never heard them mention it. I was hooked. I had to see this place.

I looked up everything I could, and hauled my then fiancé out there in late 2005. Having grown up in rural New York, he was uncomfortable about the possibility of trespassing. I, out of having grown up in the hills, being used to a lot of trespassers, or possibly just out of sheer stupidity, was unbothered. I was on fire with this place.

Getting there was arduous. I left my fiancé and climbed through shrubs and cacti. There were no trails, no indicators at all, but eventually I started seeing tiles—tiles that I recognized! I walked the length of the area, before hitting a wall of cacti. I saw tiled stairs, the outline of a small pool, alcoves in the hillside—but no spider. I couldn't see the spider anywhere. But I knew I had found something.

Weeks later, I found a picture of a woman near the little pool outline. I sent it to an e-mail address, along with a picture of what I had seen. At first, nothing happened. But a few weeks later, I heard back—there was a lot of excitement. Apparently, completely by accident, I had stumbled on the remains of the house. No one had found it before. I was thrilled to be a part of the story that had lit me up. I was glad to contribute to something that had given me so much pleasure.

But a couple of years passed, and the fact remained that I had not seen the spider. In March 2008, I packed up a camera, some nuts, and water (and a lot of loose clothing) and took to the hills. . . . I scrambled up the grassy hillside, and as it leveled out I started seeing a lot of weird debris, street signs where there was no street, old trash cans full of

tiles (and not the Spider Pool kind). . . . It was just beyond the gate of the paddock that I saw it, the white winking out of the scrubby brush. It was so sudden and such a secret, it took my breath away.

It was on the east side, so the sun wasn't on it, but it shone through the leaves and plants all around, gilding the area. The night cool still rose from the old, large-grained cement the spider was in. It was blue—the spider and the web. . . . I wandered all over the area, taking pictures, asking myself questions, scrambling over more brush to get down to the house. . . .

As much as I want to tell the story, I'm not going to tell you where the Spider Pool is. A bunch of people going up there would disrupt the area, and likely destroy whatever remains of the ruins. . . .

Now that you've read this story, you can look around this city and know that there are things hidden, things annihilated that are as strange and as bizarre as anything on Earth. And that's important. As Ken Kesey once said, "Sometimes the need for mystery is greater than the need for an answer."—*Jacy Young*

Special thanks for research, photos, and enthusiasm to Rowanart and Old Bubblehead.

Weird Adventures in Abandoned Mental Hospitals

Jonathan Crellin may be a chemistry major at Cal State Fullerton, but what this Orange County native lives for is the spontaneous unscientific joy he and his friends receive when they venture north on the 405 freeway in search of new weird adventures.

The abandoned Brentwood VA Hospital at 11301 Wilshire Boulevard is one such place Crellin and some of his friends have explored. It was used as a filming location for the Home for the Criminally Insane in the 1984 cult classic

The Adventures of Buckaroo Banzai Across the 8th Dimension. This is Crellin's story.

My interest in the mental hospital started when I made friends with someone at my school also named Jonathan. He had been there and taken some cool pictures and I was very excited to check it out.

The hospital is in Brentwood near Santa Monica. Jonathan's good friend, William, lived only a few minutes away from it. The abandoned buildings are part of the still operational Veterans hospital complex. We got some flashlights and arrived at the first of two buildings. The building was old, dark, and spooky. To enter, we had to climb down to a

basement window. Inside was cold and dark, and we nervously looked into the rooms as we made our way to the stairs to the first level.

Everywhere there were signs of past patients. Pills and needles were scattered around the floors; old beds with straps on them were sitting in corners. Some of the larger rooms were being used as storage. We saw some stairs and an elevator, but they were blocked off. We knew there was an upstairs but there was no way to get there.

Finally we decided to leave and go look at the second building. This building was much larger than the first. Again we made our way in through the basement window. Inside we heard strange noises coming from steam pipes and dripping water. We walked down a long, dark tunnel to the stairs and made our way up to the second story. My friends and I slowly walked around, examining the endless number of rooms. We were always cautious of what was around every corner, scaring ourselves into wondering if we were alone or not. Surprisingly, the old abandoned building had no signs of intruders, or any graffiti—except in one single room.

We entered a rather large room on the third floor to find a mural painting of a demonlike character with strange writings surrounding it. It was around then when we decided to leave. Over the next couple years, my friends and I make our way back to the hospital every once in a while to discover every little detail of the rooms. However, no matter how many times I have been there, it is always still as creepy as the first time.

Gay's Lion Farm

European carnival performers Charles and Muriel Gay arrived in Los Angeles in 1914. Almost immediately the young couple opened up a free lion-training exhibition on the site of what is now MacArthur Park. An amusement park dedicated to captive lions was certainly new to Los Angelenos, and huge crowds of onlookers would gather daily to view these fierce and exotic African animals up close. It wasn't long before Hollywood came knocking on the Gays' door, asking if they could use their tamed jungle creatures in various movies. The Gays' lions became famous, starring alongside Elmo Lincoln and Johnny Weissmuller in various Tarzan movies. Two other lions from the Gays' stable (Slats and, later, Jackie) became the living embodiment of the MGM logo.

The lion business was a roaring success, and thanks to the natural wonders of mating season, the Gays soon found themselves in the unenviable position of having more lions than land. In 1925, they discovered five acres of unzoned property in El Monte, just east of LA, and opened Gay's

Mr. Gay and Pluto
Gay's Lion Farm
El Monte, Calif.

Airplane View

Gay's Lion Farm

El Monte, California

Farm covers 5 Acres, has 6 large Lion Houses and 100,000 sq. ft. of Arena

MAIN ENTRANCE

Lion Farm. Here they raised the mighty carnivores in large numbers to, as they wrote in their own pamphlets, "supply the increasing demands of Motion Picture Studios, Circuses and Zoos in all parts of the world."

The U-shaped compound (inspired by African architecture) housed more than two hundred wild cats at the height of its success. There were separate cages for adult cats, a nursery, and, of course, the main stage where Charles Gay would perform the obligatory lion tamer's role and command the great meat-eating felines to do such tricks as roll over, beg, and jump through rings. One of the biggest

attractions was feeding time. The lions were fed more than a ton of meat daily, six out of seven days of the week. Mondays were nonfeeding days, and the frightening growls of a couple hundred hungry lions could be heard for miles around. Locals jokingly started referring to the first day of the workweek as Howling Monday.

The Gays also enjoyed hosting the occasional private party, and by 1927 groups such as the civic-minded Lions Club and the Los Angeles Adventurers' Club would hold banquets at the farm. According to Kim Cooper, founder of Esotouric bus tours, "These events centered around outdoor banquets set in a clearing among the animal cages, at which guests were served small samples of barbecued lion meat in addition to steak and chicken. An honored guest at these meals, toasted and encouraged to walk the length of the table, was Numa the lion." Cooper went on to say, "Charles Gay would walk Numa, his biggest lion, the length of the

table while club members shivered and their coffee spilled. Club charters were exchanged over Numa's head."

Running a corporation with human employees can be taxing enough, but when the overwhelming majority of those workers are five-hundred-pound carnivorous wild African cats, you really should have a pretty good second-in-command. Unfortunately for the Gays, their 1928 European vacation was marred when a trainer failed to secure a runway while three lions were being transported from one cage to another. The first lion ran for freedom, nearly ripping off the arm of farm manager John Rounan in the process. (Rounan received medical aid, but later died from the wound.) Another trainer, Joe Hoffman, managed to bring down the escaped animal with a single bullet to the brain, but that still left two more on the loose.

The second lion simply walked into an open cage. Hoffman slammed the door shut and went after the third lion. The remaining lion was shot in the leg and tore around the farm in a wounded frenzy, terrorizing a cow as well as a cage of lion cubs. Police arrived on the scene and opened fire on the runaway lion, bringing the great beast down in a storm of bullets.

World War II brought about rationing, and in 1942 the Gays no longer had the luxury of buying twelve thousand pounds of meat weekly. Rather than let the lions go hungry, the Gays made arrangements with zoos around the country and loaned out their lions with the understanding they would be returned to the farm after the war. Sadly, Charles Gay's health diminished during the war, and he was physically incapable of reopening the old farm. He and his wife retired to Balboa Island, along with the taxidermied remains of his old friends, Slats and Numa.

A life-sized bronze statue now sits at the overpass on Interstate 10 where Gay's Lion Farm used to be. To learn more about this and other unique pieces of Los Angeles history, we highly recommend booking a tour with the Esotouric (www.esotouric.com).

GAY'S LION FARM   EL MONTE, CAL.-75

Tail o' the Pup

In ultra-chic West Hollywood, where expensive trends start and end in the same twenty-four-hour period, it is hard to think of anything less highbrow than a hot dog stand, unless it's a hot dog stand in the shape of a giant hot dog.

Constructed in 1945, the Tail o' the Pup luncheonette was originally situated on Beverly Boulevard, but relocated in the late eighties to a block away from where it initially stood. For more than sixty years the Tail o' the Pup served its simple high-cholesterol menu to tourists and locals alike. That translates into well over five million franks, which is a lot of tube steak consumption on one street corner.

In December 2005, however, this giant hot dog with the works was ordered to go—by the owners of the land development company Regent Properties.

Apparently the bean counters at Regent Properties believed they could make more bread from condominiums than chili dogs. While this may be true, it has left lovers of "programmatic architecture" (the practice of designing a building to depict the product sold) with concern. The removal of the Tail o' the Pup is just another example of this town eating and then discarding its own history.

Hollywood legend Orson Welles is said to have had his limo driver pull up to the oversized frankfurter and place his order without ever leaving the backseat. A wall of celebrities told the stories of other show-biz luminaries who have enjoyed wolfing down the occasional lunchtime sandwich at this one-time architectural landmark.

Jay Leno, Pamela Anderson, Barbra Streisand, Magic Johnson, and Whoopi Goldberg have all partaken of the stand's beefy plumpness. The Tail o' the Pup has also made cameos in many movies, including Brian De Palma's *Body Double* and Steve Martin's *L.A. Story.*

Although the Pup is no longer serving its delicious sausage across from the stylish Beverly Center Mall, all is not necessarily lost for those who have a relish for this novelty structure. There has been talk of bringing back the kitschy eatery near the UCLA campus in Westwood Village.

If there is a lesson to be learned from this story, it's this: In this town, you may look like a pretty big dog, but there's always some giant wienie who can ruin your lunch.

The Corner of Burns and Allen

The temptations of success have taken their toll on most of the married acts in Hollywood. Cher divorced Sonny. Desi may have loved Lucy, but that didn't stop him from really, really liking a few dozen other women while still wedded to his redheaded bride. And who among us doesn't remember where they were on that fateful afternoon on July 1, 2006, a day that shocked and saddened an entire nation, if not the world. It was, of course, the day perennial newlyweds Nick Lachey and Jessica Simpson's divorce was finalized.

And so it seems there has only been one show business couple to flourish under the rigors of prosperous entertainment careers: George Burns and Gracie Allen.

The comedy team of Burns and Allen charmed the American public with a personal chemistry that shone through from their early vaudeville days to radio and film and, finally, to television. For most of their dual careers, Burns played the straight man to Allen's lovably innocent airhead. (According to Burns, Allen originally played the straight role, but the audience was naturally inclined to laugh at whatever came out of her mouth, so they quickly switched personas.)

The city of Los Angeles has a long-standing ordinance that declares that no street can be named after a living person. That edict was waived in 1986 in honor of George Burns's ninetieth birthday, and the northern end of Hamel Road was changed to George Burns Road. When Burns turned ninety-nine, the eastern end of Alden Drive became Gracie Allen Drive.

At the unveiling ceremony, the always chipper Burns quipped, "It's good to be on the corner of Burns and Allen. At my age, it's good to be anywhere."

The Brown Derby

Atop the second floor of a mini-mall at 3377 Wilshire Boulevard sits a big pink-domed helmet-y looking thing. It used to be a restaurant that was named for exactly what it looked like in its heyday. It was a different color back then and was called the Brown Derby. It's now a Korean restaurant, but the current owners didn't feel that the name "Big Pink-Domed Helmet-y Looking Thing" was going to bring in the business, so they went with the name Buzz. To some, though, that big pink-domed helmet-y looking thing will always be the Derby.

The Brown Derby Café opened its brim to the public in 1925, a few blocks away from its current location. The eatery catered mostly to the swinging Cocoanut Grove nightclub after-hours crowd hoping to sober up before hitting the road in their collective Model Ts and As.

Thirty feet in diameter and seventeen and a half feet tall, the wood and plaster building became an instant icon. Most famously, it was the birthplace of the Cobb salad. Legend has it that late one night Derby manager Bob Cobb created the popular cold savory dish while chopping up some leftover chicken breast and mixing it in with a head of romaine lettuce, avocado, watercress, tomatoes, a hard-boiled egg, bacon, chives, cheese, and French dressing. Hollywood pals Sid Grauman, Jack Warner, and Wilson Mizner stopped by the table and nibbled. The salad was such a hit that it was soon added to the Derby's menu, and it eventually became popular in restaurants the world over.

In 1929, a second Brown Derby opened on Vine Street in Hollywood, though this Derby was a Derby in just name alone. It did not resemble a huge hat, and the menu was more upscale. This was the Brown Derby that became famous for the hundreds of celebrity caricatures that adorned the walls of the bistro. This is also the Derby immortalized in an episode of *I Love Lucy*, in which Lucy accidentally knocks a plate of food on movie star William Holden.

Unfortunately, the novelty of eating inside a giant hat began to wear off by the 1970s, and on September 9, 1980, at 4 P.M., the last patron of the Brown Derby was informed that his trout dinner was on the house. Despite the hard work of those concerned with preserving Hollywood's cultural landmarks, the only piece of the original restaurant saved was the big brown domed helmet-y looking thing that is now painted pink and sits atop the second floor of a mini-mall in Koreatown.

Tor Johnson

Much of Generation X is at least aware of the legendary films of Edward D. Wood Jr. A whole new generation was introduced to this singular American auteur when Tim Burton released a biopic about him in 1994. (No, Ed isn't buried in Los Angeles; he was cremated and his ashes scattered at sea.) One of Wood's stock players was the three-hundred-pound former wrestler Tor Johnson, who played in three of his films, usually as a hulking goon or a hulking goonlike zombie.

Swedish-born Johnson made his professional debut under the stage name Super Swedish Angel and became a crowd favorite. Accordingly, he often played wrestlers in his early film roles, such as the W. C. Fields vehicle *Man on the Flying Trapeze* in 1935. Wood introduced him as Lobo in *Bride of the Monster* (1956), playing the mindless assistant to Bela Lugosi's mad scientist character. He went on to appear and sometimes star in at least twenty more films before his death in 1971. The Lobo character was so popular that Johnson reprised it in other features—not all directed by

Wood. Lobo became such a legend that when Johnson's film career tanked in the late 1960s, the actor ghouled up as the character in personal appearances. While he was still among us, a Hollywood makeup effects artist made a life mask of Johnson, which was used as a mold for an elaborate Halloween mask that is a perennial favorite.

Another famous wrestler, George "the Animal" Steele portrayed Johnson in the Burton film.

Johnson is buried at the Eternal Valley Memorial Park in Newhall in the Whispering Pines section, plot 177E. Incongruously enough, Gene "Be-Bop-a-Lula" Vincent also rests here, just down the hill in another section.

La Brea Tar Pits

If it's old, it better have some retro kitsch value to it, or you'll be laughed right out of Los Angeles. That goes for cars, fashion, and even people . . . especially people. It's more than a little unusual when you can find a building that is more than forty years old in this town, so when we're talking about a place that's been around LA for more than ten thousand times that long, you'd better to sit up and take notice.

The La Brea Tar Pits have been a part of Wilshire Boulevard since at least 39,900 years before there was a Wilshire Boulevard, and they are a much more popular attraction nowadays. That's not to say the famous cluster of tar pits didn't attract an audience during the last Ice Age—they certainly did. The problem was there wasn't much repeat business. The well-preserved fossilized remains of saber-toothed cats, mammoths, dire wolves, birds, and plants would all testify to that, if fossilized remains could talk. Of course, they can't, and that's why the Page Museum laboratory employs smart scientist types.

The oldest fossil ever to be found at the tar pits was a wood fragment, which was dated to around forty thousand years ago using the carbon-14 radiometric dating method (sometimes called radiocarbon dating).

It's pretty weird to realize that even to this day the tar pits still ooze and bubble enough asphalt to entrap lizards, rabbits, ducks, dogs, and even the occasional human—and it all happens right in the middle of one of the busiest and most modern cities in the world.

The Page Museum has a very informative Web site about how the tar pits function, and we're paraphrasing it here:

Asphalt is a particularly sticky when it is warm. The local temperatures from late spring to early fall would have provided the optimum conditions for small mammals, birds, and insects to inadvertently come into contact with the tar pits and effectively immobilized in them.

Strong and healthy animals might have escaped, but others would have been entrapped until they died of exhaustion or fell prey to passing predators—depending on its size, a large plant-eating animal might attract a dozen or more hungry meat-eating creatures, some of which would find themselves trapped too, providing even more food for other carnivores.

One such "entrapment episode," repeated once every decade over thirty thousand years suggests that there are more than a million fossils in the La Brea Tar Pits.

And now here's a Spanish language lesson, something that might make you feel even smarter than you do right now. The Spanish word for "the" is *la*. And the Spanish word for "tar" is *brea*. Therefore, "The La Brea Tar Pits," actually means "The The Tar Tar Pits."

We can't take too much credit for discovering that—it came too came from the Page Museum Web site.

Cemetery Cinema

If you've ever wondered what it would be like to watch a movie with Academy Award–winning director John Huston or matinee idol Douglas Fairbanks, then wonder no more. The good people at Cinespia have been showing seldom-screened film classics at the Hollywood Forever Cemetery during summer weekends since 2001. There, six feet above the earthly remains of some of Tinseltown's greatest personalities (such as movie and TV actor David White, below, whose best known role was as Larry Tate on the 1960s TV hit series *Bewitched*) you can spread a blanket, open a picnic basket, and sip Chardonnay on the finely manicured lawn of Hollywood's coolest graveyard.

The films are projected on the wall of the immaculate marble mausoleum that is home to Rudolph Valentino and other luminaries. Given the spooky surroundings, one might think the screenings cater to a strictly goth and horror crowd, but that is not the case. Movie night at the cemetery brings a great cross-section of cinephiles. Middle-class suburban parents attend with their children in tow. Retired couples walk across the lawn and settle down peacefully next to the same teenagers who would normally get yelled at for trampling across their neighbors' lawn, and of course the resident departed are always in attendance.

The open-air theater became an instant hit with film fans, and why not? It combines the best elements of drive-in movies, block parties, and hanging out with dead movie stars. Crowds vary in size from 1,500 to 3,000 people, depending on the movie and the weather. The audience members are mostly respectful of their fellow spectators, but if you're one of those people who demand silence during a film, may we suggest attending a showing you've seen a few times before. It doesn't matter how loudly you gnash your teeth, you're not going to drown out the inevitable chatter that comes when a thousand people mix a movie with a thousand bottles of Trader Joe's vino.

The funereal gates open at 7:30 P.M. and the movie starts at 9:00 P.M. Most arrive early to ensure a prime location, enjoy the eclectic music selections from the live DJ, and feast on the aforementioned dinner and wine. Hollywood Forever Cemetery is located at 6000 Santa Monica Boulevard.

Hollywood Forever Cemetery

Isaac Lankershim and Isaac Newton Van Nuys founded the Hollywood Memorial Park, now known as Hollywood Forever Cemetery, in 1899, but they are not buried here. Hollywood Memorial was known then, as it is today, as the final resting place for actors, writers, and directors—in other words, the hoi polloi. Lankershim and Van Nuys were both given dignified burials at Evergreen Cemetery in Los Angeles with the rest of the respectable rich folk.

The first person to be buried at this cemetery was a woman named Highland Price. Highland Avenue was named for her.

Although many think the cenotaph at Hollywood Forever dedicated to Jayne Mansfield means that she is buried there, her body (and head—she was not decapitated, as many believe) was laid to rest at Fairview Cemetery in tiny Pen Argyl, Pennsylvania.

Bianca Halstead (stage name: Bianca Butthole) was the bassist for the all-girl Hollywood band Betty Blowtorch. She had recently kicked her substance abuse problem when she accepted a ride in 2001 from Brian McAllister, an intoxicated fan. Reaching speeds of one hundred miles per hour, McAllister lost control of his vehicle, hopped a median, slammed headfirst into an oncoming car, and crashed into a guardrail, killing Halstead. Fans still decorate her unique grave.

Graphic designer Carl Morgan Bigsby is buried beneath an exact-scale twenty-foot granite model of the pioneer Atlas rocketship. In an eloquent send-off to her husband, Bigsby's wife, Constance, is quoted on the monument with the phrase, "Too bad, we had fun."

Apparently not "too tough to die," both Johnny and Dee Dee Ramone of the seminal punk rock group the Ramones are buried here. Dee Dee's grave bears the famous Ramones presidential seal logo and is often littered with guitar picks and cigarette lighters. His epitaph reads, "OK . . . I gotta go now." The sculpture of Johnny Ramone in the midst of a back-arching guitar riff is easily the most unique grave marker in the entire cemetery, and it bears farewell inscriptions from Lisa Marie Presley, Eddie Vedder, and Rob Zombie.

The tomb of Mel Blanc, the voice of Bugs Bunny, Yosemite Sam, and Barney Rubble, reads, "That's All Folks."

Col. Griffith W. Griffith, suspecting that his wife was conspiring with the pope to steal money from him and intending to kill her for it, shot her in the eye, disfiguring the woman and leaving her with only one working peeper. He received two years in prison for the crime. In an attempt to curry public favor, the colonel offered to donate $100,000 to the city of Los Angeles to build an observatory. The city declined at first, but accepted the endowment several years after his death.

The dog on the gravestone of childhood star Carl "Alfalfa" Switzer is often mistaken for the Little Rascals' pooch, Petey. It is in fact a symbol of his adult profession as an expert hunting guide and dog breeder. Switzer was killed in an argument with a client of his over $50. He was shot in the groin and bled to death.

Ex-con Jules Roth gained control of Hollywood Memorial Park just two years after he was released from prison. Over the decades, he stole millions from investors and the cemetery's endowment funds. His practice of selling the same plot over and over went undetected for years. At his other cemetery, Lincoln Memorial, he often illegally buried coffins a mere two inches below the ground, tossed headstones in the trash, and wedged children's graves along the borders of roadways.

David White, who played Larry Tate on television's *Bewitched,* is buried here, too (see previous page). At least, we hope he is dead and is not the everlasting victim of

Endora's dark witchcraft. Look for yourself, but you can't convince us that the life-size bronze bust of the actor is not so eerily lifelike that White may have indeed stumbled across Samantha's secret, and, in order to keep his silence, the comedic coven placed this ungodly curse upon Darrin Stephens's wishy-washy boss. It sounds farfetched only if you haven't seen it—believe us, it's freaky. The bust was actually a prop from a 1969 *Bewitched* episode that was modeled after White at age fifty-three.

Perhaps the most shocking story is the lack of security. All-night teenage parties in the graveyard resulted in the theft of the decomposed head of a woman from the mausoleum. The head was later discovered underneath a parked car outside the cemetery grounds.

INDEX
Page numbers in bold refer to photos and illustrations.

WEiRD HoLLyWood

ACKNOWLEDGMENTS

I'd like to thank (in no particular order) the following people for their friendship and story suggestions:

Darren Attinger, Karie Bible, J. Keith Van Straaten, Mason and Karen Brown (for allowing me to sleep on their couch one more than one drunken occasion) Dorian Frankle, David Koff, Randy Fallows, David Markland, Gina Shock (for a memorable night of drinks). Chris Doyle (because I know what it means to him to have his name in the same book as Davy Jones), Davy Jones, Brooke Seguin, Paul Petersen, Scott Hennelly, Brian Mulligan, Count Smokula, Harry Perry, Mr. Blackwell, Skip E. Lowe, Gary Owens (the guy wouldn't even let me pay for lunch) Rich Kuras (for allowing me to sleep on his couch on more than one drunken occasion) Claire Partin, Eric Soto, Patton Oswalt (for at least writing me back and saying he would if he could) Bonnie Vent, David Liebe Hart, Robbie Rist (for fulfilling a childhood dream of getting drunk with a Brady—of sorts) Andrew Koenig, That guy with the thing, Eliot Hochberg, Butch Patrick, Frank Stallone (hope to interview you for the next book, Frank), Stan Wells, Dennis LeBlanc, Scott Rubin, Deborah Vancelette (for allowing me to sleep on her couch on more than a few drunken occasions), Angelyne, Clint Howard (for bringing coupons to lunch – a truly down to earth guy), Mira Wilder, Sandeep Parikh, George Barris, Huell Howser (for calling personally to decline, even though he would have been great), Jennifer Wenger, Christopher Dennis, Jess Harnell, Johnnie Whitaker, Mamie Van Doren, Melissa Burech, Melrose Larry Green, Michael Lindsay, Dennis Woodruff, and everyone else I forgot who feels they should be included here.

And of course, Jennifer, Jessica, and Hannah.

PHOTO CREDITS

SHOW US YOUR WEIRD!

Do you know of a weird site found somewhere in the United States, or can you tell us about a strange experience you've had? If so, we'd like to hear about it! We believe that every town has at least one great tale to tell, and we're listening. It could be a cursed road, haunted abandoned site, odd local character, or bizarre historic event. In most cases these tales are told only in the towns in which they originated. But why keep them to yourself when you could share them with all of America? So come on and fill us in on all the weirdness that's lurking in your backyard!

You can e-mail us at: Editor@WeirdUS.com,
or write to us at:
Weird U.S., P.O. Box 1346, Bloomfield, NJ 07003.

www.weirdus.com